# Juvenile Nation

# Juvenile Nation

## Youth, Emotions and the Making of the Modern British Citizen, 1880–1914

Stephanie Olsen

**B L O O M S B U R Y**
LONDON • NEW DELHI • NEW YORK • SYDNEY

**Bloomsbury Academic**

An imprint of Bloomsbury Publishing Plc

50 Bedford Square          1385 Broadway
London                     New York
WC1B 3DP                   NY 10018
UK                         USA

**www.bloomsbury.com**

**Bloomsbury is a registered trade mark of Bloomsbury Publishing Plc**

First published 2014

© Stephanie Olsen, 2014

**British Library Cataloguing-in-Publication Data**
A catalogue record for this book is available from the British Library.

ISBN: HB: 978-1-7809-3695-6
ePDF: 978-1-4725-1009-9
ePub: 978-1-4725-1141-6

**Library of Congress Cataloging-in-Publication Data**
A catalog record for this book is available from the Library of Congress.

Typeset by Newgen Knowledge Works (P) Ltd., Chennai, India
Printed and bound in Great Britain

*For my family*

# Contents

# List of Figures

# List of Abbreviations

| | |
|---|---|
| AP | Amalgamated Press (led by Alfred Harmsworth, Lord Northcliffe) |
| BL | British Library |
| *BOP* | *Boy's Own Paper* (RTS) |
| CETS | Church of England Temperance Society |
| *GOP* | *Girl's Own Paper* (RTS) |
| NSPCC | National Society for the Prevention of Cruelty to Children |
| RTS | Religious Tract Society |
| RTS ECM | Religious Tact Society Executive Committee Minutes |
| WYAS | West Yorkshire Archive Service |

# Acknowledgements

In many ways, this is a book about coming of age. In the writing of it, I feel I too have gone through a personal process of development and fulfilment, frequently asking myself 'which path should I take?' Without the help of great friends and colleagues, I doubt I should have found the way. Elizabeth Elbourne, Brian Lewis and Michèle Cohen have given me superb direction, assurance and confidence. Joy Dixon and Ian Gentles provided me with my first wonderful experiences studying British history. Stephen Heathorn provided me with excellent comments in the course of this project's development. I thank them all.

My colleagues at the Max Planck Institute for Human Development, Center for the History of Emotions, have given me a warm welcome and have encouraged me to think about my research in new ways. I am especially grateful to Ute Frevert, Margrit Pernau, all of the wonderful research staff and graduate students past and present, and the most helpful support staff anywhere.

The research for this book was generously funded by the Social Science and Humanities Research Council of Canada, the Max Planck Society, the Fondation Ricard, the Department of History at McGill University, the Friends of the Princeton University Library Research Grant Program and Harvard University. Together they have made the research and writing process truly enriching and global in scope.

Many thanks to the helpful staff at the British Library, SOAS, York Minster Library, Lambeth Palace Library, the Bodleian Library, the West Yorkshire Archive Service (WYAS) at Bradford and Leeds, the Norfolk Record Office, Birmingham City Archives, the National Archives of Canada, the Osborne Collection, Fischer Rare Books at the University of Toronto, the McGill libraries, Cotsen Children's Library at Princeton University and especially Judith Crowe at the Institute of Alcohol Studies (London) who could not have been more helpful. Thanks to Katelyn Fricke and Fabian Steininger for the research assistance during the final stages of this project. Emily Drewe, Frances Arnold and Claire Lipscomb at Bloomsbury have been marvellous.

The book was developed at many conferences and seminars around the world, but I reserve special mention for the Montreal British History Seminar, under Bob Tittler's capable command, and the Northeast Conference on British

Studies, both of which represent the strength and warmth of the British history community in that region. The year I spent at the Minda de Gunzburg Center for European Studies at Harvard University was enormously stimulating, with particular thanks to Arianne Chernock and the British Study Group, and to Judith Surkis.

Due acknowledgement is given to Men's Studies Press, Palgrave Macmillan and *Women's History Review* for granting me permission to reproduce material from: 'Daddy's Come Home: Evangelicalism, Fatherhood and Lessons for Boys in Late Nineteenth-Century Britain', *Fathering* 5, 3 (2007), 174–96; Adrienne Gavin and Andrew Humphries, eds, *Childhood in Edwardian Fiction: Worlds Enough and Time*, 2009, Palgrave Macmillan and 'The Authority of Motherhood in Question: Fatherhood and the Moral Education of Children in England, c. 1870–1900', *Women's History Review*, 18, 5 (November 2009), 765–80.

I owe a debt to friends and colleagues who shared their expertise and sympathy on the long and sometimes frustrating road: Harriet Atkinson, Nick Attfield, Swapna Banerjee, Cynthia Belaskie, Justin Bengry, Juliane Brauer, Jodi Burkett, Alexandre Dubé, Heather Ellis, Greg Fisher, Michele Haapamäki, Jane Hamlett, Dan Horner, Hartmut Lenz, David Meren, Raul Necochea, Christiane Reinecke, Matthew Roberts, Dan Rueck, Cheryl Smeall, Noémi Tousignant and Karen Vallgårda. Tom Brydon is sadly missed. Sir Brian Harrison, Joanna Bourke and Natalie Zemon Davis have been inspirational, both in conversation and by example.

My parents, Inge Rumler Olsen and G. W. Olsen, have always been supportive and encouraging, and provided me with a nurturing intellectual environment and a love of history. I cannot ever hope to repay all their help and faith. Rob Boddice has patiently read every draft, providing me with keen insights and faultless judgement along the way. He is a constant source of intellectual and emotional sustenance.

# Introduction

Sometime after the conclusion of hostilities a young father reads together with his daughter about the history of the Great War. She sits on his knee and points at the pictures in the book. The setting is safe, comfortable, a domestic cliché. At the father's feet a little boy plays with toy soldiers, rehearsing manoeuvres of cannon and infantry in a childhood fantasy of glorious war. Suddenly, the little girl asks her father a question that causes him pain and remorse. Emasculated, he cannot answer. The question, 'Daddy, what did *YOU* do in the Great War?' has hit upon his greatest shame.

The scene I describe is that of the First World War propaganda poster on this book's cover, one of many that played on the sensibilities of young men in order to compel them to enlist. What is striking about it is its framing of the young man's future as a domesticated father, and his perceived failure – his shame – in that role because of his lack of military engagement. The respective contexts may seem jarring. This book sets out to explain how the image of home life and fatherhood was central to the fin-de-siècle ideal of manliness, which in turn ultimately explains why posters like this one were able to appeal to a sense of domesticated duty – to frame the national war effort, and the individual's part in it, with the family.

*Juvenile Nation* concerns the emergence of a modern conception of childhood and the coming together of a broad swath of society as informal educators from the 1880s. It examines the generation of boys for whom army-enlistment propaganda would become directly pertinent in 1914, the endpoint of this study. The modern boy, how he was to be made a 'fit' citizen in a 'great' civilization, is a principal concern. The book examines the training of emotions in the building of moral character, and the perceived dangers of failing in this regard. I argue that in this period the father was reinvigorated as moral leader, home and family were at the centre of a consensus concerning citizen formation, the 'adolescent' emerged as a pathological problem-child of a certain age, and childhood ideals were exported to imperial realms. In sum, this book asks what was the child expected to become in this period? What kind of adult? What kind of citizen?

Towards the end of the nineteenth century, children (especially boys) of all areas and social backgrounds were thought to be failed by the various institutions of formal education (be they the elite public schools or the new schools springing up since the Education Act of 1870). Equally worrying, it was feared that certain moral imperatives were being inadequately met by the nation's parents. Stressing the continuity of religious influence in the everyday experience of children throughout the late Victorian and Edwardian period, *Juvenile Nation* charts the agreement established between disparate groups on the importance of disseminating Christian values for the task of raising the nation's boys into manly, domesticated men and good fathers. This emphasis on family life is crucial, since it broadens the current historiographical focus on the imperial connotations of elite education and the supposed middle-class 'flight from domesticity'.[1] By showing that masculinity was not only about patriarchal or imperial outlooks, but also about emotional attachment and loyalty to family, the meaning of fatherhood in the period is explicated, stressing the continuing importance and validation of men as fathers and of the boy 'as father to the man'. This message was also extended to colonial subjects. Mass outpourings of militaristic fervour in 1914 can alternatively be seen as habitually restrained emotional outpourings based on association to family, to community and often to Christian cultural continuity, even in a so-called secularizing society. Framing a study of the generation before the First World War in the context of the war will lead to some fruitful new thoughts on the reasons why so many young men volunteered to go to war, in a country with no tradition of standing armies, and why so many did not.

The key contribution made by *Juvenile Nation* is to show how the incipient man's development occurred through what I term *informal education*. Particularly important here are the building of character and morality through the mode of emotional training. Lying in the realms of church, voluntary association and social institutions, the periodical press, and the family, this history of informal education has a bearing on the histories of religion, social reform (state legislation for the child) and emotions. In an era thought to be defined, at least in part, by the absent father, the attempts of psychologists, temperance activists, evangelical advice-column writers and moral publishers to educate boys to *be*, rather than simply to behave, can be understood as the building of future fathers who would ensure the passing on of these lessons. Acting in a sense as surrogate fathers, these activists asserted a consensus on the form of Britain's future citizenry, located its germ in the child and attempted to cultivate it, eliminating numerous 'wrong paths' as they went. Appeals to emotion, emotional control and the shaping of 'correct' emotional responses were key to the shaping of the next generation of men. *Juvenile Nation* ties the historical study of emotions to an examination of some of the moral foundations of society and the individual's place in it: family, religion and citizenship. It links the development of the individual and his place in the nation and empire with contemporary understandings of the meaning of both, amid fears of degeneracy and, conversely, assumptions of natural racial superiority.

The combined efforts of this disparate group of 'educators' necessarily had implications at the level of the State, and required a new rhetoric or 'science' of expertise. There are important links between the cultural media, social policy and emerging science. New discourses of 'storm and stress', or the scientification of adolescence, led by G. Stanley Hall, drew upon prevailing cultural ideas of the emotional and character-based education of boys. Increasing intervention of the State in domestic affairs was consistent with the idea of the family as the basic unit of the nation, its guidance being critical to the proper development of the nation's citizenry.

These central arguments are developed through the pursuit of the following questions. First, what part did education (outside of school) play in the cultural formation of (manly) men from boys? To what extent was there consensus on what being 'manly' meant? Was there also a concomitant consensus on appropriate emotions, both inwardly (inspiring action or abstinence) and outwardly (influencing conduct or demonstrating restraint)? It has been widely understood that manly ideals were generated from within the elite, and it is worth pursuing the question of whether, as Kelly Boyd has stated, these 'elite ideas [were] repackaged for a youthful audience', or whether manly ideals also flowed from the bottom up.[2] One of the major arguments of this book centres on the society-wide and pan-class consensus about what manliness meant, its ties to an emotional profile of restraint and the embodiment of morality, and about how these things should be taught to boys. Nevertheless, there is a question of the degree to which there were conflicting ideas on the informal education of boyhood. How did secular and religious tendencies differ in efforts to raise boys and change the attitudes of fathers? Further, what were the connections between working-class and middle-class attempts to train and educate boys and their fathers, and to what extent did they result from autonomous working-class movements? Similarly, it is important to draw out the connections among labour, temperance and education reformers and reforms for boys.

## Childhood, youth, adolescence

Current social scientists who study children are critical of their disciplines' past failure to recognize and encourage the possibility of child agency in child development. Though the question of agency itself is increasingly becoming problematized, the critique is valid:

> The child was regarded as 'becoming', rather than 'being', and it was the very materiality of childhood – the fact that children do grow into adults, physically, psychologically and socially – which permitted childhood socialisation to be conceived of as 'the way to give the desired shape and order to future adults and to future society'.[3]

But if twentieth-century childhood expertise has been criticized for employing 'a rather crude developmental understanding of "the child"', it might derive further criticism for having arisen largely before and independent of the discipline of psychology.[4] *Juvenile Nation* situates the enormous growth of professionals concerned with childhood development, and the principal idea that the child could be 'socialized', as having arisen from firmly within traditional discourses of Christian moral teaching. Childhood was thought to be malleable, and left to nature the shape might take on immoral, Godless proportions; hence the concerted effort to shape the child, to nurture character, duty, patriotism, piety. This was not about simply imposing the will of adults and experts from the top down, but an attempt to engage the child and, through the process of reflection in his/her own reading, to have the child become a direct (if limited) agent in his/her own moral development. An additional element in this scheme, and one that *Juvenile Nation* discusses at length, was the possibility of the child exemplar. Far from removing all agency from the child, these reformers forecast that the child exemplar, pure of heart and noble of spirit, could shape not only his child peers, but also the adults in his life. Only in the translation of decades of informal education into 'professional' child psychology and child welfarism did the idea of the child exemplar and child agency get lost.

Inspired by Ellen Key, juvenile advocates believed the twentieth century to be the century of the child.[5] Throughout our period childhood (and later, adolescence) were ideally distinct times of life, free from adult responsibilities during which young people were to cultivate knowledge, abilities and moral understanding for their future adult lives. This was a popular echo of philosophical ideas, in large part Rousseauian, about the nature of the child and his/her unique and desirable qualities. This fin-de-siècle preoccupation with childhood and its protection also had more pragmatic foundations. Britain was concerned about the encroachment of European rivals and sought to maintain its pre-eminence as much (if not more) through its future adult population than through its current one. An educated future workforce would ensure Britain's economic position vis-à-vis its competitors; a healthy population would combat fears of racial decline. New attention was paid to children of both sexes, and all social classes. Girls, primarily seen as future mothers, were to be physically healthy and morally equipped to take on their future roles of raising young Britons and of taking care of their physical, educational and spiritual needs. While a broad definition of citizenship embraced female Britons as moral guides and educators of 'Britishness', a more narrow definition only really focused on males. Boys were of the utmost concern as, unlike girls, they were to be Britain's future citizens, leaders, workers and heads of families. Attention was paid to boys of all social classes for whom it was necessary to instil the correct kind of conduct and values, perhaps already absent from men of their fathers' generation.

The years between around 1880 and the beginning of the First World War were a period of enormous change in Britain. The fin de siècle saw a growing awareness of the challenges that Britain had failed to meet: in the 1880s the extent of poverty was revealed, and political reform had failed to heal the rifts among different parts of society. Worries over recruitment during the South African War (1899–1902) led to fears of degeneracy, a flirtation with eugenics and the establishment of organizations (the Boy Scouts being the best known), in order to create a more virile population and thus a stronger country.[6] In the years immediately before the war this flirtation intensified into a perceived imperative as labour activism, Irish protest and suffragette militancy threatened major social upheaval, exacerbated by aristocratic inflexibility.

Many factors promoted this increased interest in boyhood and the new, age-specific strategies designed to address it. These came from manifold origins on the local, national and international levels. The coming of adult male democracy in 1885 and the politics of class interest created a growing concern that Britain's male citizens be educated to exercise their vote with diligence. Furthermore, the spread of industrial and technological modernization in Britain required an increasingly trained workforce. From the 1870s onward, and with accelerating speed, the spread of these modernizations beyond Britain fostered the rise of pressures for 'national efficiency' and market consolidation within Britain.[7] There was also a worry about the rise of juvenile delinquency that had emerged in the Victorian era, but had not subsided by the turn of the century when the paucity of jobs for boys became a topic of debate. M. J. D. Roberts argues that in later nineteenth-century culture there was a 'decay of assumptions about the capacity of individuals to "master their own destiny" by exercise of "character".[8] Though perhaps there was less belief in the power of the Smilesian good character and self-improvement in the formation of successful men than hitherto, this rhetoric continued to be widely used in publications for boys that addressed the 'modern' concerns enumerated earlier. Boys were the hope of the nation and much interest was focused on them, their development and their reading.

The broad period of the fin de siècle (1880–1914) shares defining and distinctive characteristics about ideas concerning boyhood and methods to address the 'problem' of boyhood. Many of the problems and concerns about boys contained within the periodicals studied here were certainly not novel, nor was their discussion new at this time. The Rev. J. Tunnicliff, founder of the Band of Hope movement, wrote as early as 1865 that 'The boy is father of the man. And what you are while young, if you persevere in that way, you are likely enough to be all through your life.'[9] This sort of statement could have been made decades earlier or later. Yet this study marks change as well as continuity. At the beginning of the period, a great boom in publishing for boys started, in a market that continually changed to appeal to, and also to shape, its readership.

By the end of the century, adolescence was also carved out as a distinct, and dangerous, stage in the lifecycle and the British boy, no matter his social class, became the focus of intense attention.[10] His behaviour, his education, and particularly his bad habits and the temptations he faced, aroused concern and seemed to demand active intervention at parental, institutional and governmental levels. Many organizations, both religious and secular, were especially concerned with juvenile drinking, smoking, masturbation and other bodily vices, and they made vigorous appeals against them.[11] Despite a lack of exact knowledge of its nature, duration or causes, many attempted to solve the 'problem' of adolescence. Its deleterious effects, if left unchecked, seemed certain, obvious and odious. The loss of boys to the wrong path in their process of emerging as men threatened the national body and contributed to contemporary fears of national and imperial decline.[12] These campaigns led to a profusion of literature for boys, and to successful movements for social and legislative reform. 'Experts' agreed that it was far better to prevent boys from becoming delinquent in the first place than to resort to punitive or controlling measures.

The periodical press may have 'sought to constitute the adolescent as a cultural phenomenon', but in doing so they also sought to alleviate his difficulties.[13] The solution to the problems of adolescence, according to contemporary thinking, could be found in appropriately constructed reading matter. The moral training of youth would thereby take care of itself, as if naturally. This would compensate for the shortfalls of formal education. Writers in the 1880s complained that even boys with the best public-school education knew nothing that would aid them in the professions or in the 'business of life':

> Thus at the age of seventeen – and often, indeed, at eighteen – the young man has to be sent to some cramming establishment, where the special knowledge which is necessary to enable him to enter upon active life is packed into his brain in such a manner, and under such conditions, as that in less than a year it is found to have all oozed out, and left the brain in a state of confusion – if not of absolute disease.[14]

If school could not lock in 'special knowledge', it was widely assumed that informal methods could.

## Informal education

The establishment of compulsory, universal education is an important result of the desire to shelter modern childhood from the world of adults, with several Education Acts in Britain from 1870 leading to this goal. The history of education, however, does not belong only to formal settings such as schools. There is, in addition, a history of children being taught informally, through the work of organizations and youth groups, through reading material designed for the purpose, and through the everyday interactions of children with each other and with their parents and other authority figures. These informal influences are at least as important as formal channels of education for our understanding of the history of education, but have been significantly underdeveloped in the historiography. They are perhaps even more important in the context of the Raj, where a system of universal schooling was never established. Many nineteenth-century educators and moralists believed that informal education had a far greater reach, and was far more efficient and effective, than formal education. It at least served to fill important gaps where schooling was found to be lacking, particularly in emotional and moral education.

Roland Barthes famously noted that educational practices can be classified and compartmentalized into three broad categories: *teaching*, *apprenticeship* and *mothering*. To Barthes, these were distinct forms of knowledge transmission. Informal education, however, encompasses all three of these practices: knowledge is transmitted 'by oral and written discourse' (like *teaching*), it is can be introduced through *praxis* (like the *apprenticeship*) and, equally, it can be taught through nurturing (like *mothering*, and I would also add *fathering*).[15] Informal education can in fact take many forms.[16] At its broadest, it could be defined as anything that serves to educate outside of a formal school setting. This could be through a vast and systematic network administered by large religious or social authorities, or it could be as minute as a gesture or a look to tell a child that his/her behaviour does not conform to the norm. Education in informal contexts often lacks a framework of rigorous disciplinary codes and punitive consequences, unlike much formal education.

All educational systems are expressions of power, the most overt expression of which is the State's enforcement of mandatory schooling. Informal education also expressed power relations, but in more subtle forms. Children were ushered into youth groups by their parents and peers, but also often found informal educational avenues themselves. The power of informal education in this regard was to serve to fill the gaps left by the formal educational curriculum, providing the lessons (religious or alternative) that the formal system would not provide, while appealing to wholesome pleasures and 'positive' emotions like joy. This book probes further by asking how informal education was conceptualized and put into practice. It suggests a holistic approach to childhood experience for historians of education, incorporating analyses of children's literature (especially children's magazines and periodicals) and of extracurricular institutions and practices established respectively to take care of children's welfare, morality, religious adherence and spirituality, and bodily health and fitness. Specifically, it connects informal education to enculturation and the acquisition of the 'correct' emotional toolbox. It argues that if historians of education wish to understand where values come from, how children were emotionally and morally educated, then they need to shift their critical gaze also to include informal channels of learning.

The tenor of this informal education stressed the positive actions of sobriety as well as the negative action of staying away from bad influences. Crucially, both hinged on the 'right' kinds of emotions, of being 'Unselfish, true and tender' and of mustering up the 'right' emotions at the 'right' times, delaying false happiness for future 'real', domesticated, happiness.[17] An appreciation of the joys of home life was especially important. Informal moral education was not just about correct emotional exploration, but also about teaching boys emotional control. This last lesson was particularly emphasized in warning against intemperance and sexual exploration.[18]

Morality, patriotism and good conduct were key goals of the state education system.[19] The same was true for the British public-school boy, about whom much has already been written. The distinguishing feature of elite education was its tailoring to cater for an elite group – the cultivation of leaders, esprit de corps, and empire builders and safeguarders. So much is well known.[20] Nathan Roberts has suggested that both elite and mass education emphasized 'the construction of an environment in which young citizens were guided towards the achievement of character through indirect, though pervasive, disciplinary influences'.[21] The principal goal, through a discourse of character, was to transform pupils 'into citizens of their community and nation'.[22] We shall see that the informal education in the publications studied throughout this book complemented these goals. The correction of juvenile vices, seen to be more tempting and more dangerous in modern, urban times, became a focus of the informal education provided by the periodical press for boys and their families, plugging potential gaps left by schools and homes at all social levels.

A network of important and influential youth-minded groups held enormous sway in the periodical market. The evangelical Religious Tract Society (RTS), the reform-focused Church of England Temperance Society (CETS) and the Band of Hope are all major focuses here. They increasingly attacked the dominant view of secular, muscular and imperial masculinity which emerged at the turn of the century, stressing instead the continuing importance of the role of the father in the home. An equal focus lies upon the seemingly opposite force of secular educational publications for boys. It will discuss Alfred Harmsworth's (1865–1922)[23] endeavours to address the perceived new secular and educational needs of boys in his AP publications and his often similar constructions of masculinity and the importance of family and home. Surprisingly little work has been done on the AP's boys' papers, while a scholarly focus on the sensational serial story has given the impression that the moral messages contained within the papers (especially in the editorial sections) were insignificant or even disingenuous. Yet within the context of the AP's own declaration of an 'adherence to the policy of doing all in its power in all its publications to build up the security and stability of family, home and Empire', its boys' papers reveal much about the consensus of opinion in the juvenile publishing market.[24] In the period from the 1890s to the First World War, the AP dominated in the publishing industry for boys. Harmsworth's constructions of masculinity were not so secular, muscular and imperially directed as they have been characterized to be, and in fact they were similar in message (at least in the editorial sections) to the periodicals of the major religious organizations.

The content of the periodicals, although largely comprised of serial stories, was not entirely fictional: it was a product of wider societal preoccupations and change. Their advice was often placed in the broader framework of a moral nation, constituted of pious, domesticated and loyal male subjects. This concept was encapsulated in the notion of the 'Briton', a trope commonly used to denote the characteristics required of the male citizens of a self-styled great nation. But it was more significant in instructing boys in 'proper' emotional responses and in their behaviour at home, within their families, in school and at work. The popular periodical was thought to be crucially formative in this regard, and the imperative of disseminating the 'right' message was summed up by George Orwell, in a passage on the boys' weeklies, written as late as 1940. The 'worst books', he said, 'are often the most important' because they are 'read earliest in life':

> It is probable that many people who would consider themselves extremely sophisticated and 'advanced' are actually carrying through life an imaginative background which they acquired in childhood. . . . If that is so, the boys' twopenny weeklies are of the deepest importance. Here is the stuff that is read somewhere between the ages of twelve and eighteen by a very large proportion, perhaps an actual majority, of English boys, including many who will never read anything else except newspapers. . . . All the better because it is done indirectly.[25]

Indeed, according to Claudia Nelson, late Victorian editors envisioned 'the child consumer as a powerful agent requiring cajoling rather than homilies. An excessively authoritarian text, like an excessively authoritarian parent, would prove counterproductive. Rather, boy and text are constructed almost as equals; they change each other . . . in mutually beneficial ways.'[26] It is clear that for the most part, however, the publications had conservative messages for their young readers to internalize, often evangelical or temperance, or both. This was certainly not the avant-garde of publishing in the late nineteenth century. Yet the editors and writers of these publications did respond to more modern ideas about families, gender relations and new opportunities for women. The reaction was not universally negative. It is also important to note that conservative elements in the late nineteenth-century British press were not simply repeating stale messages from earlier decades: they adapted their publications to current realities, while reinforcing traditional gender roles (albeit with some important modifications). This is visible both in their non-fictional and fictional accounts.

Many British men and women were enculturated (in part by the publications considered here) at an early age to understand their roles as adults as centred upon family life: first that of their parents, and later on their own. In this context it is easier to understand the content of publications for boys. While these contained little direct discussion of family life, they contained many lessons that would be useful to boys in their future roles as husbands and fathers. These lessons were both practical and moral, involving their relations with men and women and, of course, with God. Similarly, teachers and conductors within youth movements like the influential Band of Hope were, men and women alike, encouraged to nurture childhood emotions. For female temperance workers, their 'real and tender love for little children' might seem stereotypical, but such phrases were not meant to exclude male tenderness to the same degree. One male temperance teacher solemnly declared: 'I love the children. I want everybody to love them, and I want them to prove their love by watching over them with a more than parental regard.'[27]

Callum Brown makes an important observation with regard to juvenile literature and masculinity, remarking on what he calls 'the evangelical code'. 'It was this code', he said, 'that established the appetite for the literary boom of the late nineteenth and early twentieth centuries which almost universally used that code, providing Britons with the primary format in which they learned, explored and negotiated their own individual life destinies.' The kind of stories to which he refers were the crucial element in juvenile constructions of their own idealized lives. They were central in the construction of a 'conception of religiosity' in young people and served as a 'guide to behaviour'.[28] Militarized youth movements which epitomized muscular Christianity were, as far as Brown is concerned, 'not changes to masculinity as such, but rather "sub-discursive" struggles going on in the shadow of an overarching opposition between the conceptions of piety and masculinity'.[29] This book focuses on non-military movements like the Band of Hope, and in particular on the literature that drove them, sweeping boys along in great numbers. It aims to reconnect piety and masculinity and to show this connection in the positive light in which it was generally seen, and preached, in fin-de-siècle Britain.

## Emotions, character, morality and manliness

The notion that there is an emotional basis to morality – that the knowledge of the right thing to do and when to do it occurs in the body as a feeling – was more prevalent in the eighteenth and nineteenth centuries than it is now, although the principle retains influential adherents.[30] Although there have been differences over the centuries concerning how the emotional basis of morality worked, at the core of the idea is a fairly continuous understanding of sympathy – be it God-given or evolved – that distinguishes human civilizations from one another and from other animals.[31] Charles Darwin and Adam Smith ultimately shared a view of sympathy, placing it at the centre of moral life. Sympathy – there by nature – effectively encapsulated the Golden Rule. Likewise for both, where sympathy was corrupted – and both knew that it could be – the Golden Rule, and thus civilization, were placed under threat.[32]

If sympathy and all the other benevolent emotions and virtues were correctly instilled, an individual could be said, in Victorian parlance, to have 'character'.[33] The term indicated a composite of sound emotional adjustment and a well-orientated moral compass – not just knowledge of what to do, but the fibre to do it. This was the intellectual background into which informal educators approached the moral education of the child.

In an 1880 article in the *Fortnightly Review*, Frances Power Cobbe – Unitarian and social activist – encapsulated this Victorian preoccupation with the training of character. Under the title, 'The Education of the Emotions', Cobbe wrote of the dangers and benefits of emotional contagion. Basic sympathy among men rendered them open to the emotions of other men. What society looked like, what it felt like, depended very much on the kind of contagion going on. While fear was said to spread 'through whole armies with such inexplicable celerity', in more mundane affairs the 'contagion of sentiments' often spread 'from one individual of a family or village to all the other members or inhabitants'.[34] In such lay the foundation of mutual happiness and coexistence, as well as the rise of prejudice and bigotry: 'Even the strongest wills are bent and warped by the winds of other men's passions'.[35] Although a great deal seemed to hang on whether emotions were good or bad, it was hopeless, so Cobbe thought, to try to impose an emotional regime. Since sympathy was the inescapable source of contagion, 'We must *give* the feeling we desire. We cannot possibly *impose* it'.[36] So began Cobbe's programme for the education of the emotions, which involved not only 'giving' those emotions that were desired, but also the holding back – control or suppression – of those that were not: '[P]arents duly impressed with the importance of the subject would carefully suppress, or at least conceal, such of their emotions as they would regret to see caught up by their children'.[37]

Cobbe's article, with its explicit foregrounding of the language of emotional management, summed up the programme of informal education being taken up by the juvenile periodical press and the raft of youth organizations detailed in this book. In many ways she also forecast the language of early twentieth-century child psychologists:

> Every good father desires his son to respect his mother. . . . Yet how do scores of such well-meaning men set about conveying the sentiment of reverence which they recognise will be invaluable to their sons? They treat those same mothers, in the presence of those same sons, with such rudeness, dismiss their opinions with such levity, and, perhaps, exhibit such actual contempt for their wishes, that it is not in nature but that the boy will receive a lesson of disrespect. His father's feelings . . . can scarcely fail to impress the young mind with that contempt for women . . ., which is precisely the reverse of chivalry and filial piety.[38]

Cobbe extended the warning to include the potentially malignant influence – the 'moral poison' – of ill-charactered teachers, whose words would steer 'the young men and women who are the hope of the nation'.[39] Cobbe was clear on the threat. It was not 'opinion' that put children at risk, but 'the contagion of his emotions'.

The important elision being made here, not untypically, as this book will bear out, is that of emotions and morals. A salubrious emotional atmosphere led to moral character: right-feeling boys would also be right-acting. An atmosphere filed with anger, contempt, lust and hate would lead to 'moral corruption'.[40] It was not sufficient, for the late Victorian moralist, to *do* good. One had to *be* good. *Being*, it seems, began with the emotional disposition. Thus, due to the 'high-minded Masters' of great public schools, the alumni thereof 'will despise lying and cowardice and admire fair play and justice'. So much could be 'taken for granted' and celebrated as a 'grand . . . foundation for national character'.[41] Those left to the vagaries of life's baser influences were in moral peril. Cobbe knew, just as the generation of informal educators of children knew, that literature held the key. If it were good, literature could 'awaken the most vivid feelings', promoting the 'contagion of piety, patriotism, enthusiasm for justice and truth, and sympathy with other nations and other classes'. If bad, however, it could 'light up baleful fires, of the basest and most sensual'.[42] Cobbe took aim at Zola; the rest of her generation set their sights firmly on the penny dreadful.

The moral life was not seen as an end in itself, even, perhaps surprisingly, for religious youth leaders. Rather, moral education was viewed as an emotional upbringing and maturation, in which boys would discover true fulfilment, happiness and pride in doing their duty towards their families, communities and the nation. 'Manliness' was the umbrella concept which described this emotional maturation. Negative moral exhortation, shame, guilt and fear, so effectively deployed in earlier generations among British evangelicals (their cultural legacy extending far beyond those who shared their faith) had transformed into something radically different. Positive emotional appeals now predominated: future happiness and respect in manhood would be attained through sacrifice and abstinence in boyhood. This was a black-and-white emotional choice – future happiness/sadness – replete with moral guidance associated with the dichotomy.

The conceptual closeness of morality, character and manliness has been historiographically underappreciated. Character is now seen as an essential cultural concept for understanding the late Victorian and Edwardian periods,[43] but manliness is too often dismissed as a quality only understood in elite athletic or imperial terms.[44] According to Michael Roper, in mid-twentieth-century memoirs of public schooling, men were increasingly viewed as 'the emotional victims of a training in manliness'.[45] Yet historians of masculinities have pushed manliness aside as an analytical concept.[46] John Tosh reduced manliness, by and large, to a distinctly limited category referring to the character of mind, not to masculinity related to the body, nor to masculinity related to sex.[47] But if, as he points out, this 'dominant code of Victorian manliness' chiefly emphasized 'self-control, hard work and independence', then the category is reanimated for the historian of the emotions.[48]

As an ideal way of conceptualizing men and their place in society, manliness predominated in this period, which began in 1879 with Thomas Hughes' vigorous defence of manliness precisely in Christian, character-based, emotional and moral terms. 'The conscience of every man', Hughes wrote, 'recognizes courage as the foundation of manliness, and manliness as the perfection of human character'. If the absolutism of this statement was at all at odds with Christianity, Hughes opined, then 'Christianity will go to the wall'. But Hughes could find no contradiction between manliness and Christianity because the 'perfection of character' was 'reached by moral effort in the faithful following of our Lord's life on earth'. The 'necessary condition of that moral effort' was the 'constant contact and conflict with evil'. The full explication of Hughes' reasoning was designed, fittingly, as a course of 'Sunday readings'.[49]

Sarah Williams has found echoes of these sentiments in the popular beliefs of working-class lives, which stressed the importance of 'teachings in Christianity' for the 'formation of individual character'.[50] Following this impetus, *Juvenile Nation* presents a complex account of manliness, demonstrating its multiclass distribution, its allusions to the physical *and* moral states of incipient men, and the emotional component of a 'training in manliness' for boys beyond the public school.[51] In particular, the book reveals that there is nothing 'inevitable' about studies of manliness privileging the elite.[52] I agree with Nathan Roberts in his revision of this interpretation, demonstrating that the cultivation of character reached far beyond the elite culture.[53] Rather it was seen as a goal for *all* young Britons to be 'instilled with those qualities of citizenship that would guarantee the vitality and efficiency of the social organism'.[54] This statement, if pushed, has important implications for the study of manliness in this era. Indeed, it seems to have lost little of its relevance, even for today's youth.

*Juvenile Nation* argues that character and manliness were codes for a certain set of accepted emotions and emotional norms. In sum, they were the building blocks of morality, which was to come from an inner feeling of right and wrong, rather than from an external or penal imposition. This is therefore a history of the (informal) education of emotions and emotional responses. This nuances William Reddy's idea of 'emotional regimes'.[55] Emotional regimes (if we want to call them that) are not just those of the nation-state. Religious entities or maybe even lifecycle groupings (like youth or adolescents) can operate in a similar way, determining for their members appropriate emotional reactions through informal education. Furthermore, emotional communities are not only social communities, as Barbara Rosenwein maintains, but they are also communities of shared interests and goals (even though they might not share many social characteristics in common).[56] The role of moral education is crucial. Through this education, children were meant to carve out their individuality. For the groups described here, this was not believed to be ready-made at birth but rather was to be cultivated so that boys would in time discover that it was in their interests to feel and consequently to behave in certain ways that conformed to the standards of the 'community'. The book reveals the extent to which character formation (or reformation) was thought to be the key to success on the individual and societal levels, producing productive and responsible citizens.

The extent of male piety could best be judged in the familial context. Popular religious journals with strong moral messages were not directly at men only; models of male piety were only to be found in magazines for families or for children. According to Callum Brown, these were 'truly exploratory of male religiosity, for it was in men's relations to the family that the key to issues of their piety and impiety lay'.[57] In the case of the family magazine, its form of multiple readership promoted men's piety in a familial context. Its form, therefore, was as important in promoting moral values as its content.

For evangelicals, an important part of male identity was piety and proper religious adherence. The RTS, for example, thus saw one of its roles to be the education of boys to be the future moral and spiritual leaders of their families. The temperance movement also placed great emphasis on reaching boys while they were still young enough to adhere to the lessons taught within its periodicals and before they developed bad habits, which were said to be falsely regarded by boys as making them 'manly'. It was important for these papers to teach boys and their families of all classes their version of 'manliness', one based on familial responsibility and piety. This was in no way a certain goal in an age where many men were feared to be increasingly neglecting their duties towards their families.

## Fatherhood, home and family

Scholars generally describe mothers as the most powerful guides to piety and to morality.[58] Fathers, by contrast, have been given secondary roles at best, after the high point in male domesticity in the 1840s.[59] As Judith Rowbotham states, 'the nineteenth century invented the tradition that it was the women who were the "natural" guardians of morality and standards, and the teachers of these to the next generation.'[60] This was based on a rather unbending understanding of the idea of separate spheres for men and women. Martin Francis provides a more complex assessment:

> [T]he nineteenth-century cult of motherhood invested moral authority in the female, untainted as she was by sexual desire and the beastliness of public life. As women usurped the moral and religious instruction of children, men now foregrounded practical education, sharing with (especially male) children their thoughts on business or politics. In a significant linguistic displacement, fathers' responsibility for their children was recorded as 'influence' instead of authority.[61]

Tosh provides a revised image of the Victorian father, showing that 'the nineteenth century witnessed both the climax of masculine domesticity and the first major reaction against it.'[62] He acknowledges that a substantial number of fathers followed the dictates of male domesticity, but he maintains that the late Victorian period, marked by contested masculinities in social, economic and sexual arenas, triggered in many men at least a temporary 'flight from domesticity'.[63] By stressing the 'flight from domesticity' at the end of the nineteenth century, Tosh largely neglects the significant emphasis on domesticated masculinity during this period, as exemplified by Frances Power Cobbe, who did not:

> hesitate to affirm that all that is best and soundest in public opinion in England is derived, first, from the private opinion of English firesides. It is the fathers who teach, the mothers who inspire, those sentiments and judgments on moral questions which their children in later years (perhaps, after some revolt and oscillation), as a rule adopt and formulate as their own convictions.

As a consequence, Cobbe wrote, 'the great Public Opinion of England is broadly moral, honourable, and religious, and stands out, in these respects, above that of the other countries of Europe.'[64]

As *Juvenile Nation* shows, RTS, CETS and Band of Hope publications for boys and for families reveal Christian efforts to counter the 'subversive' influences of the late nineteenth and early twentieth centuries: sexuality and feminism, secularization, worldliness and pleasure seeking. RTS publications displayed three linked types of fatherhood, a new trinity: the heavenly, the earthly and the surrogate father, a powerful prescriptive weapon in maintaining religious adherence and societal and familial continuity. In contrast, Harmsworth's publications embraced a new Edwardian reality, and yet still saw fathers as central to the family and boys as future fathers. For Harmsworth, the RTS, the CETS and the Band of Hope, the formation of masculinity for working and middle-class boys was intended to develop them as independent, self-sufficient, physically strong and sober men. This also included the ability to manifest and strengthen traditional Christian values.[65] Fathers passed on their notions of manhood to their sons, in ways which obliged them, more or less, consciously to accept or reject these parental prescriptions. Fathers themselves were products of their boyhood environment and contemporary discourse, and boys' literature had a part to play in instilling these masculine and fatherly characteristics.

This should lead us to rethink women's roles in relation to men and masculinity in the domestic sphere. Sean Gill's entreaty that 'we need to go beyond the oversimplified generalizations implied by such labels as "The Angel in the House" or "Muscular Christianity" as if they represent a straightforward mirroring of Victorian Christian understandings of gender', is critical.[66] It is important to see them as part of a complex and often contradictory pattern of cultural discourse. The focus on women's centrality in the home has made difficult a nuanced understanding of men and of women. Robert Roberts, in his autobiography of working-class Salford, serves a reminder of the importance of male domesticity as a desired ideal in the Edwardian period:

> Home, however poor, was the focus of all his love and interests, a sure fortress against a hostile world. Songs about its beauties were ever on people's lips. 'Home, sweet home,' first heard in the 1870's, had become 'almost a second national anthem.' Few walls in lower-working-class houses lacked 'mottos' – coloured strips of paper, about nine inches wide and eighteen inches in length, attesting to domestic joys: EAST, WEST, HOME'S BEST; BLESS OUR HOME; GOD IS THE MASTER OF THIS HOUSE (although Father made an able deputy); HOME IS THE NEST WHERE ALL IS BEST.[67]

This was not only true of the slum child, but was a prevalent theme throughout popular sources for boys and for families of all classes. This reflected a continued cultural theme of home and ideals of boyhood conduct, which, as Roberts' example shows, were often tinged with nominally religious messages. These themes in popular fictional and non-fictional literature, as this book documents, had far greater significance than simply conveying a cosy ideal of domesticity. They also had substantial national import. As Stephen Heathorn has noted in the context of formal education for working-class children in this period, 'the home was held to be not merely an oasis from the pressures of the public realm', but was central to the cultivation of a feeling of national belonging and citizenship.[68]

## Nation, empire, citizenship

It has been asserted by some that 'modern conceptions of childhood' signalled the exclusion of children 'from full community membership as citizens'. James and James have claimed that 'the apparent benevolence of . . . 19th century reforms and the establishment of children's rights to welfare and educational provision can be shown to have worked, ironically, to disable and disenfranchise children as citizens.'[69] This is in part based on a reading of T. H. Marshall's tripartite definition of citizenship in 1950, where civil citizenship pertained to the rights of free speech, justice, personal freedom; where political citizenship centred primarily on the franchise; and where social citizenship encompassed 'access to welfare and education', but also the 'duties and obligations an individual has to society' in return for such.[70]

James and James, agreeing with Marshall, assert that children were subjected to 'a very particular kind of age-based social exclusion.'[71] There were 'citizens *in potentia* only'.[72] The problem with such a view is that the attempt to categorize and differentiate these types of citizenship only took place in the middle of the twentieth century, from the vantage point of universal suffrage and the welfare state as reality. In the nineteenth century, official definitions of citizenship had been tied to (limited) enfranchisement, but the discursive concept of citizenship remained mutable and messy, open to claimants and liable to exclusions, according to the dynamics of civil life. There was certainly citizenship beyond the vote. Insofar as the qualifications for it can be nailed down at all, this book argues that it began at home, in the family and with fatherhood especially. The multivalence of citizenship also structures the imperial framework of the book, by examining to what extent colonial boys and their identities were shaped by imperial concerns. Beyond the capacity to vote lay a notion of citizenship that encompassed an idealized set of moral and emotional qualities that were dispensed, in the first instance, through parents. Moreover, it laid the emphasis on the individual's duties and responsibilities to family, nation and empire, rather than on the State's responsibilities to ensure an individual's 'rights'.

This casts the nineteenth-century child reforms in a different light, for if by 1950 Marshall could see the child as citizen in potentia, this would have satisfied most of the reformers and campaigners discussed in this book. They were activated by a fear that, left unnurtured, the child would fail to be a worthy citizen as an adult. This fear had arisen from a sense of previous failure, in the midst, to late Victorian eyes, of the clear signs of degeneracy and immorality among parents, inveterate and hereditary intemperance among fathers and boys especially. The whole end of the widespread consensus to 'train the child, save the man' was to influence not so much what children were as children, but rather what they would become as adults, as citizens.

In a period where most men had the vote, informal education had, ultimately, to have citizenship as its end.[73] As Stephen Heathorn has noted, 'the good "citizen" was presumed to be male, and in large part "good citizenship" was the civic code of an approved form of masculinity.'[74] Derek Heater, conjuring with T. H. Green and Arnold Toynbee, concurs, pointing out the centrality of character – the living of a 'cultivated, considerate human life' – and religion – since 'there must also be something of the spiritual in this character' – to citizenship.[75] To examine the historical forces at work in connecting these notions of masculinity, civic code and good citizen – the process of enculturating young men to recognize the 'natural' affinity of this grouping – is one of this book's overarching aims. Training in boyhood was clearly also associated with citizenship, in addition to, but also through the ideals of individual character and morality. As Nathan Roberts has observed about formal education in this era, 'If a child was to grow into a useful citizen, his will had to be "fashioned" or he would become "vacillating, untrustworthy, and ineffective": the negative image of the ideal liberal subject."[76] The recognition of boyhood and youth as distinct categories from manhood necessitated a moral education specific to boys. To that end, disparate groups tended to agree on the importance of disseminating Christian values for the task of raising the nation's boys into manly, domesticated men and good fathers. As *Juvenile Nation* shows, components of this consensus included positive exhortations related to morality, good conduct, politeness, religiosity and respect for family; and negative prohibitions regarding bad conduct and perceived vices such as drinking, smoking, gambling, masturbation and too-early romantic attachments (to perhaps put it euphemistically). And this was delivered in a package designed to appeal to an emotional understanding of right and wrong, while at the same time ensuring that such an emotional understanding was positively instilled.

Children, and especially, boys, were the incipient citizenry of a future Britain in a time preoccupied by worries about efficiency and racial decline. These were not merely concerns about the physical health of Britons, although popular fears of national degeneracy were indicated by the rise of eugenic ideas and figured prominently. Crucially they were also concerned with the moral welfare of the population. This placed a powerful emphasis on children as the 'hope of the race'. The purity of childhood served as an example to an unfit adult citizenry, whose shortcomings were both physical and moral. Raising boys incorrectly was dangerous to the family, nation and the nation's imperial projects, when these boys became men. This message was exported to various colonial settings, where it was adapted and either actively embraced or rejected. Arguably, the urgency of the moral and emotional education was greater in potentially unstable colonies like India.

Contemporary concerns and perplexity regarding youth, especially in times of crisis, are certainly not new. Late nineteenth-century reformers, policy makers and parents also had many questions to ask about youth behaviour and feelings; but they thought they had concrete answers to provide, based on a shared understanding of morality and masculinity. Though they might not have been any more successful in shaping youth to their mould, especially those who resisted that shaping, they nevertheless developed a working consensus on what form this informal education should take, and on its emotional value and weight.

# 1

# Stakeholders of Youth

Children and youth are obviously the most important stakeholders in their own lives, yet their voices are notoriously difficult to hear. Adults concerned with these groups, and their interventions on their behalf, are much more present in the historical record.[1] Yet children's own agency can sometimes be detected in their choice whether or not to buy a paper or to attend a youth group. That youth workers of various stripes believed in the power of children's agency is also apparent in their attempts to appeal to them directly, in ways that were subtly adapted over the years to address them effectively, and affectively, in order to make 'positive' changes in their own lives and to influence their families and peers.

As childhood increasingly became isolated from the rest of the lifecycle, with its special expectations and occupations, adults became more preoccupied with children and youth who did not fit into the mould of what childhood should be. Increasing numbers of youth experts and groups intervened in this 'problem', in an effort to make their concept of childhood universal (though class specific).[2]

## The juvenile publishing industry

According to M. J. D. Roberts, in the 1870s the moral status of self-denial in middle-class culture began to be questioned. This encouraged religious and voluntary leaders to reconsider their ways of functioning.[3] One result was the increased attention by diversely motivated groups on juvenile publishing. In addition, advances in printing technology, railway distribution, the penny post, the repeal of 'taxes on knowledge' and increased government spending all had a material impact on the great profusion of newspapers and periodicals in the second half of the nineteenth century.[4] With the market expanded by increased literacy after the 1870 Education Act, in the early 1880s, over 900 new juvenile books were issued annually and 15 secular boys' periodicals competed for boys' attention.[5] There was a boom in the number of juvenile periodicals beginning at the end of the 1870s. Patrick Dunae estimates that there were only 59 such periodicals in 1874 (none was recorded in 1863). Numbers increased substantially to 100 in 1884 and continued to accelerate to 218 in 1910.[6] John Springhall notes that 'Fortunes were certainly made and lost by London's publishers of cheap juvenile fiction, suggesting the scale and significance of a business catering specifically to the popular end of the juvenile market.'[7] Products of this business atmosphere, all of the papers discussed in this book were backed by major publishers, to whom we will now turn.

## The Religious Tract Society[8]

The RTS was a product of the Evangelical Revival that had begun in the mid-eighteenth century. Evangelicalism was a social as well as a religious movement, concerned with ensuring 'real' rather than formal Christianity through individual conversion. Like the other major organizations of the evangelical movement, the RTS, a widespread non-denominational society throughout Britain and in missions around the world, was created to disseminate spiritually improving literature to an expanding audience of Christians and the 'unconverted'. The Society's founder, the Rev. George Burder of Coventry proposed the establishment of a non-sectarian society for the preparation and circulation of evangelical tract literature at the London Missionary Society Anniversary Meeting in 1799. To that end, the RTS committee was formed, consisting of 12 members, both clerical and lay. According to the RTS's own official history, published at the end of the nineteenth century, good tracts contained 'pure truth', 'some account of the way of a sinner's salvation', and plain, striking, entertaining and idea-driven content. They should be adapted to various situations and conditions, 'for the young and for the aged, for the children of prosperity and of affliction, for careless and for awakened sinners, and for entering into the reasonings, excuses, temptations, and duties of each, and pointing to the way of the Lord'.[9] In its first year, 1799–1800, the RTS sold 200,000 tracts, a number which rose to 800,000 in the Society's second year.[10] The RTS quickly expanded, publishing increasing numbers of books and periodicals, all with the same high moral tone.

Throughout the 1850s, several cheap religious periodicals were established in an attempt to benefit from the growing family-reading market for weeklies.[11]

So-called improving magazines, many of them published by the RTS, dominated this market.[12] At mid-century, the RTS began publishing two one-penny weeklies, the *Leisure Hour* (1852–1908) and the *Sunday at Home* (1854–1940), both edited for many years by James Macaulay, with his colleague and successor, W. Stevens. According to the Society's late nineteenth-century chronicler, Samuel G. Green, the most important step in the provision of popular literature was the introduction of the *Leisure Hour*, which aimed to treat all topics of human interest 'in the light of Christian truth'.[13] Both magazines sought to reach the widest audience possible, including most of the literate working classes. The magazines were also issued in monthly parts for five pence each. Along with these two periodicals, the Society began to publish cheap religious periodicals for the popular, family weekly market, although a distinction between weekly and Sunday reading was maintained.[14] These publications were cheaper than their biggest secular competitors for readership. At two pence, Charles Dickens' weekly, *All the Year Round*, was double the price of the RTS family publications.[15]

By 1850 Evangelical enthusiasm was less pronounced, but the cultural legacy of the movement remained powerful, particularly in the intertwining of Christian values and middle-class mores. Though magazines of the non-improving variety grew, particularly from 'the 1890s, the bulk of the domestic literature of the British family remained strongly evangelical in origin at least until the 1910s'.[16]

The *Leisure Hour*, and even more the *Sunday at Home*, reflected the much larger Sabbatarian movement, devoted to preserving Sunday as a day of rest and of religious observance. This movement was important for members of the RTS who wished to set aside Sunday as a day when fathers could abstain from work outside the home and spend time with their families, to combat the perception that fathers were increasingly becoming 'strangers' in the home. The RTS clearly targeted the family circle, as is indicated in its magazines' subtitles: the *Leisure Hour: A Family Journal of Instruction and Recreation*, and *Sunday at Home: The Illustrated Family Magazine for Sabbath Reading*. Both periodicals often led with fiction, and included at least one large illustration in each issue. As a Sabbath magazine, *Sunday at Home* was more sober in its presentation and contents than the weekly *Leisure Hour*, providing appropriate reading for all ages on the day of rest. This periodical was more overtly religious, but was still intended to be non-denominational.

Most aristocrats resisted militant Sabbatarianism, and many members of the working class could not strictly adhere to it. But for the middle classes, Sunday tended to be quiet, and at least an external observance of Sunday was regarded as a normal requirement of respectability.[17] By the 1880s, this was beginning to change. Gradually the taboos on Sunday recreation were being lifted.[18] Yet by providing entertaining family reading, the RTS encouraged men to remain at home on Sunday with their families, instead of the often morally dubious activities of pub-going or the increasingly popular homosocial environment of the club. The *Sunday at Home* continued to be published even as middle-class interest in Sabbatarianism waned, since RTS members wished to preserve Sunday as a day of rest and family time in which the father could be an active participant. According to one article in the *Sunday at Home*, 'There can be no doubt that there is a wave of unbelief and ungodliness passing over this country. According to reports from the clergy the Archdeacon declares that it is more difficult to get men to church on Sundays, in town and country.'[19] The remedy to increasing ungodliness was for fathers to lead family prayers every day.

Though historians like Callum Brown now see late nineteenth-century fears about secularization as exaggerated, it is clear that many Britons at the time were concerned about declines in religious adherence, especially in church attendance and piety, and the consequent effect on morality and on the family.[20] The RTS was a prime location for these kinds of concerns. In a history of the RTS published by its current incarnation, the Lutterworth Press, in 1949, author Gordon Hewitt described the challenge the RTS faced in the late nineteenth and early twentieth centuries:

> The secularization of English society which had begun in the closing decades of the nineteenth century became more marked in the early years of the twentieth. Church attendance fell away, Sunday Schools declined; the Christian religion was not openly repudiated or aggressively attacked, but it came to be commonly assumed that a man's religion was his own affair, and that he was a competent judge of it without making reference to the specialists and without making any practical experiments.[21]

This secular trend, though perhaps overestimated in significance, created serious problems for a society that had been founded primarily to promote Christian evangelism at home. As Hewitt concluded, 'The old tracts appealed to the Bible as an ultimate authority accepted alike by writer and reader, but acceptance on the reader's part could no longer be assumed.'[22] At the fin de siècle, because of these external societal pressures and increasing competition from 'secular' publishers, the RTS focused less on tracts (its former mainstay) and more on its periodicals for families and girls and boys. It also attracted children by giving away many prizes awarded for proficiency in Bible studies classes. As it realized that the acceptance of religious messages could no longer be taken for granted, the Society adapted the content of its periodicals to suit the tastes of a more 'modern' reading public.

The RTS claimed to have an enormous influence in this domain. In the autumn of 1900, for example, the society sold more than 100,000 copies of the annual volumes of its leading magazines. It was estimated that each of these actually exerted 'some influence upon the mental and spiritual development of from ten to fifteen readers', as the magazines were placed in libraries and reading-rooms, given away as presents or sold second-hand. Thus, the estimated readership was from a million to one-and-a-half million. 'And when it is born in mind', according to one *Sunday at Home* article, 'that the ultimate purpose of all this reading matter is not only to amuse and instruct, but, if possible, to benefit directly, both morally and spiritually, all who read its pages, the tremendous power of this agency becomes at once apparent.'[23] Sales income peaked in 1885 at over £180,000 a year.[24] Such a massive increase in sales was made possible by the new publishing programme, with its broader appeal particularly among the middle- and lower-middle classes with spending power. The high point of the programme was the launch of the *Boy's Own* and *Girl's Own Papers* in 1879 and 1880, which were voted the most popular periodicals among youth in 1888, and which greatly boosted sales income.[25] The *Boy's Own Paper* (*BOP*) provided evangelical messages of purity. It served as the antidote to other papers for boys and families. Even religious leaders admitted that the 'proper' message could be dull, dry and sanctimonious, noting that 'anything evangelical was rather flat-footed, and lacking richness and variety'.[26] In order to increase readership, religious papers were promoted as having interesting topics for boys that were pervaded by a Christian tone, rather than containing doctrinal religious teachings per se.

By the end of the 1870s, the RTS committee was convinced of the need to provide improving literature for both boys and girls. In the 1879 Report, the committee expressed the urgency of creating a periodical specifically directed at boys:

> The urgent need of such a periodical had been long and deeply felt. Juvenile crime was being largely stimulated by the pernicious literature circulated among our lads. Judges, magistrates, schoolmasters, prison chaplains, and others were deploring the existence of the evil, and calling loudly for a remedy, but none seemed to be forthcoming. The Committee, fully admitting the terrible necessity

of a publication which might to some extent supplant those of a mischievous tendency, yet hesitated to enter upon the task.[27]

The Society believed that it was outside its scope of operations to produce a paper that was not largely religious in its teachings, yet acknowledged that an overtly religious periodical would do little to challenge the profusion of 'penny dreadfuls' that emerged after the 1870 Education Act provided universal schooling.[28] 'It was thus forced upon the Committee to attempt an enterprise from which others shrank' and the first edition of the *BOP* – a 16 page and one-penny weekly – appeared in 1879.[29] Its founder and editor was G. A. Hutchison, who had an interest in the Sunday School movement and other juvenile educational activities; James Macaulay acted as supervising editor. According to the editors of the *BOP*, 'True religion, in their view, is a spirit pervading all life, in work or in play; and this conviction, rather than any purpose of direct doctrinal teaching, gives a tone to the Paper, which has already met with very wide and cordial acceptance.'[30] It was also important to demonstrate that the papers had the support and cooperation of authority figures like ministers, parents and schoolmasters. As part of an important evangelical organization, the goal of the *BOP*'s editors was to bring it to the attention of every boy in the land, of all classes. In return, they promised to employ the best writers and artists for the *BOP*'s content, 'and neither pains nor expense will be spared to render the BOP the most complete and attractive journal for lads ever produced'.[31] In its first two years, the *BOP* estimated a readership of 600,000. The RTS was printing over 500,000 weekly copies by the late 1880s. Patrick Dunae estimates that this actually indicates a readership of one-and-a-quarter million, as on average two to three boys read each copy. He points out that total circulation might have been even higher as the RTS later printed closer to 665,000 weekly copies.[32] In fact, the *BOP* had the largest circulation of any boys' paper, also surpassing many popular adult magazines and newspapers of the era.[33]

Most of the *BOP*'s competitors had been sensational in tone and poor in quality, for example, E. J. Brett's *Boys of England*. By 1900, however, most of the old rivals had disappeared and were replaced by Alfred Harmsworth (Lord Northcliffe)'s AP boys' papers, the *Boys' Friend*, the *Boys' Herald* and the *Boys' Realm*. These papers were more robust and seemingly more appealing to working-class boys. This new and aggressive competition may have accounted for some of the *BOP*'s difficulties. Whereas since its creation the *BOP* had been profitable for the RTS, after 1900 it relied on the Society's financial subsidy.[34] Since the RTS believed that the paper made a valuable contribution to the moral welfare of boys, it continued its support of the *BOP* for altruistic rather than for financial reasons. This was a unique situation – the boys' periodical market was generally competitive and capricious. Though potentially lucrative, most publishers faced financial ruin if they did not accord with the changing interests of potential juvenile readers.

Yet, the RTS did concern itself with the business side. In 1912, when the *BOP* showed a substantial loss, the RTS appointed a new subcommittee to scrutinize the paper's affairs. One of the suggestions of the subcommittee was to appoint a less elderly vice-editor, a competent man who would eventually become editor.[35] Hutchison then became consulting editor until his death in 1913, and Arthur Lincoln Haydon took over the editorship until 1924. RTS editorial control over content was strong, especially over the *Boy's Own* and *Girl's Own*. The minutes of the RTS Executive Committee frequently record questions over the moral appropriateness of content of the juvenile papers.[36] Where there was a dispute between the editor of the *Boy's Own* and *Girl's Own* and the Executive Committee, the Committee asserted its authority. In the most extreme instance still on record, the Committee expressed its 'displeasure' that the editor of the *Girl's Own Paper* (*GOP*) permitted morally objectionable replies in the 'Answers to Correspondents – Medical' section, culminating in one article that apparently referred 'to a criminal operation' (probably abortion). The editor was instructed to decline further contributions from the writer in question and to discontinue entirely the section.[37]

## Lord Northcliffe and the Amalgamated Press

In Robert Roberts' opinion, school stories had more impact on working-class youth than anything else (including the Boy Scouts). They internalized the public-school ethos better through these stories than by the teachings of their secular and religious leaders. Older boys graduated to reading AP papers like the *Gem*, the *Magnet* and the *Boys' Friend*.[38] Roberts opined that AP founder, Alfred Harmsworth was successful because he simplified the style of written English to make it appealing to working-class readers.[39] The papers were also cheap enough for most boys to afford, yet the wholesomeness of their content was often called into question. Starting in the early 1890s, Harmsworth's papers were called the 'halfpenny dreadfuller', implying that they were simply a cheaper and nastier version of the infamous 'penny dreadful'.[40] The AP published many papers of interest to boys. In 1912, for example, its papers, all for 1d each, could keep boys busy all week long, with the luxury of choice on some days:

*Boys' Friend* (Tuesday); *Magnet* (Tuesday); *Marvel* (Wednesday); *Cheer Boys Cheer* (Wednesday); *Gem* (Thursday); *Boys' Herald* (Thursday); *Sports Library* (Thursday); *Union Jack* (Friday); *Pluck* (Saturday); *Boys' Realm* (Saturday). The AP also produced other publications, such as the *Harmsworth Self-Educator Magazine*, which were directed at youth.

In contrast to the other organizations discussed here, Alfred Harmsworth's publications eschewed discussions of religion. For example, an insert in the first volume of *Harmsworth Self-Educator Magazine*, depicting Holman Hunt's 'The Light of the World', an illustration of Christ, is discussed merely as an example of symbolism in art.[41] Harmsworth believed that popularizing secular education was going 'to change the whole face of journalism'.[42] He recognized a great need at the turn of the century for improved education as a means to personal betterment, a need that was not being met at home or at school. As he wrote in 1884, 'The Board Schools are turning out hundreds of thousands of boys and girls annually who are anxious to read. They do not care for the ordinary newspaper. They have no interest in society, but they will read anything which is simple and is sufficiently interesting.'[43]

The AP became the dominant publisher of boys' papers in the period from the 1890s to the First World War. Kelly Boyd maintains that at this time

> [A] new type of hero emerged as well. No longer were the heroes aristocratic or even from a broader elite. Now skilled male workers were often the heroes and the manly virtues they exemplified were not just about leadership, but about concern for the group and responsibility to family and employer.[44]

This focus on working-class heroes manifested itself in Harmsworth's more utilitarian and educational publications as well. The *Self-Educator* (1906) aimed to equip the lower middle and upper working classes with precise fortnightly instructions, from typing skills to Biology, for negotiating the needs of modern life.

The controlling and actual editor for all of the AP papers discussed here (except the *Self-Educator*) was Robert Hamilton Edwards. He was also a director of the AP. Hamilton Edwards and Harmsworth had a close, if rocky, relationship. Their correspondence varied from the affectionate to the openly hostile and mistrustful. Hamilton Edwards left the AP in 1912, apparently to make boots.[45] The end of their saved correspondence occurred in December 1920, when Hamilton Edwards wrote in affectionate terms, from a hospital prison in Dublin, describing prison and trial conditions.[46] He had taken control of the *Freeman's Journal* and moved to Dublin in 1919.[47] Robert Hamilton

Edwards' wife Madge later sent Harmsworth two letters requesting money, with a postscript: 'I do not know his reason for leaving me or the Amalgamated Press . . . but it was hard for me.'[48] While he was in charge of the AP papers, his influence on the boys' papers was huge. By far their longest serving editor, his tenure lasted for the majority of the papers' run.[49] Though he hired acting editor W. H. Back for the *Boys' Friend*, *Boys' Herald* and *Boys' Realm* in 1907, Hamilton Edwards wrote serial stories for these papers and, most significantly for our purposes here, his authorship is attributed to the editorial sections of all the boys' papers. Whether Hamilton Edwards actually wrote these editorial replies to readers remains in doubt,[50] but what is clear is that the tone of the editorial section certainly changed after he left the AP, indicating that at least he played a large role in the tone of its content. During Hamilton Edwards' time at the papers, the letters selected to be answered within the papers were personal and moral in nature. The majority were from boys who sought advice on their daily problems. The replies took on a paternal voice. This was in stark contrast to the *BOP*, the top-down educational style of which was 'written exclusively by adults', allowing no room for the words of children in the correspondence section.[51] Though the AP papers are usually characterized as secular, Hamilton Edwards repeatedly called himself a Christian; the writing attributed to him reflected this stance. After he left in 1912, however, both the questions and answers were almost exclusively related to the content of the papers, and could be categorized as promotional in nature. It cannot be confirmed whether the letters printed in the AP boys' papers were genuine. In many issues, Hamilton Edwards maintained that they were. To prove their authenticity he printed a letter from a boy who said that he really enjoyed the paper and hoped that his letter would be published in order to prove to his friends in the neighbourhood of Shepherd's Bush that the letters are real.[52] Edwards also boasted about the vast quantity of letters he received, a number far too great to print in his papers, around 500 to 700 every week.[53]

Hamilton Edwards frequently published letters ostensibly from parents (especially fathers) and other authority figures (like schoolmasters and Sunday School teachers) who praised the high quality and the moral tone of his papers. He wanted to assure boys that his papers were far from 'trash' or penny dreadfuls, and that they could take the papers home without admonishment from parents. One 1911 letter from 'a scoutmaster, Sunday-school teacher, secretary of honoured institutions, and a church officer', said that the *Boys' Friend* interested him as much as it did in his teenage years and that he would never have taken it had he thought it was a penny dreadful.[54] Another letter, not at all unusual, says Hamilton Edwards, was from Henry William Hill, a father who felt it was his 'duty' to give the editor 'a little encouragement to keep up the standard of excellence and purity which has always been the dominant point in your papers'. Hill went on to say that as he had a lot of experience with boys' papers, he could come to the conclusion that the *Boys' Friend*, the *Boys' Herald* and the *Boys' Realm* 'contain the best literature the British boy can possibly want'. He asserted that not only boys read the papers, but also 'grown-up men, who have the responsible positions of training up children of their own'.[55] Hamilton Edwards published the thoughts of Alfred Luker, a 64-year-old Nonconformist Sunday School superintendent who recommended the *Boys' Friend* to his young male charges as a clean and manly paper. In fact, Luker said, 'it is the ideal paper to teach boys to be manly and independent, to fight their way in the world.'[56] The tone of these letters is remarkably similar to that attributed to Hamilton Edwards in his editorial sections. Whether or not these letters of support were genuine, they demonstrate the great effort involved in making the AP papers seem as wholesome and moral as their 'religious' counterparts.

If the AP can be trusted in reporting its own numbers, the reach of its publications was enormous:

> The combined net sale per issue of those only of the Amalgamated Press journals which accept advertisements is nearer six million than five. They reach every corner of these islands. In ninety-eight per cent of the homes of England, Scotland, Wales and Ireland, some one or more of them is read regularly. In the extent and variety of their appeal they stand quite unrivalled. There is no class of public, and there are very few interests, not covered by one, or two, or three, or by a large group of Amalgamated Press publications. More than that, from the point of view of the advertiser, their circulation is an effective one. Each copy is read sometimes many times. It reaches the home of the millionaire, the professional man, the typist, the artisan, and the working woman. It passes from hand to hand throughout the family and sometimes outside.[57]

These estimates do seem reasonable for 1925, judging by a 1909–10 chart that was slipped in with the Harmsworth/Hamilton Edwards correspondence, recording sales of more than 3 million for the papers controlled by Hamilton Edwards alone.[58] The combined sales per issue for the *Boys' Friend*, *Boys' Herald* and *Boys' Realm* were substantial at 133,628, having overtaken the *Boy's Own* around the turn of the century.

# Temperance organizations and their publications

## The Band of Hope

The Band of Hope was an influential multidenominational, mainly working-class national temperance movement in Britain, with a specific focus on children.[59] Though there was widespread concern in the middle and upper classes of the period about working-class moral and physical degeneracy, it would be too simplistic to say that the Band of Hope was a top-down reform movement. Rather it was driven by working-class people who recognized that moral and physical reform needed to take place within their own communities, starting at a young age. There were also less-successful attempts to enrol middle- and upper-class children. The first Band of Hope was founded in Leeds in 1847, with the aim of instructing boys and girls as to the properties of alcohol and the consequences of its consumption. Bands organized midweek meetings with music, slides, competitions and addresses on the importance of total abstinence. By 1855, there were so many local bands that a London Union was formed and in 1864 this was expanded to become the UK Band of Hope Union.

The story of the creation of the Band of Hope has become almost mythical. The founders, Mrs Ann Jane Carlile and Rev. Jabez Tunnicliff, each had something resembling an evangelical conversion story. Both personally encountered the devastating effects of children's drinking and decided that they would dedicate their energies to juvenile teetotalism. In Carlile's case it was a little girl named Mary whom she met doing voluntary work at Newgate Prison. She took Mary home and witnessed her lapping up spilt whiskey off the floor, after having been influenced by her imprisoned mother's drinking.[60] Tunnicliff was a young Baptist minister when he visited a former Sunday School teacher who was dying of an illness related to drunkenness. He asked the minister to 'warn young people about the danger of the first glass'.[61]

The pace accelerated after 1870, when most new Band of Hope societies (and County Unions) were formed.[62] Important regional unions were also formed, such as the Lancashire and Cheshire and the Yorkshire Band of Hope Unions. The increased support for temperance by churches and chapels of all denominations gave the children's organization a great impetus to expand, particularly starting in the 1880s. By the end of the century, the movement claimed a total of 26,355 societies and over 3 million members in the United Kingdom.[63] In the estimation of Lilian Shiman, 'In terms of numbers, no one could deny the success of the

Band of Hope.'[64] Its success in shaping future citizens, specifically the success of its publications in this regard, is a more open question.

In answer to the question, put by the Greenwich and West Kent Band of Hope Union, 'Why are you a Member of a Band of Hope?', four reasons are provided: 'I want to be strong; healthy; good; and Christlike.'[65] Yet the main purpose of the organization was of course to promote the temperance movement among the young. Though the temperance movement among adults was controversial, there was little debate that it was necessary among children. In 1886, Parliament forbade the sale of liquor to children under 13 years for consumption on the premises, but there was still concern that children were being given alcohol at home, either as a beverage or as a remedy. Frustrated at the slow speed of supportive legislation, temperance reformers saw the most effective way of creating a temperate society was through the education of the young. As the Band of Hope National Secretary, Robert Tayler, argued in 1946, 'A new race of citizens had to be created, who were fully aware of the evils of drinking, and could eventually create the public opinion without which Temperance reform could never be achieved.'[66]

The Jubilee year, 1897, was an important time for the UK Band of Hope Union. It secured the patronage of the Queen. It also created a Jubilee programme, which it submitted to its workers in the United Kingdom and in the dominions, with three main components: (1) a commitment to securing greater public recognition for the movement through sermons (in every denomination), addresses in Sunday Schools and public demonstrations and meetings; (2) the 'Million More Jubilee Scheme'; and (3) the raising of funds, both on the national and local levels, for the building of a new national headquarters. On three Sundays, Jubilee Sermons were estimated to have been preached in ten thousand Church of England and Non-conformist churches and chapels throughout the United Kingdom. The Official Jubilee Sermon was preached at St Paul's Cathedral by Frederick Temple, the Archbishop of Canterbury.[67] Thousands of Band of Hope addresses were also given at Sunday Schools and Bible classes (for older pupils).

'The Million More Scheme' was the most ambitious of the Jubilee endeavours. A commitment was made to add a million new members to the Bands of Hope, by the visiting of more than a million homes by volunteers. This was a huge undertaking, requiring extensive organization and coordination. On Saturday, 16 October, for example, more than 53,000 mostly female volunteers visited more than 1,500,000 homes in every part of the United Kingdom. They encouraged the parents they visited to allow their children to join Bands of Hope, or at least to permit them to sign the temperance pledge on the provided forms.

Each visitor left a letter by the president, and made a second visit during the week.[68] The UK Band of Hope Union reported that in 1913–14, Bands of Hope and other organizations of a similar kind numbered 34,045, with an estimated membership of 3,788,969.[69] At the local level, success was measured not only by membership numbers, but by attendance at weekly meetings and by unbroken temperance pledges. The Bedford Institute (Spitalfields) Band of Hope, for example, was deemed to be 'a flourishing society': in 1883 it had a total of 586 members, with a weekly attendance of 349. Some 218 junior and 167 senior pledges had been taken during the previous year. The visitation of absentees was a systematic practice, and it was found that of those visited only 17 had broken their pledge.[70]

According to Charles Wakely, the General Secretary of the UK Band of Hope Union, the age of membership differed in various societies, but in most Bands of Hope the members were received at 7 years of age, and at 14 were drafted into a senior society, where the proceedings were adapted to their 'increased intelligence and altered habits of thought'.[71] Membership was conditional upon giving a written promise of abstinence, and upon compliance with the rules that governed each society. The declaration in general use was the following: 'I promise to abstain from the use of all intoxicating drinks as beverages.' The pledge was central to the Band of Hope. 'It makes the signatory feel that he is one of many who have banded together in a crusade. When later in life he tries to keep his promises and overcomes temptation, he is strengthened in his moral and spiritual character'.[72] After several months of keeping the pledge, the member could purchase an ornate certificate, often replete with gilt printing, which served as a permanent reminder of the values associated with the pledge (Figures 1.1 and 1.2).[73]

It was argued that children thus strengthened would be less likely to succumb to other vices like smoking or gambling, and more likely to become manly men. The emotional bonding with other children and with leaders, most of whom were pledge takers as children, was considered to be vital. United feeling and combined will encouraged pride and happiness when individuals adhered to the moral precepts of the movement, amplifying negative feelings when a child strayed from the ideal. This was probably accomplished through personal interaction within the group and the community, but was certainly strengthened rhetorically in the movement's publications and recitations for its members. This feeling of community might also explain the 'emotional hold of the church on individuals' in later life.[74] In addition to negative emotions linked to individual conscience, many stories, songs and recitations also attempted to trigger

**Figure 1.1** Band of Hope Pledge Card, 1886. 'Train up a child in the way he should go'. Courtesy of the University of Central Lancashire, the Livesey Collection, Preston, UK.

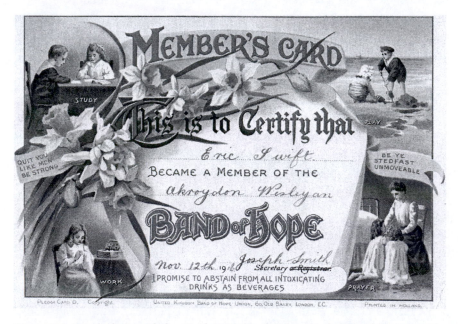

**Figure 1.2** Band of Hope Pledge Card, 1916. 'Study, Play, Work, Prayer'. 'Quit you like men. Be strong, be ye stedfast, unmoveable'. Courtesy of Hans Swift.

embarrassment, pity and fortitude in children whose parents (especially their fathers) strayed from the moral ideal.

Young people became members without fees, but usually paid a weekly contribution of one halfpenny, if possible. In most cases, members received a monthly temperance magazine (often *Onward* or the *Band of Hope Review*), and admission to the entertainments, tea meetings and annual outings. The written consent of at least one parent or guardian was necessary in the case of children under 14 in order to counter any claims of interference in parents' sphere of influence or indoctrination of the young. Parental consent and involvement were crucial to the movement's success.[75]

There were many publications associated with the Band of Hope movement. The best in terms of quality and content and the most widely distributed were the *Band of Hope Review* (1851–c.1936), published in London by S. W. Partridge & Co. and connected with the UK Band of Hope Union, and *Onward* (1865–c.1964), published in Manchester by the Lancashire and Cheshire Band of Hope Union.[76] Brian Harrison estimates that in 1861 the *Band of Hope Review* had a circulation of over 250,000.[77] Although it is difficult to measure the success of these papers, the impressive time span of their publication is an indication of their usefulness in the Band of Hope movement. Many of these publications were distributed to current and future Band of Hope members. If not an indication of the appeal of these papers to the young members themselves, then it certainly indicates the enthusiasm of Band of Hope workers, who welcomed the stories and lessons contained within as a supplement to, and sometimes a replacement for, Band of Hope meetings. Various local bands and unions also had their own monthly or quarterly papers, containing stories borrowed from larger Band of Hope or temperance papers, often with more local news and reports.

Fund-raising at the national, regional and local levels was an important part of the movement. For example, the National Band of Hope Bazaar, held in Exeter Hall by the Band of Hope Union in 1890, proved 'a great success', adding £4,200 to the funds of the Society. The event proved so popular that it was extended by a day over its planned run and the proceeds on that day largely exceeded the previous days'.[78] A popular annual event, the Band of Hope Choirs performed at the Crystal Palace. In 1886 there were 15,000 singers divided into 3 choirs appearing on the same day on the same stage.[79]

Activities like these not only raised much needed money; they also served to increase awareness of the organization among the mostly working-class target audience and among the elite, from whom the movement drew its honorific leaders. As mentioned, Queen Victoria was the patron of the UK Band of Hope Union, along with a range of aristocratic and other elite supporters and benefactors. Prestigious support was also to be found at the more local level. For example, the Earl of Carlisle of Castle Howard was the president of the Yorkshire Band of Hope Union.[80]

The various Band of Hope organizations also raised money to pay for temperance speakers in schools. The UK Band of Hope Union raised £10,000 in 1889 to pay for 7 scientific and medical lecturers to give talks wherever schools would permit them. The speakers had to attest to their own 'personal fitness, abstinence, and moral character', the same qualities the Band of Hope sought to instil in its child members.[81] By 1893 this London-based union had 29 agents and lecturers, though not all were qualified to visit schools. Other Band of Hope unions in the provinces hired their own school lecturers to work within the locality.[82] Speakers' plans were drawn up by the unions as an aid to the local groups. The unions introduced new ideas and broader visions by providing outside lecturers to speak to local Band of Hope children. This part of union work so increased in importance that, by 1895, the Bradford union claimed to have 137 names on its speakers' list and to have made an average of 30 appointments a week for speakers to talk to various organizations in the area.[83]

The unions took seriously the task of hiring and appointing temperance lecturers and Band of Hope workers. While most school lecturers were male and had some educational and/or scientific credentials, many Band of Hope meeting leaders were female, sometimes drawn from the ranks of the older membership. All were required to uphold high standards of personal conduct.[84] Skill and knowledge at imparting scientific lessons became increasingly important but the religious and moral qualities of these workers were always paramount.

The movement had a far greater impact than its membership numbers indicate. By 1946, over 20 million children had heard the scientific total abstinence lectures of Band of Hope representatives.[85] Their lectures were focused on the effects of alcohol from a scientific point of view, leaving aside the moral and spiritual components so often explored in the movement's periodicals. School lectures, however, were deemed less effective than Band of Hope attendance. Only 'systematic teaching in a Band of Hope' could engender a 'lasting loyalty . . . in the heart of the child', a loyalty 'strengthened by the signing of the pledge'.[86] Throughout the nineteenth century, temperance teaching for children was increasingly based on 'scientific', rather than on moral, precepts.[87] But even the scientific teaching of temperance concerned a cultivation of the emotions. 'Love' for temperance in all things and the 'dangers' and 'evil' of intemperance were still stressed. To paraphrase William Axon in a paper he read at the Manchester Teachers' Guild in 1891, learning is empty if it does not guide the heart.

Temperance education was introduced into the curriculum of day schools to help 'the men and women of the future to brighter lives and happier homes than some of those in which they have been reared'.[88]

Wakely thought that the teaching of the Band of Hope was 'grounded on the principles of religion, morality and science', presenting these contrasting principles seemingly without tension.[89] A religious tone was supposed to pervade the entire movement, although there was fear that this was sometimes lost in entertainments and recreational activities. Band of Hope instructors were told to sustain the children's interest from week to week by various means, such as magic lantern shows, object lessons, dissolving views, chemical experiments and physiological charts, and to make every possible effort to render the meetings engaging and attractive.[90] Band of Hope instructors and lecturers were often devoted to the cause. In fact, Tayler claims that 90 per cent of the leaders of the Band of Hope (in 1946) were members in their childhood.[91] They had a 'sacred and definite' mission.[92]

The Band of Hope Union reported yearly on its work in day schools. It maintained a fairly constant schedule of visiting around 3,800 schools per year.[93] These were of all varieties: Council, Voluntary, Industrial, District or Workhouse Schools, Evening Continuation Schools and High Schools. It also visited Orphan Asylums, Deaf and Dumb, and Blind Schools. Institutions of every kind for the ordinary education of the young, no matter the class or sectarian peculiarities (Roman Catholic and Jewish schools included), were offered and accepted the free services of lecturers. The main feature of the work was the delivery of addresses, invariably illustrated by charts, diagrams, specimens and experiments demonstrating the dangers of alcohol. The lectures, usually around 40 minutes long and during school hours, were given to the older children, who, in the estimation of the report, welcomed 'the addresses as a pleasant break in the routine of their school work, and who showed, by the intelligence with which they answered searching questions, and by the fullness and discrimination of their written reports, that they had secured a grasp of the subject calculated to prove most useful to them in after life'.[94]

There was much mutual sympathy and collaboration between the UK Band of Hope Union and other influential temperance organizations (and their associated juvenile branches and periodicals). In 1891, for example, the CETS held two conferences on the topic of alcohol and childhood, with all the influential representatives of the movement present. The morning conference was chaired by Frederick Temple, Lord Bishop of London, and the afternoon's by the Duke of Westminster. Much of the discussion was focused on the Band of Hope, its impact and how its influence might be increased. Rev. J. R. Diggle, chairman of the London School Board, gave a talk on 'Temperance in the Schools', during which he claimed that eight out of ten Board school children in London belonged to a Band of Hope, in large part because of visits by temperance lecturers during school hours. He praised the efforts of the UK Band of Hope Union in providing school lectures – 'The teachers like it, and the children like it' – and encouraged plans for the CETS to set up its own involvement in schools throughout England.[95]

There were tight connections between the juvenile temperance movement and Sunday Schools. The Band of Hope sought to tap into the already well-established Sunday School movement. One report estimated in 1894 that there were over 6 million Sunday scholars, and 674,000 teachers in the United Kingdom.[96] According to the Honorary Secretary of the Junior Division of the CETS, the Sunday School and the Band of Hope had members who belonged to both institutions; they both met in the same rooms, had workers who were enthusiastic about both or 'one common object in training up the children in the way they should go'.[97] He added that 'what is wanted is that every Sunday School teacher and superintendent shall clearly recognize that he has a duty to perform towards the temperance work, even when for any reason he may be unable personally to take active part in it'.[98] Recommendations to teachers included keeping track of individual Sunday School children's participation in the Band of Hope and examining their Band of Hope attendance cards; and obtaining parental consent for children who were not already Band of Hope members. Sunday School instructors were told that each lesson must be taught by one clear, graphic illustration. At least one text (but not more than three or four) was to be learnt with each lesson, the child committing to memory 'words which will live in the days when the stress and strain of temptation will try him very hard'.[99] Clergy were encouraged to introduce temperance principles to Sunday School children who did not attend the Band of Hope and to promote the Band of Hope in Sunday School.[100]

Charles Wakely encouraged greater cooperation between Sunday Schools and the Band of Hope. This support was sometimes lacking, he argued, because of a false idea that drinking in moderation was beneficial.[101] Yet the Band of Hope was promoted as a valuable auxiliary to the Sunday School, encouraging increased attendance in Sunday School of children who were already Band of Hope members. It also provided a place with religious influence to meet during the week, and not merely on Sundays.[102]

Rev. C. A. Davis of Bradford took a tougher approach. 'There exist in the land such gloomy buildings as prisons and reformatories. In their cells can be found forty thousand persons: *six out of seven* of these have been Sunday scholars!' To the question, 'How did they get there?', he answered that they did not pass directly from the Sunday School to the Prison; 'they went through the public-house.'[103] The solution to this dramatic problem was twofold. It was the responsibility of fathers to provide a temperate example to their sons. Sunday School teachers were to do the same. The second part of the solution would be to teach temperance lessons in Sunday School and to create closer ties between it and the Band of Hope, with the goal of creating new Band of Hope societies attached to every Sunday School.[104] Using the example of his own church, Davis also maintained that the Band of Hope increased the spiritual power of the Sunday School, as five-sixths of the new members of the church were from the Band of Hope section of the schools.[105] This claim coincides with evidence from other clergy members. In Charles Booth's survey of the 1890s, for example, a Presbyterian mission minister divulged that accessing young people through the Band of Hope was a strategy to ensure churches' more regular membership.[106]

The UK Band of Hope Union provides one view of the movement as a whole, being responsible for national lobbying and campaigns, providing expensive resources to local societies, and publishing the main juvenile periodicals. Large regional unions, like the Lancashire and Cheshire Band of Hope Union, had similar functions. Yet, since the movement was loosely associated and individual Unions and societies had much local control, examining a local Band of Hope Union and associated societies provides quite a different view. The Bradford Band of Hope Union began in 1851, with individual Bands founded as early as 1849. It was the first Band of Hope Union in the United Kingdom.[107] This Union was the organizational centre for the local Bands of Hope, and later had links to the much larger Yorkshire and UK Band of Hope Unions. It consisted of a 14-member male-only executive committee with annual elections. Candidates were chosen from the various local Bands of Hope; there were also about 50 delegates who attended each meeting. In the late 1880s and early 1890s, this Union had 163 societies, with 28,724 members; 8,250 of these members were over 16 years old. This was an active Union, with wide participation. In 1891–2, a profitable bazaar was held and the 'Million More Scheme' adopted, because of which 7,607 home visits were made and 3,987 pledges secured.[108] In 1897, there were 2,700 Band of Hope workers in Bradford. In the same year 3,105 meetings were held, with a total average attendance per week of 11,286. The local agent spoke at 198 engagements, with a total attendance of 31,941. In addition, 135 voluntary speakers made visits to 1,623 meetings. Temperance Sunday was observed and 223 sermons were preached and 176 Sunday School addresses were made.[109]

It is also revealing to examine the situation even more locally, at the level of individual societies. The Sion Band of Hope and Temperance Society, Harris St Bradford, was one of the original five societies which formed the Bradford Band of Hope Union. This is an example of a well-run and successful organization, which cooperated with other local societies.[110] All of its programmes were planned well in advance. It often had festivals and competitions to attract new members and increase awareness in the local community. These events were usually reported in the local newspapers. For example, at its forty-fourth annual festival, held in the large schoolroom, on Good Friday, 12 April 1895, the society had Tea at 5 p.m. (Adults 5d, Children 4d), which was incentive to attend the (free) meeting. After tea, there was an address by Mr E. W. Pike, Agent of the Yorkshire Band of Hope Union. Attendance at the meeting was impressive at 400. At the Annual Festival on Good Friday, 16 April 1897, there was a Grand Concert with songs, recitals and an address. The annual report and balance sheet were also presented.

Competitions were regularly held. In the junior Recitation Competitions each competitor had to render two pieces, one being taken from the 'Prize Reciter'. The first prize, a sterling silver medal donated by the United Temperance Council Prize Committee in London was awarded to Master John Wilfred Mason, who in addition to the test piece, 'What Can Children Do?' recited 'A Story of an Apple'. The second prize went to Master Joe Squire for the test piece and 'Little Roy' and the third prize was secured by Miss May Saul, for the test piece and 'Incorrigible'.[111] The recorded attendance was of 120 members and the event details were published in the local newspaper. Sion's weekly meetings were generally well attended. On 'Boys' Night', 16 November 1904, the attendance was an impressive 250. At another meeting a few months later, with recitations on the theme of boyhood, there were 130 participants.[112] Magic lantern lectures seemed to be popular and attracted 250 members.[113]

The Girlington Congregational Band of Hope was a younger organization having joined the Bradford Union on 12 November 1890. This organization had a rocky start. According to an organizer, D. B. Scott, 'More workers, better entertainments, more enthusiasm and financial help and the Band of Hope Girlington will be as fine a society as any in Bradford.'[114] These were challenging areas to improve, and the society suffered from a lack of interest by adult workers, declining juvenile membership and some 'rough and unruly boys who were a source of great trouble and annoyance'.[115] The Report of the 1895–6 session puts a positive spin on low interest by highlighting the generally good attendance (average of 42), and good behaviour, considering the small number of adults at the meetings. The entertainments, though 'much the same as usual' were lacking, and were blamed for poor order and attendance.[116] The January lantern entertainment was more successful. During the same session, only 6 out of 15 appointed speakers kept their appointments. The November Children's Social was more of a success, as 90 people attended, perhaps thanks to the coffee and parkin served. There was, however, a net loss even at this relatively successful event. The conclusion of the organizer was that in the five years of its existence, this Band of Hope had not made any real improvements in membership numbers or finances and had suffered a decline in volunteers (from 28 to 8). Various changes were made, and by 1900, the Girlington Band of Hope was in a stronger position. It had more organized and stable leadership (all members 16 years of age and older were members of the committee), a sound financial footing and better attendance by members at regular meetings (average attendance in the winter was 80, with the highest attendance being 115). There were also more events to attract new members: magic lantern lectures and entertainments, prizes for good attendance (oranges), annual summer excursions and concerts. One concert, for example, held on 22 February 1902, featured a ventriloquist, a blind pianist, dialogues and refreshments. It was well attended and even made a profit of 5s.7d. Girlington also had a Sunday School and participated in large gatherings in Bradford like the 'Jubilee of the Bradford Sunday School Union', a celebration in Peel Park in July, 1901, at which 10,476 teachers and scholars marched.[117]

St Andrew's Presbyterian Church of England on Infirmary Street in Bradford started a Band of Hope in 1888. In the first year, it had 143 members, representing a moderately successful start.[118] The number of children who attended on a weekly basis, however, was significantly lower. In its second year, for example, its largest weekly attendance was 56, but the average was 32. In 1893–4, the total numbers were down to 114, but the average weekly attendance was up to 60 children. In 1901–2, there was a lack of interest and the session closed at Christmas, but by 1907–8, the average attendance was back up to 52, and the organizers were reporting that despite 'many other counter attractions in the neighbouring district', the interest for the Band of Hope was kept up, with the lantern shows an especially attractive feature of the meetings.[119]

In 1894, of the 86 schools of the Bradford Sunday School Union, 26 were without a Band of Hope, but vigorous attempts were made to rectify this situation.[120] The St Andrew's Presbyterian Church Band of Hope was tied to the church Sunday School, but despite assumptions that the relationship of Sunday School and Band of Hope would be mutually beneficial, the Sunday School had declining attendance through the 1890s, to a low of less than 100 pupils. The only exception, remarkably, was the Young Men's Class, which increased in numbers. A report stated that these meetings were well attended, and 'much enjoyed and appreciated by all'.[121] The numbers for this group, though increasing, appear to have remained small, as in 1909–10, the Young Men's Class's membership increased from 23 to 27, with an average attendance of 16. Significantly, the linked Third Bradford Company Boys' Brigade suffered a similar fate to the Sunday School and was reported to be suffering from a lack of interest and dwindling numbers in 1903–4, with 35 boys on the roll. The report confidently stated that an investment in new uniforms and musical instruments would help enlarge the company.[122]

The details listed in the local Band of Hope reports and minute books are perhaps inconsequential in themselves, but when understood in the context of the broader movement, they provide examples of the daily trials and successes of diverse local communities. They demonstrate that local churches and chapels of various denominations struggled to attract and maintain the interest of the youth in their areas, and attempted numerous strategies towards their goals. For boys, manliness was a key word for these goals and included the disciplining of their passions, the shunning of vice, and the building of character and religiosity. Band of Hope workers approached their tasks with evangelical missionary zeal. In the words of Charles Wakely,

> Let us bear in mind that we are not simply labouring for the present, but the future, not for this world only, but for eternity. Realising this, we shall be progressive and aggressive, striving to ever enlarge our borders, and letting no day pass without endeavouring to win over fresh recruits for the great army of abstinence, which by God's help, shall at length, through the children, become invincible and victorious.[123]

## Church of England Temperance Society and its Juvenile Division

The CETS helped persuade Anglican and other educators to introduce temperance lessons for children for which the CETS often provided classroom materials.[124] It sponsored annual prizes for students most knowledgeable about the glories of temperance and the dangers of alcohol, and formed its own Bands of Hope.[125] CETS publications for youth included special newspapers, handbooks for workers in juvenile branches and extensive textbooks extolling the physiological, genetic, moral, social, economic and even historical benefits of abstinence.

Founded at Lambeth Palace in 1873, the CETS was 'the most far-reaching, prestigious, and influential temperance society in Victorian and Edwardian Britain, and one of its most extensive voluntary societies'.[126] It replaced the Church of England Total Abstinence Society (founded in 1862), which had been largely unsuccessful. By 1877, the CETS was financially strong and was represented throughout the country.[127] By 1898 there were 451,446 known juvenile teetotallers in parish societies, about four and a half times the number of abstaining adults.[128] More than half of English bishops abstained.[129] This success can be at least partially explained by the CETS's 'dual basis' policy, teetotalism mainly for the working classes and for those who wanted to provide them with an impeccable example, and moderation for the rest of the supporters of the movement.[130] This policy was not, however, entirely class based. As Mr H. T. James of the St John's (Middleton) Band of Hope explained during an entertainment for family and friends of that band's members, 'total abstinence was the only means of saving the drunkard, but moderate users of wholesome alcoholic drinks could also be earnest workers'.[131] There was general agreement, however, that this principle was not to be extended to children, rich and poor, and that they ought to be taught teetotal principles early in life. The CETS aimed to accomplish this through its periodicals, through the establishment of branches of its Juvenile Division and Band of Hope societies at the parish level, and through the association of temperance teachers.[132]

After 1908, the Cradle Roll even enlisted infants in the movement. The 1910 CETS manual stipulated the entry age for the Band of Hope as 8. Young graduates of the CETS Junior Division passed into the Intermediate Division at 15, moving to the Adult Division at 19 years of age. Many passed directly from the Band of Hope to the Adult Division between the ages of 14 and 17. The age of passage from youth to adult was sometimes considered to be 16, the legal drinking age after 1872. Similar to other Band of Hope organizations, the CETS developed a full set of presentations to mark various stages of membership in the parish branches.[133] A new member was presented with an illuminated card. After six months, the child earned a white metal badge and annually, for the first four years, a bar which could be turned in at the end of five years for a bronze badge or long-service star, to be supplemented by bars until a silver badge was earned for the tenth year, after which, silver bars marked each year (Figure 1.3).

This sort of visible reward system for good membership was common in youth organizations of the period. From the founding of the Boy Scouts

**Figure 1.3** Advertisement for UK Band of Hope Union Medals and Badges, at the back of *The Band of Hope Manual* (London: UK Band of Hope Union, 1894).

in 1908, badges were awarded to members for attendance, good behaviour and the accomplishment of tasks, and would have already been familiar to children and their parents who had been involved in the juvenile temperance movement.

The Band of Hope movement was far more successful with working-class children than with those of other classes. This was not through want of trying. In 1895 the CETS admitted that though 'the children of the upper classes need as much enlightenment on the temperance question as the children of the masses', they had largely been neglected.[134] Put another way, children of the 'educated classes' had been less inclined to join Bands of Hope than working-class children. According to the CETS, 'The victims of intemperance are to be found among those who pride themselves on their ancestral relations and blue blood, just as among those, who occupy the humbler stations in society, for alcohol is no respecter of persons'.[135] CETS Women's Union organizers worked hard to convert privileged children to teetotalism. In 1881 they founded the Juvenile Union to alert 'better-class' youth to drink's evils with special events in parishes, public schools and other educational institutions.[136] The Juvenile Union and its twentieth-century successor, the Young Crusaders' Union, were, however, the least successful CETS youth efforts. The Juvenile Union was established probably in no more than 150 parishes.[137] With a subscription fee of at least 1 shilling per year, the Young Crusaders' Union was more costly at the outset than regular Bands of Hope. Unlike the dual basis of the CETS for adults, the Young Crusaders' Union had a pledge of total abstinence from alcohol. The failure to attract 'better-class' youths to teetotalism was blamed on 'the prejudices and opposition on the part of many parents' to a movement that might have made 'little prigs' of their children.[138] After 22 years of work among middle- and upper-class juveniles, the Women's Union admitted in 1903 that 'the children of the working classes receive far more definite instruction in elementary scientific temperance than any others', a confession made less disappointing in light of the special CETS mission to reach Britain's working-class majority while they were young enough to be influenced.[139] In 1891, Walter M. Gee asked Archbishop E. W. Benson of Canterbury to patronize the new CETS Church Lads Brigade, a paramilitary teetotal organization for 'some of the poorest boys in London' and elsewhere.[140]

CETS worker, H. F. Clarke, admitted that it was difficult to retain Band of Hope members after they reached a certain age. There seemed to be an almost inevitable drifting away of members when they started to earn their own living. This was also the period when they were judged to be most at risk since they were newly exposed to various temptations. Starting around the age of 14 or 15, boys were of special concern in this regard and in need of 'wise and continual supervision and guidance'.[141] In order to keep older members, several strategies were recommended. Transfer papers for members who moved from one parish to another were one way to keep track of youth who might otherwise have drifted away from the movement. Older members were often given increased responsibilities as junior officers or as visitors to younger absentee members. Clubs for youths, and Church Lads' Brigade and Senior Bands of Hope also encouraged young people to stay within the Band of Hope movement. The management of the senior societies, in which the teaching was more advanced and the evening meeting times more suitable to young working people, was left much more to the members themselves, providing them with leadership opportunities for future adult temperance work.[142] This system of self-management was also set up for fear that young people would bristle under the authority of adult workers. That weekly meetings based on temperance only may become 'tiresome', and that 'no Band of Hope will ever compete with the popular amusements and resorts of the day' were acknowledged.[143] In the tradition of informal self-education, readings and lectures of general interest were therefore to be presented on subjects like history, science, music, commerce and poetry. Letters from Senior Band of Hope workers show that all of these recommendations were implemented in individual societies.[144]

Industrial Bands of Hope were set up in many locations as a way to attract older, mainly working-class, boys.[145] The CETS saw this as an effective way to keep them involved in the temperance movement with the aim of joining the adult society. The goal was to teach them practical skills while providing moral influences and teetotal principles. There was some debate whether this sort of more practical twin purpose should be permitted, as it could be seen to detract from the religious and moral messages of the movement. According to one Industrial Band of Hope leader, one more practical disadvantage of this organization was the bad behaviour of some of its (mostly male) members, especially with tools and hot glue. The most effective solution was judged to be the keeping of a black book for misbehaving members to be excluded from free admission and charged a fee for the next Band of Hope entertainment.[146]

The St John's (Middleton) Band of Hope, or Juvenile Union, in connection with the Durham diocesan branch of the CETS was provided by CETS organizers in the early 1890s as a model of an Industrial Band of Hope. Founded in 1889, at the end of its first session there were 235 members and 28 teachers, about one-fourth of the population of the district. At the start of the next session the membership was reduced to 107, as only members who were not in arrears and had not frequently misbehaved were readmitted.[147] Boys had classes for learning joinery, fretwork, painting; girls had classes for various kinds of needlework. Spelling and geographical bees were also introduced. Members gave entertainment evenings for parents and friends with songs, instrumental pieces and recitations, which 'were rendered with much spirit'.[148] A sale of the members' handiwork resulted in £9 in proceeds. By the end of the 1890–1 session this Band of Hope was out of debt (the start-up costs had been considerable at £7, plus a sum nearing £5 for advances from shareholders). It also had a large stock of materials and tools and about £2 worth of unsold goods.[149]

The CETS had numerous publications, but the salient ones here are the *Church of England Temperance Chronicle*, the *Illustrated Temperance Monthly*, the *Young Crusader* and the *Young Standard Bearer*, as well as other occasional pamphlets and Band of Hope material produced for children and young adults. At one halfpenny monthly, The *Young Crusader* and the *Young Standard Bearer*'s lack of success cannot be blamed on the price. The second paper had by far the worse quality of artwork, printing and paper. The *Chronicle* contained many entries for the Band of Hope and Juvenile Union. The *Illustrated Temperance Monthly*, directed at all classes, had a section on the Juvenile Division. Reports of progress from the Juvenile Division and comparative results of inter-diocesan Band of Hope examinations were also contained in every CETS *Annual Report*.

The CETS *Annual Reports* also provided updates on the organization's magazines, publications and juvenile sections. The magazines department section tells of the uncertain progress of the *Young Crusader, Illustrated Temperance Monthly* and *Temperance Chronicle*. The *Young Crusader* suffered losses of £126 during its first year, explained by the advertising required to promote a new paper, and the copies used for free circulation, as well as by the increasing cost of printing.[150] By the following year, the annual report announced a large advance in circulation, as the publication was adopted as the localized Juvenile Organ in the Dioceses of London and Manchester and in the Rural Deanery of Croydon. Increased sales were expected in 1894.[151] In that year, improvement in the circulation of the *Illustrated Temperance Monthly* did not take place as expected,[152] but the *Young Crusader* fared better, at least temporarily. Its circulation increased rapidly and it was then also localized by the Liverpool Diocesan Society. The Council hoped that many other Dioceses would adopt the *Young Crusader* and that it would 'become a profitable property to the Society. There has been a considerable margin of profit on this year's work, and there is no reason why the circulation should not continue to increase.'[153] Yet in 1903, the *Young Crusader* was still not selling as well as the Council wished and it entered into new arrangements with the London Diocesan Board for its localization, hoping that this would finally lead to an improvement in the circulation of that magazine.[154] In 1907, the *Young Crusader* was 'remodeled to some extent' to suit the needs of the Bands of Hope and circulation increased.[155] In 1912, the Council complained that the circulation of the *Illustrated Temperance Monthly* was still not satisfactory, although the paper received much praise. That year they also made an appeal to their branches:

> In the *Young Crusader* the Society has a halfpenny monthly for Band of Hope children, which deserves far greater appreciation than it receives. Beautifully illustrated, and consisting of pretty Temperance tales, The *Crusader* – which is sold for 3s a hundred – should, in the judgment of the Council – be taken in some considerable quantity by every Band of Hope. The Council cannot but fear that the fact of the magazine not being more widely circulated is due to apathy. When a recent circular, urging the support of the *Crusader*, was sent to the Bands of Hope from the Central office, one branch of some standing wrote: 'Please send us a specimen of the *Young Crusader*. . . . We have never heard of it.'[156]

By 1913, the CETS Council was complaining of 'general neglect' of both the *Young Crusader* and the *Illustrated Temperance Monthly* by the branches.[157] Because of this 'neglect' and because of added wartime publishing and distribution difficulties, the *Young Crusader* ceased publication in 1915. Yet in that same year, the Junior Division was continuing to administer Band of Hope examinations. There were 11,184 candidates in 778 parishes, which was considered a good number in wartime.[158]

The CETS was plagued by increasing financial difficulties. According to G. W. Olsen, 'The CETS' tendency to expand its operations more quickly than its income eventually forced a curtailment of activities for monetary reasons, especially after 1891 when increasing CETS identification with the British Establishment demanded more business-like practices.'[159] The conviction of the Publications Department manager for keeping a bawdy house demonstrated the challenge of insuring morally upright staff in a time of declining funds.[160]

# Conclusion

The juvenile publishing industry and the temperance organizations for the young worked to eliminate what they considered to be the most dangerous vices, which were seemingly untouched by a system of formal education. They feared that, left unchecked, the future of the nation was in jeopardy. The tenor of their approach in implementing their informal education on the nation's boys was heavily influenced by the context in which they worked. Alongside their own particular moral or religious stamp, these organizations drew heavily on new notions of childhood, and particularly of youth/adolescence, as distinct times of life with their own sets of particular problems and emotions. Moreover, they employed to their advantage material and discourses gleaned from sociological, psychological and State-driven initiatives to investigate the causes and consequences of, and solutions to, what was perceived to be a growing tide of parental neglect, widespread immorality and physical degeneracy. All of these factors will be explained in detail in this book.

# Moral and Emotional Consensus

The groups outlined in Chapter 1 are many and disparate, but they shared an attitude towards the upbringing of boys along certain moral and emotional pathways. This can be demonstrated through a comparison of the messages from evangelical and so-called secular papers. Contemporary socialist papers manifest further evidence of a remarkable degree of continuity in this regard. This chapter encompasses an analysis of the activities of the social groups related to these publications, often based around the principles of temperance. It reveals how these groups encoded emotional ideals and appealed to 'correct' emotional responses.

What is striking about the groups and their respective publications is their shared 'language of emotion', framed in terms of moral action and its effects on conscience, and the building of character. Sympathy, caring and love in domestic life were to be part of a boy's emotional toolbox in becoming a man. Forethought, sensitivity and kindness to women were considered vitally important characteristics for developing men. Yet informal moral education was not only about correct emotional exploration, but also about teaching boys emotional control. The chapter explores the ways in which positive emotional responses to youthful temptations – drinking, smoking, masturbation, cruelty – were thought to be triggered, making for a moral character. Through the inculcation of positive responses, negative responses could be diminished. Boys were taught to control their negative emotions and delay gratification of their positive emotions by abstaining from bad habits in order to promote future happiness. Problems only emerged if wrong choices were made, all of which were thought to be avoidable. In sum, the correct moral 'feeling' was thought to determine the path of development towards adult uprightness.

These sets of moral responses to stimuli were thought to comprise a whole mode of being that in turn defined how an ideal citizen would be, rather than simply how he should act. This moral 'prescriptive citizenship' was therefore rooted in emotional education, the tenor of which was held in common by religious and secular 'educators' alike. This moral and emotional consensus is presented as a major contribution to the understanding of childhood, and therefore to notions of Britain's future, at the fin de siècle.

## Real dangers

While it would be misleading to argue for an all-encompassing general societal consensus regarding boyhood and youth in this era, it will be argued that the most widely spread and influential juvenile papers, and their associated societies, did agree on how to view boyhood and on the strategies involved in promoting the 'right' kind. Encouraged by the apparent popularity of this particular view of ideal boyhood in the juvenile periodical market, the publishing industry maintained a similar message throughout the period. The late Victorian and Edwardian boy was the subject of abundant discussion and intense scrutiny in the juvenile press. He was also the subject of grave concern. Gordon Stables, the flamboyant and prolific writer on health matters for the *BOP*, remarked that boys faced dangers that were 'very, *very*, real'.[1] He advised that:

> The very first stepping-stones to good health and success are the giving up of bad habits, whether school vices or smoking and the declaration made to yourself and before Heaven in your own chambers that *you will not read sensational or impure literature again*. You thus bid fair to purify your minds and bodies also, and remove the most dangerous obstacles to your advancement in life.[2]

The religious and secular press both promoted the same view: a boy's life course was fragile, and the few years before adulthood would make a significant difference in producing either the next generation of responsible citizens and heads of family, or moral and physical degenerates. Disparate groups, which one might otherwise expect to be at odds with one another, agreed that better than encouraging boys to cease the practice of bad habits, was to prevent them from ever starting them.

Since the popularization of Rousseau's ideas, childhood increasingly was set aside as a special, sacred time, one ostensibly free from adult responsibilities and temptations. The reality in the period 1880–1914, however, was that many children of all classes faced adult pressures before their time. Of these, childhood exposure to alcohol, in particular, came under attack by reformers and publishers in innovative ways. Gambling, questionable morality and lack of religiosity were often linked to drinking. These pressures were thought to be especially perilous for boys, held under the misapprehension that it was manly to drink. Smoking was also widely believed to be unacceptable for boys and young men before the age of 21. New and growing concerns for males, in a phase between boyhood and adulthood indicated an increasing fear that young men would not be fit for a modern Britain, their manliness and their morality in question. Perceptions of declining rates of religious adherence and fears that many men were shirking their familial responsibilities for the homosocial environments of the Empire and the club,[3] drove organizations to promote the informal education of the next generation of young men, in the hopes that they would be better husbands, fathers and citizens.

Of course, temperate and 'good' wives and mothers were also required, based on a typically gendered understanding of women's roles in the home and their special vocation as moral guardians and teachers of children, through their superior emotional cultivation. Girls were certainly a focus of the Band of Hope and in some bands they formed the majority; it was also more shocking for females to be intemperate and to stray from the feminine ideal. As one Band of Hope worker put it, 'a godless woman is a greater anomaly, a sadder failure even, that a godless man'.[4] Yet boys, as future men and citizens, were the primary focus of the movement, as they were less sheltered and thus presumably more open to temptations.

The widespread consensus in British opinion on boyhood behaviour, even among seemingly disparate organizations, both secular and religious, is evident in the publications by Alfred Harmsworth (later Lord Northcliffe) and his AP, the RTS, the CETS and the Band of Hope movement and will be briefly compared to socialist periodicals for children. The common discussion in popular periodicals for boys can be mapped demonstrating how this consensus was shaped. This survey is by no means exhaustive, but aims to provide a broad sketch of popular cultural and intellectual opinion on the importance of fin-de-siècle boyhood.

The consensus on boyhood education and enculturation involved an understanding that the future of society and the nation depended on reaching children in time. This view was stated unequivocally, especially by temperance advocates. As the Lancashire and Cheshire Band of Hope Union stated clearly, 'The Future of the Nation *is* with the Child'.[5] The *Workers Onward*, the publication for Band of Hope workers containing temperance news and information, blackboard addresses and a 'hints and helps for the work' column, published a photograph of a huge juvenile temperance rally held on 10 October 1908. The focal point of this photograph was an enormous banner draped across a balcony, which read 'Train the Child, Save the Man',[6] as did a song sung at the Jubilee of the Band of Hope in 1897: 'As the hope of the earth is the spring-time, So the Hope of the race is the Child'.[7] Advice to the Lancashire and Cheshire Band of Hope workers made this clear: 'To train the child is easier, safer, and its results more permanently abiding than to reclaim the man. With the untrained, unreached children of to-day will be found the drink-problem of to-morrow.'[8] While the motivation for educating boys on temperance in particular was clear, the principle was far more pervasive. The Band of Hope had to combat the widespread idea that being rough and intemperate was manly;[9] the movement's image of masculinity contrasted to a far greater extent with popular, conventional ideas than did its understanding of femininity. For both sexes, however, this informal education was an appeal to the emotions – to be able to learn to feel what behaviours were moral, to be able to delay immediate happiness for greater future happiness. Indeed, it is essential to remember that 'temperance' referred first and foremost to a virtue of character, defined by moderation, restraint and even-temperedness. It was this self-control that alcohol put under threat, subjecting the drinker to animal passions. The director of the National Society for the Prevention of Cruelty to Children (NSPCC), Robert Parr, made clear that children, since they were the 'central figures in religion' and 'the moving force in the home', and even more crucially, 'the main hope of the nation', should be a central responsibility of the nation.[10] The extension of this argument was also widely expressed: attention ought to be focused on boys in particular since they themselves were the future holders of responsibility in matters of familial, community and national concern. One typical recitation, 'The Coming Men', asserts that boys ought to be prized as future teachers, preachers, voters and statesmen, positively influencing their families, communities and the wider nation. It associates temperance, Christian religiosity, family and effective manhood and citizenship.[11] The idea of promise in boyhood was common.

The argument here might seem surprising. That there was a consensus of opinion about the moral upbringing of boys within periodicals and their associated organizations is not an obvious conclusion. These organizations had sometimes opposite points of view politically, theologically and commercially. They were also targeted at different classes, based on their prime motivations for change within specific groups. In the messages these papers directed at boys and at their parents, however, there was far more similarity than ideological friction.

It will be shown at the end of this chapter that socialist papers also promoted the same views. For children of all classes, abstinence from alcohol and tobacco, gambling, masturbation and impure thoughts were all essential. Furthermore, there was a strong emphasis, even in so-called secular papers, on religious faith, fair play, sensitivity, sympathy and kindness to women and children. All of these positive attributes were tied in with the view that boys would become men; they were to be trained to become the 'right' sort of men: citizens who were at the centre of domestic life, with fidelity to family, to country and to Empire (in that order). Most importantly, all of these widespread publications emphasized that the boy, and the crucial life stage between boyhood and manhood that would become 'pathological' – adolescence – were of utmost importance to the family and the nation. As boyhood and, increasingly, adolescence came to be recognized as phases of life distinct from manhood, there was an increasing perception of the need for a moral education specific to boys. In an era of universal schooling, this sort of education was seen to be lacking in formal settings of school, church, chapel and home. Perhaps it was also deemed better to teach these moral lessons more subtly and informally, through a popular medium that young readers could enjoy while absorbing deeper messages.

Raising boys correctly was given to mean nothing less than the advancement of the British race. According to one commentator, 'What the nation will be in thirty years hence depends chiefly on what the children of the present decade are. The world makes its progress on the little feet of childhood.'[12] Raising them incorrectly, or in other words, not using all possible means to inculcate the right sort of behaviour and beliefs, might cost the family and the nation dearly, when boys became men.

Boys were informally educated through the stories in popular periodicals to become responsible men and caring fathers. This moral fiction aimed at correcting the 'immoral' pulp of penny dreadfuls was an important undertaking at the turn of the twentieth century when, as Martin Francis and John Tosh have outlined, a rapidly changing society provoked questions about the place of men in the family.[13] The legislation of this era is indicative of a heightened concern for the rising generation's physical and moral health. Several key acts demonstrated a new concern for children in their own right, and not as possessions of their fathers (see Chapter 6). Since many late Victorian and Edwardian boys were falling short of modern physical, educational and moral standards, organizations (the Boy Scouts being the most influential after 1908) were formed to ameliorate these shortcomings. The juvenile periodical press was a key player.

Many constants remained regarding childhood in the Victorian and Edwardian eras. A preoccupation with boyhood especially dominated the prescriptive writings of the whole period. That the future of Britain depended on the proper upbringing and education of boys was not in doubt. What was in doubt was whether boys were being adequately taught at home and in school. Victorian publishers had begun to fill that gap; Edwardian publishers sought to refine this informal education in a changing market, making the boy's paper serve religious and moral ideologies, and advance Christian truths.

## Boys will be men

The *Young Crusader's* 'Temperance Lesson' addressed more holistic life choices than simply abstaining from alcohol. Though total abstinence was viewed as an essential component for boys' development into moral manhood, it was not sufficient. The following list of negative habits and influences could have been published in any of the papers:

1. Beware of swearing.
2. Beware of lying.
3. Beware of disobedience to parents.
4. Beware of scoffing at the Bible.
5. Beware of gambling.
6. Beware of bad company.
7. Beware of the first glass.
8. Beware of the first pipe.[14]

The emphasis was placed on making sure that these bad habits were not even tried, rather than on reforming boys who had already strayed. This view promoted goodness in potentially corruptible children, rather than on reforming their already corrupted parents. Bad habits were condemned as having disastrous effects on the body. Disobedience to adults (especially to parents) and lack of piety or honesty were also bad habits of the spirit. The two were mutually propagating. Bad influences, found in the home, the street, the gambling den or the pub, could either be the first step towards the moral and physical corruption of the young, or could lead to further degradation in those already seeking out a bad habit.

The periodicals of late Victorian and Edwardian publishers were structured with serial stories as the strongest component, while there were usually also illustrations, aspirational biographies and advice columns. The advice sections urged boys to read the *right* kind of story, and to understand what lessons to draw from their reading. What was promoted in the periodicals? In short, it was the message that boys should be trustworthy, honest, hardworking, punctual, polite, unselfish, justly independent and self-reliant and abstain from bad habits.[15] There was some latitude in terms of the extent to which 'bad' habits were proscribed. Robert Hamilton Edwards, editor of the AP's boys' papers, did not want to be called a 'rabid teetotaler', but he did advocate for every British boy to be not only an abstainer from alcohol, but also from 'cigarettes, swearing, and every other bad habit'. He maintained that if boys were total abstainers during their youth, there would be far more abstinence among adults.[16] That 'the British race would be all the better for it' was agreed by all concerned groups, with varying degrees of 'rabidity'.[17]

The early Victorian emphasis on strict evangelical messages was certainly becoming unpopular, in favour of more subtle moral messages which would be more palatable to the late Victorian and Edwardian young. Yet, even in so-called secular papers (as Harmsworth's are understood to be), a strong Christian foundation can be uncovered. The values promoted in the texts were Christian in origin, though it would be far too simplistic to dismiss the papers as relics from an evangelical past. They were certainly of their age, competing in a modern publishing industry and with the modern reader in mind. Boys were no longer miniature adults: they were often viewed as naturally good and pure and could be moral beacons for adults, but their good qualities could easily become polluted under the wrong influences. Boyhood was a distinct and crucial phase of development, one in which boys were trained in the serious matter of character building for manhood, while also catering to their specific pastimes and fantasy world. This new and growing concern for boys was indicative of an increasing fear that many men were not fit for a modern Britain, with their manliness and their morality in question.[18] Evidence from the major boys' papers shows a strong concern for training boys in an informal and indirect way: while there was an abundance of explicit moral instructions in these papers, it was common for the educational value to be implicitly loaded into the morals of stories, and into the general tenor of the publications over this entire period. Moral training was therefore not reducible to one or other particular story, but was formed from a general and long-running appreciation, in the reader, of the whole. Boys were given advice on how to prepare for a modern career and how to provide themselves with a healthy lifestyle. More important than these outward attainments, they were also instructed how to lead a manly life.

The inner qualities of manliness were actively taught. As John Tosh puts it: 'It was the consistent aim of boys' education to internalise these moral qualities – to make them second nature so that they could be expressed in action instinctively and convincingly. Virtue was held to be inseparable from manliness.'[19] To this extent, morality, virtue and manliness were felt qualities, trained emotional dispositions that would ensure boys responded in the right ways at the right times. Both religious and 'secular' organizations made clear in their informal teachings for boys that the attributes of a 'real' man, of a real gentleman, were open to any class. It could be put simply, as in one 1914 *Band of Hope Review* piece, that 'the boys who keep on trying have made the world's best men', regardless of class.[20] Equally, *no* boy should be drinking, smoking, gambling or physically 'impure'. Real success was in becoming a 'real' man, one who took seriously his responsibilities to his family and to his country. Hamilton Edwards clearly expressed this in 1903: 'I want them all to remember that success in life, is, after all, not so much about the mere making of money, as the making of one's self a useful, honest citizen of our great empire.'[21]

The juvenile publishing industry had long recognized its potential influence. As early as 1886, Edward Salmon, a journalist who wrote extensively on juvenile literature, had made the connection clear, emphasizing that morality was not merely a code concerning appropriate actions, but a 'sense' or a state of mind. Reading had an influence on 'national character and culture' that was 'impossible to overrate', for, he said, 'Mind, equally with body, will develop according to what it feeds on.' The development of a 'moral sense' depended on whether reading matter was 'pure' or 'foul'.[22] The moral of a story was to be reified in the boy; his thoughts, actions and moral sense were to be shaped by reading as much as by his contact with the world around him.[23] While the juvenile press had different motivations, they all recognized the importance of the boy to society, and in the words of one commentator, 'to the character and well-being of the nation and the state'.[24] Thus, in the late Victorian and Edwardian period, 'frantic educational and religious dashes' were made at boys.[25] This urgency to reach boys was clearly seen by the RTS. Earl Cairns (1819–85), a supporter of numerous evangelical causes, was chair of the RTS's Eighty-Fourth Anniversary meeting in 1883:

> The urge for increased support is drawn from the home life and the young life of this country. It has ever been the grandest feature of the Society that influenced for good the life of our country in its most sacred and influential spheres. Guard home and young life, and you take the best method of establishing religion and righteousness in the land. Keep these pure, and you purify the whole nation.[26]

This was to be accomplished by publishing uplifting periodicals and other reading material for the young and for families. Other anniversary meeting speeches carried similar messages, such as Chairman Sir T. Fowell Buxton's[27] for the Eighty-Eighth Anniversary, 'This Is a Reading Age',[28] or the Hundredth Anniversary speech, 'The Antiseptic Power of Good Literature'.[29] All were especially concerned with providing the young with pure and uplifting reading material. Home and the young were the keys to a better future for Britain.

For all the papers, boys, rather than girls, were the centre of attention. As one *BOP* writer declared in 1910, 'People say, "Boys will be boys;" but they are wrong – boys will be men. And to prepare for their manhood not a day is to be lost.'[30] There was a new sense of urgency in the late Victorian and Edwardian papers: modern life was comparatively fast-paced and the years before adulthood so few that moral guidance, as well as the education required for a modern workforce, needed to be passed on effectively and efficiently. This was in line with received opinion, which the papers were keen to reference. For example, on the back cover of the June 1910 issue of the *Seed Time and Harvest*, there was an advertisement for David Williamson's new book, *From Boyhood to Manhood*. The contents of this book addressed the same issues as the papers and reflected a continuity of message throughout the period, with a focus on character and manliness: 'starting work', 'lodgings', 'clothing', 'doing work well', 'changing employment', 'reading', 'the simple life', 'ambitions realised', 'a true gentleman', 'keep eyes open', 'friendships', 'building character', 'keeping on', 'debating and speaking', 'keeping accounts', 'acquiring knowledge', 'the soul life'.[31]

Positive images of masculinity were mixed with warnings against the temptations of modern life. It was feared that the 'ugly thoughts, wicked memories and unclean pictures' of bad books would etch themselves into boys' hearts.[32] One young reader of the *Band of Hope Review* wrote in 1908, 'If a boy reads rubbish he nearly always thinks about it afterwards, and feels inclined to do the same things himself. And it robs him of strength of will, and care for his character.'[33] Gordon Stables and countless other writers of the period blamed 'penny dreadfuls' for boys' descent into vice and violence, which produced immoral, ungodly and unproductive lives. Ruined lives were thought to be redeemed only with difficulty, and only through moral influence and example. It was thought far better positively to influence the young before they 'ruined' their lives. The fear, however, was that the publishers of penny dreadfuls and even the producers of newer inventions like cinematography understood the weaknesses of the boy, and could therefore influence his moral behaviour and his upbringing more than 'the Sunday-school teacher and the Band of Hope lecturer, and better even than the woman who bore him'.[34] Yet there was hope that with the availability of the 'right' sort of reading material the fin-de-siècle boy would know what to choose. Hamilton Edwards believed this to be true of his own papers. He wrote in 1912 that 'The present-day fellow carries plenty of common-sense in his head, and when he reads a thrilling story, he wants it to be thrilling in a sensible manner, and not a mass of blood-curdling improbabilities'.[35] The advice to boys was clear: 'Do not load up your heart then with hateful things you must carry with you to the last; load up rather with thoughts that are beautiful and true and lovely: these will lend you wings to help you mount higher and be happier'.[36] Morally correct reading was prescribed, that 'good books' would be inscribed on boys' hearts and influence their emotions.

## Defining the path

By generally focusing on concepts and objects – man, nation and Empire – with which readers from different backgrounds could all agree and identify, and by boiling down the religious, moral and physical precepts to their essences, the papers attempted to provide messages that could be universally understood. Diversity of perspective and of opinion in late Victorian and Edwardian life were therefore minimized in order to provide boys with a clear, fairly uniform prescriptive pattern of manhood. Far more important than class, status or social manners were the inner qualities of the boy, which were to be cultivated for manhood. As the *Young Standard Bearer* pointed out, what a man said or did was not as important as 'what a man is'.[37]

In the CETS paper, the *Young Crusader*, a short story called 'Uprooting the Passions' shows the intent of this prescriptive genre. In this story, a young boy who is walking with an old man is asked to pull up increasingly bigger shrubs. He pulls up the first ones with ease, but the task becomes more difficult, until he can no longer move the roots at all. The old man then makes the connection to the passions clear: when young, it is easy to 'pull out' passions with a little self-denial, 'but if we let them cast their roots deep into our souls, then no human power can uproot them – the Almighty hand of the Creator alone can pluck them up'.[38] This boy had a good role model in the wise, older man. The *Young Crusader* played the wise old man for its own readers. The periodical press became the late Victorian and Edwardian child's moral guardian and emotional guardian.

Moral guidance was easily and consistently encapsulated in pictorial form. In the March 1908 issue of the RTS's publication for its workers, *Seed Time and Harvest*, for example, a pictorial story appeared titled 'Which Path Will You Take?', demonstrating the importance for young boys of taking the right path while young enough to influence their ultimate destiny (Figure 2.1).

This was a greatly reduced facsimile of a 'striking' banner that had recently been published by the RTS to be purchased by teachers in elementary schools, Sunday Schools, mission halls, boys' clubs and similar institutions. It was also made available as a postcard. In short, it was to be shown anywhere in Britain where groups of boys were gathered for moral instruction or character building; it was also translated into many different languages for missionary purposes abroad. The title, according to the RTS, 'seems to us well calculated to be of service in the training of the rising generation'.[39] The pictures received support from educational and religious leaders. The Bishop of Manchester, Edmund Knox, believed that it would teach boys honesty and industry. The Rev. Canon Denton Thompson wrote that 'It will not only attract the eye and impress the

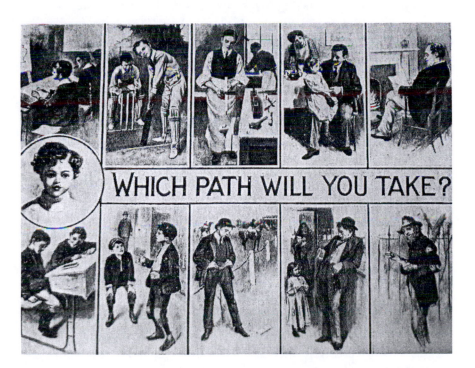

**Figure 2.1** 'Which Path Will You Take', *Seed Time and Harvest*, March (1908): 17.

mind, but also be retained by the memory, and as such, I am sure it will prove a potent force in the development of moral character.'[40]

The moral of the image is typical of its type. In the top sequence the boy goes through the life stages appropriate to a young Briton who will take up his rightful place as citizen and head of family. He is attentive at school; practices fair play at cricket; learns a respectable trade in the presence of a wise master; provides for a comfortable home; takes pride in his family; and retires to a quiet life of dignity and refinement. The other path demonstrates what could go wrong if boys were not properly guided: the young boy falls asleep at his lessons; gets into mischief in the street where he comes under the attention of the police; gambles on horses; neglects his family in favour of drink, exposing his pleading children to the immoral environs of the pub; and ends up a beggar on the street. The social status of this boy is ambiguous, signalling the relevance of the story's weighty message to boys of different social classes. According to this scheme, the building of moral character, in conjunction with a commitment to work and family, allowed boys of merit (regardless of standing) to reach the higher echelons of society; conversely, a poor work ethic, disregard for morality and the authority of the father, drinking and gambling, would lead to poverty and depravity. Many stories showed boys that they had a choice: they could be real men, or they could let poverty overwhelm them and lead them into lives of vice. Manliness could be manifested outwardly: 'in an upright bearing in business engagements, in public duties'; and inwardly and emotionally: 'in the private delights of friendship and love'. For boys of all classes, manliness was seen as encouraging 'growth of inner life, of intellect, of character'.[41] This manliness, and its emotional expression, was fundamentally tied to Christian faith.

The Band of Hope typified this emotional emphasis, not least by its explicit association to hope. This hope was both personal, for the individual futures of the young members, and collective, for the hope of the nation. In addition to hope, other positive emotions were promoted and cultivated in the young, always with reference to the Christian foundations of the movement. Love, joy, kindness and enthusiasm were all emotions that children were to develop, both in reference to God and to their families. Many stories in Band of Hope publications were dramatically written accounts of lives lost to vice and the devastating impact on family and surroundings. These stories were meant to rouse the public's emotions: to feel disgusted by ruined lives; to feel love and hope for little children who were innocently involved; and to fear drink. The goal was that these emotions felt in reading would lead to action to promote total abstinence both in the home and in the wider world. Parents were to 'lead them straight', meaning that they should not have alcohol in the house if they did not want their children to associate drinking with positive emotions in the home. Band of Hope outline addresses, written for teachers to use in meetings, frequently discussed the difficulties of emotional education in, for example, promoting the 'right' sort of joy within the home. In one, 'Does Temperance Interfere with Family and Social Joy?' teachers were instructed to focus on the difference between the real joy of feeling strong and responsible with an eye to the future, and the false joy of sociability with alcohol.[42]

'Which Path Will You Take' was not particularly innovative, and might have been reproduced in any of the juvenile periodicals, regardless of denominational or political outlook. Analogously, 'The Child – How Will She Develop', published in the *Girl's Own* in 1894, revealed the 'dangers' of militancy to girls (Figure 2.2).

The picture was originally published in two vertical columns over two pages, with accompanying text in the middle. The images here have been compiled to fit on a single page, the top two rows being the virtuous path, the bottom two the path of militancy and misery. The first path shows the girl conforming to traditional expectations: she is loving, caring and nurturing. Though she does get an education, she chooses marriage and maternity over a career. The second path shows the girl choosing the life of the 'New Woman'. She is self-sufficient and intellectual, yet discontented, miserable, wanting in sympathy and alone. Whether intended to teach lessons to girls on the dangers of female emancipation, or to boys on the dangers of vices and character faults, these images provided children and young adults unequivocal messages on acceptable development. The messages were to be internalized in the full sense of that word. The development of character would proceed as it were 'naturally', based on an appropriately disciplined disposition. Training the character, so prevalent an idea in the religious and secular press, found new life among emerging discourses of comparative psychology and eugenics (see Chapter 6), where its surface was peeled back to reveal 'scientific' insights about its composition. According to C. W. Saleeby, intermingling his interests in science and the cultivation of a moral, temperate youth in the *Harmsworth Self-Educator*, and conjuring with Herbert Spencer, 'The great discovery which we have to recognize is that what we call *instincts* are the obvious aspects of emotions. Not only do the two go together, but they are essentially one.'[43] If instincts could be trained, then, by definition, emotions were also trained. Indeed, the cultivation of the correct emotional profile in the young was the essential precondition for the building of a desirable character.

THE CHILD:—
HOW WILL SHE DEVELOP?  AT SCHOOL.  FRIENDS WITH ALL.  AT COLLEGE. CONGRATULATED.  DEVELOPMENT OF HEART.

THE INTRODUCTION.  GOOD HABITS AND PLEASANT FRIENDS.  WEDDED.  MATERNITY.  HAPPY OLD AGE.

THE CHILD:—
HOW WILL SHE DEVELOP?  AT SCHOOL. DISLIKED BY MOST.  WASTE OF TIME.  THE FALLING AWAY.  WANT OF SYMPATHY.

BAD HABITS AND BAD FRIENDS.  READING HER OWN PRINTED PHILOSOPHY.  DISCONTENT.  A MISERABLE END.

WOMEN! ARISE !!! TO SUPPRESS THE ENEMY — MAN !!!! WE SLAVES

**Figure 2.2** 'The Child: How Will She Develop?' *Girl's Own Paper*, 16, no. 6 (1894): 12–13.

## Masturbation: A delicate touch

Whereas the periodical press' treatment of alcohol abuse could appeal to observable social problems as highlighted by the temperance movement, other problems tapped into a persistent societal fear which necessarily resisted any form of empiricism. The 'problem' was, nevertheless, no less real to its critics. Throughout the period, some physicians wrote prolifically about the devastating link between masturbation and impotence later in life.[44] One physician maintained that males were no more passionate than females, and that therefore, boys ought to be raised as sexually pure as girls: 'Yet how few are! How many of the female sex never know or understand the pleasure of sexual congress until after they are fully grown and married, and how many of the male sex are weakened and exhausted before reaching the age of maturity!' He encouraged a comparison of the number of cases of female and male impotence in order to understand the influence of 'early sexual excitation'.[45]

In a lecture delivered in London to an audience of 1,200 men, Alfred Dyer, the Quaker publisher, Contagious Diseases Act repealer, White Cross League supporter and author of the best-selling *Plain Words to Young Men on an Avoided Subject,* made it clear that men as well as women should be pure, and that the passions should be controlled even in marriage. He presented the opinion of a medical doctor, who, in response to the question 'Would the bringing up of boys in a more moral atmosphere diminish physical passion for sexual indulgence?', replied that it unquestionably would and that this was one of the 'most pressing difficulties of the age'.[46] Using a religious tone throughout, Dyer also advised total abstinence from alcohol and tobacco, in part because of their stimulating effects. Further safeguards against immorality and licentiousness included a 'well-occupied mind, plenty of out-door exercise, and a resolute avoidance of vicious companions'.[47] Dyer also advised against impure literature or art and quoted John Angell James, an eminent preacher and advice manual author, as saying in his pulpit:

> Twenty-five years ago, when I was a boy, a school-fellow gave me an infamous book, which he lent to me for fifteen minutes. At the end of that time I was to return it to him, but that book has haunted me like an evil spirit ever since. I have asked God on my knees to obliterate that book from my mind, but I believe I shall carry down the damage of those fifteen minutes to my grave.[48]

Masturbation, or self-abuse, was a persistent and delicately touched issue for boys' papers. All agreed that it was harmful, for both moral and physical reasons. It was supposed to destroy boys' manhood before they had even attained it, and even to lead to early death. The *Boys' Herald* cautioned readers that it causes 'spots before the eyes', if not much worse and that it should be ceased immediately.[49] Hamilton Edwards provided a more candid than usual response to one reader, 'Very Sorry' from Plymouth, who was the 'victim of foolish practices', though these practices were still not named. The boy is said to have given up these practices, but not before they damaged his 'physical system'. Although Hamilton Edwards is clear that he will not go into detail about what this damage entails, he provides advice for this reader and the many others who require similar counsel. Citing this advice in length will provide a good sense of the tone and attitude of Hamilton Edwards and the writers of the other papers regarding masturbation:

> The boy who has been guilty of stupid practices need not suppose that the mere giving of them up is going to restore him to his former condition of good health. He will have to take care of himself, and he will have to give himself time to remedy the damage which he has done. Moreover, he will have to give Nature some little assistance in repairing the harm which his own foolishness has caused. Plenty of open-air exercise, clean living, clean thoughts, are essential. In addition, a good tonic is a very useful thing.[50]

The *BOP*, in articles by Gordon Stables, provided advice on how to prevent such a habit from forming in the first place. In addition to getting straight out of bed into a cold bath every morning, followed by lifting dumb-bells, 5 to 10 minutes in the open air, and a healthy breakfast, he encouraged boys to 'Think, . . . before it is too late. Think – and pray.'[51] Echoing the more straightforward advice of the papers' other sections, these religious, moral and physical precepts were the core tropes of juvenile fiction in these periodicals (a tradition stretching back to *Tom Brown's School Days* (1857)), which consistently emphasized bodily exercise and private prayer. They were also the subject of recitations, whose repetition could only serve to emphasize the weightiness of the message of keeping all 'animal appetites' at bay:

> Boys are wanted whose breaths are sweet,
>
> The pure air undefiling;
>
> Who scorn all falsehood and smooth deceit
>
> That lead to a soul's beguiling.
>
> Boys who in scenes that are glad and bright,
>
> Feel their pulses beat faster,

But who hold each animal appetite

As servant, not as master.[52]

The boys' papers all agreed that that boys should be encouraged to avoid dangerous habits if they wanted to grow up to be upstanding husbands, fathers and citizens. This disciplining of 'animal appetites' was the essential first step in this process of growing up.

## Socialist messages for the young

So far we have seen that this 'consensus' included the Evangelical (of various denominations), the Anglican, the for-profit secular and the temperance presses. The socialists, too, who were mainly Christian socialists in this period, focused on educating the young. This education served to promote socialist principles, but also to inculcate general moral fundamentals, much like the other papers discussed here. There were many socialist papers for the young, often associated with the socialist Sunday School movement. A prominent example is the *Young Socialist: A Magazine of Love and Service*, owned by the Glasgow and District Sunday School Union and edited by John Searson.[53] This magazine discussed the progress of the schools, the movement and the links forged with socialist children within Britain and in other countries. It printed stories and poems with socialist and moral messages. The *Young Socialist* also tempered its socialist teachings, so that its tone was much in line with the moral messages and the development of character found in the other papers:

> If you have learned to be kind, sincere, helpful, the little seed has been planted which will grow up and bear fruit. We have all to do what we can, whether that be little or much. A little spite, a little angry word, makes enemies of those who were friends. A little selfishness helps to drive love out. A little kindness brings us nearer each other, and a little knowledge wisely given may change a boy or girl's thoughts, bringing light where there was darkness.[54]

As with the leitmotiv of their evangelical counterparts, socialist papers for youth emphasized the cultivation of an emotional foundation, on which the structure of morality could be built, first driving out spite, anger and selfishness, and installing in their stead love, selflessness, courage and kindness. With titles like, 'Helping One Another', by Lucie from Huddersfield School, the *Young Socialist* tried to promote considerate and sympathetic action in children.[55] These values supported socialist views, but they were also much broader values, equally promoted by the non-socialist papers.

As with the other papers, these messages were sometimes couched within fatherly lessons to children. The last verse of the song, 'What Daddy Told Dolly', provides a good example of the socialist/paternal tone:

'And must this ALWAYS be?' asked Dolly,

Looking very sad –

'Is there no cure for poverty and misery, dear dad?

Must people ALWAYS work and work, and be so poorly paid?'

'Oh, no!' said daddy, as he stooped and kissed his little maid.

Chorus – 'There are brighter days in sight, Dolly dear,

Dolly dear!

When these wrongs shall be put right, that is

clear, Dolly dear!

SOCIALISM is the cure

For the ills the poor endure,

And it's coming, slow but sure,

Never fear, Dolly dear!'[56]

Teachings had to be adapted to suit children in particular. Providing a familial context helped to make socialist ideals more familiar. 'Joy and gladness' were central to socialist writings for children.[57] Dour messages of class inequality were seen as far less effective for children than were hopeful messages of future happiness and equality.

Socialist papers for adults also contained articles and stories for children, often within dedicated children's sections. Important examples are the *Yorkshire Factory Times*, the *Labour Prophet*, the *Labour Leader: A Weekly Record of Social and Political Progress* and the *Clarion*. These papers had the support of socialist leaders, who sometimes wrote themselves for the papers' children's sections. In the 1890s, Keir Hardie, founder of the Labour Party, wrote many serial stories for children, frequently published in the *Labour Leader*, the paper he edited.[58] Some of these stories were reprinted in the *Young Socialist* in the 1910s.[59] They clearly show Hardie's devotion to socialism, but also to temperance and to Christianity. Hardie had been a temperance supporter since he was a boy and was a convert to Christianity and a lay preacher in the Evangelical Union Church.

Robert Blatchford (or 'Nunquam'), founder of the Manchester Fabian Society, author of *Merrie England* and editor of the popular socialist newspaper, the *Clarion*, also wrote stories for children. Blatchford and the *Clarion* thought that the moral education of children ought to be the priority, since it related directly to politics. This view was widely held among socialist writers and publishers. As with the non-socialist papers, moral education was linked not only to domestic and personal satisfaction, but also to good citizenship. The *Clarion* promoted the view that 'Education is the next essential – moral education more than any other kind.' Extending the franchise would be useless unless voters were not only wise enough to use their vote 'properly', but also 'honest' enough to go through with it: 'You can no more make a man a good citizen by giving him a vote than you can make him a good carpenter by giving him a basket of tools.'[60] Boy and girl readers were often addressed together in these publications, but they generally followed predictable gendered prescriptions for childhood and future adult behaviour and action. While girls were encouraged to take on a supporting role, boys were described as future leaders of the movement. As with the other papers, socialist boys were taught what it meant to be a man. Robert Blatchford wrote that 'When you meet a *man* he will tell you to respect *everybody*; but he will also tell you to respect yourself. And he will tell you that unless you respect yourself you will never respect other people. You will only *fear* them. Which is a very different thing.'[61] This idea of manliness was consistent with the teaching in the other papers in its elimination of debilitating and negative emotional states.

As with many of the other papers for children, the socialist papers helped to promote socialist Sunday Schools, and were intended as reading material for such gatherings. The *Labour Prophet*, for example, provided its 'Cinderella supplement' free of charge. An announcement for a socialist Sunday School meeting in the *Clarion* made clear that socialists, like their non-socialist juvenile publishing counterparts, regarded this sort of education for the young as crucial for the future of the family and the nation: 'Comrades, our hope for the future lies with the children of to-day. Help us help them.'[62] Many such socialist Sunday Schools (which met on Sunday afternoons) were founded in the 1890s in London and across Britain, including one in Fulham started by Uncle Archie, regular contributor to the *Young Socialist* and to the children's section of Hardie's *Labour Leader*. By 1911, one source counted about 120 Socialist Sunday Schools in Britain with an attendance of about 7,000 children and 1,500 adults.[63] It was recognized that attention ought to be focused on educating children to be morally solid adults, trained in socialist thinking. As John Trevor, founder of the Manchester Labour Church (1891) and the editor of the *Labour Prophet* noted:

'The children, rising up into a world which will be theirs to renovate, must be gathered into our great movement.'[64]

In addition to the socialist Sunday Schools, there were socialist summer camps and other gatherings that focused on children. As part of the annual May-Day Socialist Festival at Alexandra Palace in 1903, children could obtain *The Children's May-Day Souvenir* in which was written: 'The children are to Socialism what the flowers are to Spring. In their happy faces we already get a glimpse of the victory the future holds in trust for our cause, and every earnest Socialist feels a duty in fitting with the coming generations to make Socialism a living reality throughout the world.'[65] The aim of this festival and its accompanying booklet, as well as the socialist papers and their associated socialist Sunday Schools was to promote the socialist movement among the young. Like their counterparts in other parts of the political spectrum, socialist children's workers believed that it was crucial to educate children while they were still young enough to be moulded, rather than attempting to change the behaviour and beliefs of adults. One poem asked that pure childlike qualities be promoted for all: 'O, give me my child-heart – My child-hope again.'[66] As socialist teachings were promoted for children, it was hoped that adults might also be taught by children.

It would be difficult to argue that this 'consensus' of moral teachings for children was understood that way in the early twentieth century. There was much opposition to socialist Sunday Schools, and by extension, the papers in which their lessons were contained. Traditional (Christian) Sunday Schools were praised, and contrasted with the socialist schools, which were seen, by groups like the London-based Children's Non-Socialist League, to undermine religious teachings and pervert Christian terms with their 'The Ten Commandments, The Hymn, The Red Catechism, The Declaration, Socialist Saints, the Socialist Doxology'.[67] These teachings were denounced as a 'Sacrilege!' and a 'Travesty of the Forms of Christian Worship Taught to Children on Sunday Afternoons'.[68] The 'awful evil' done by these schools was seen to be increasing.[69] Some argued that it was urgent to save the faith of the 7,000 children who attended these schools, since as adults they would not be able to accept Christianity if as children they were trained to despise it through agnostic teachings. This could not be allowed to happen in 'Christian Britain'. This kind of judgement of socialist Sunday Schools was clearly exaggerated for the purposes of polemic. In fact, since the 1890s socialist Sunday Schools had had a theistic and Christian socialist view in promoting values to children.[70] It was not until after the First World War, when the Communists joined up with the socialist Sunday Schools, that the ideas promoted within them became more radical and less palatable, even to many socialists.[71] Until that point, however, even if the various opposed groups (from the evangelical RTS, to the secular AP, to the various socialist groups) could not acknowledge it, there was a marked similarity and consistency of moral message among them.

## Conclusion

C. E. Schwann, an MP from Manchester, was quoted as saying that 'From the age of fourteen to eighteen a boy was a *queer sort of creature*. He was scarcely a boy, and yet not a man, and it was easy for him to get off the right path.'[72] This was precisely the concern of the groups mentioned in this chapter, and the popular education associated with them in the juvenile press; it also serves as a reminder of the message of the 'Which Path Will You Take' cartoon discussed earlier. There was a common agreement among the juvenile publishers to fill an educational gap left by the inadequacies of school and home life with moral instruction for this liminal stage of life. This chapter highlights the existence of a broad consensus in late Victorian and Edwardian Britain regarding the coming generation of male citizens, even among seemingly disparate 'secular' and religious movements.

The first verse of a poem in the 1914 *Band of Hope Review* neatly sums up the preoccupation of authors and publishers of late Victorian and Edwardian boys' periodicals:

If boys should get discouraged

At lessons or at work,

And say, 'There's no use trying';

And all the hard tasks shirk,

And keep on shirking and shirking,

Till the boy become a man,

I wonder what the world would do

To carry out its plan.[73]

The late Victorian and Edwardian juvenile periodical press and its associated youth movements, although varied in their methods and motivations, provided a unified message for boys of various classes. They facilitated the transmission of common values and of expected behaviours, in order to educate boys on their future roles as men, husbands, fathers and Britons. They also promoted improvements in their physical health and work-related skills. This education was informal, not too heavy-handed or didactic, and often catered to boys' desire for fun and play. It created a space for boys to be morally instructed outside of the stricter confines of church, chapel, school or even home, forging close ties with a diverse range of boys' associations with similar aims. Most importantly, this education was to affect boys at the level of the heart, that morals and values would be felt, duties and responsibilities carried out as if by second nature. The consensus on informal education can be reduced to this emotional landscaping of the inner boy, that the desired result – a temperate, manly citizenry – would arrive straightforwardly. The next generation of strong and moral men were to be capable of heading their families and of being good citizens, in peace time and in the increasing likelihood of a European war.

# Domestic Bliss? Husband, Wife and Home

Chapters 3 and 4 explore in detail the parameters of the key characteristics of the prescribed citizen, as put forward by the moral consensus. Chapter 3 focuses in particular on the relationship between husbands and wives, the primary importance of home life, and the question of moral leadership and domestic authority, as they were presented to youthful readers through the medium of the periodical press. The specific identification here of citizen with father leads to a reassessment of the importance of fatherhood as a locus of moral education within the domestic realm in the late nineteenth century. Working against notions of motherhood as the sole moral compass within the home, I arrive instead at a definition of the domestic ideal that put the father at the centre of notions of racial survival and national greatness. Yet this father-centredness still stressed the importance of marriage, fidelity, temperance, duty, religious adherence and morality.

With this in mind, the boy as future citizen was necessarily also a future father. This section details informal educators' work in ensuring that boys understood the importance of fatherhood and the authority of their own parents, before assimilating precise instructions on how to become good fathers themselves, once they were men. Moral and emotional education for boys, it is argued, was essentially education for how, eventually, to be fathers and citizens. Boys were taught that a real man was one who would not be led by peers, but would keep in mind his real duties to God, his family and his country. He was taught to develop sympathy to consider the feelings of those around him – his family, his peers and his community – and those who might be important to him when he became a man: his future wife and children. The chapter concludes briefly by examining the threat posed to the domestic ideal by the rise of the 'New Woman' and the attempt among the stakeholders of youth to co-opt this newly empowered figure into a pre-existing arrangement of domesticity.

## Home politeness

In a 1911 *Boy's Own* article, 'Mother and Home', a clean-cut Christian young man is reported as having said that he had been one of the worst boys in town, but seeing the example of a boy from a good home who was respectful to his mother, he decided that he would try to be the same to his own mother. Though he is mocked for his new behaviour, his whole life begins to improve and the narrator comments: 'thus one boy's kindness to his mother is still bringing forth good fruit in the life of a man.'[1] The *Young Crusader* also emphasized the importance of placing the family and home above wider pursuits. In one 1897 article a young man is described as having been discontented with his home, and consequently having enlisted as a soldier. He had wanted to see the world, have adventures and wear a red coat. Five years later, he learned that 'be it ever so humble, there's no place like Home.'[2] Such stories served to instruct readers to be accountable to God, to their families and to themselves.

Robert Hamilton Edwards told boys, many of whom left home to work at an early age, to write home regularly, thereby fulfilling a duty to their parents. 'I need hardly say that nothing brings greater happiness in after life than the knowledge that you have been a good son to your father and mother, and have spared them all needless worry and anxiety'.[3] A letter from a young female reader (many girls also read the AP's boys' papers) asks for advice for her brother who wants to be a scout, against the wishes of their father. These papers clearly promoted the Boy Scouts, but in this case, emphasizing duty to family took priority. Hamilton Edwards replies that though the boy should attempt to talk to his father about the merits of scouting, he should be obedient to his father always. He then used the opportunity to teach readers about their debt to their parents: 'their parents feed, clothe, and educate them from the time that they were tiny babies'. He also notes that in the 'vast majority of cases, until they are at least fourteen, none of them ever bring a shilling into the house'.[4] Though Hamilton Edwards was making the point that boys owed their parents obedience and kindness for their financial support, he also relates to his working-class readership by appealing to their own realities.

In the religious and temperance press as well, politeness to father and mother indicated that a boy had good manners to everyone else. A boy who was not polite to his parents might seem courteous to others, but, as one 1884 *Band of*

*Hope Review* article stated, he 'is never truly polite in spirit, and is in danger, as he becomes familiar, of betraying his real want of courtesy'.[5] Emphasis on good manners, originating in the home, but also projected onto society, was part of boys' training for a modern workforce, and was tied in with more concrete new skills like bookkeeping or typing. Modern business skills, without a concomitant transformation of manners, would be useless in working-class boys' advancement. In a similar way, middle-class boys were taught moral ways of comportment in society in order to ensure that they too would advance, or at least not descend from the position of their parents.

Though various periodicals were primarily read either by parts of the working or the middle classes, there was a consistent message for all. According to the *Young Standard Bearer*, a Mr Burns, when addressing the boys and girls of the Anerley District Schools, 'gave some excellent advice, which applies to all classes of society'. He instructed the boys 'when they went out into the world to shun gambling and strong drink'; and he said to 'the girls that to boil a potato well was better than playing a piano badly, and to nurse and dress a baby was far preferable to overdressing themselves'.[6] Such talk of the preservation of 'traditional' gender roles helped bridge the gap between what young people were exposed to in their reading material and in their moral formal education in school. Essentially, boys were to prioritize family above all else and obey their parents, even if they felt their advice unreasonable or outdated. 'No matter how keen their desire may be to see the world outside, their first duty is to their parents.'[7]

## Marriage

It's very clear that all of us

Good wives intend to be,

And how we carry out our plans

Some day I hope you'll see.

And when folks look on our bright homes

And pleasant, healthy lives,

They'll say 'tis plain that Temperance makes

Good husbands and good wives.[8]

The above stanza is from a long recitation for eight girls called 'Temperance Wives', from the CETS paper, the *Young Crusader*, published in September 1898. This piece is an exemplar of Victorian social thought, emphasizing the 'naturalness' and comfort of the ideology of separate spheres and of a gendered separation of labour. The pervasive view of contemporaries and of scholars is that 'females were seen as ordained by God to be dutiful wives and mothers, guardians of the home and family.'[9] Though the family conjured up in the imagination of little girls reciting this piece is humble, it follows the aspirations of 'middle-class' domesticity. The wife will make a pretty little house and her husband, when he comes home at night, will be proud. She will be neat and cook good meals. She will send the children to bed early so that she can sew and mend as her husband reads to her. They will be snug and happy. They will have a little garden, where her husband will like to go after work; he will never want to go to the pub. If the wife is kind and gentle, the husband will want to stay at home. In return for her contributions to their domestic bliss, she hopes that he will help her. This is the ideal picture of a companionate marriage, for little girls.

Targeted at middle-class children, it did more than to show the virtues of temperance in the working classes. It was intended to reinforce and confirm in the minds of its young readers 'correct' gender relations in their future lives as men and women, no matter their social status. They were taught that they should not aspire to wealth for its own sake, but should seek a happy and comfortable home. It will be shown that these 'middle-class' domestic values were far more pervasive than rigid class distinctions allow. Publications targeted at working-class audiences also provided this sort of image of domesticity, but framed in terms with which their readership could identify. This was no mere imposition of gender norms from above. Moreover, mainly middle-class papers also stressed domesticity as a goal for men, perhaps because of a perception that many middle-class men found the home a far less appealing prospect than in previous generations.[10] In fact, often stories targeted at one class would feature characters from another class, thereby creating ambiguity in the directional flow of the messages among social classes. This was certainly due to wider readership aspirations of the publishers, but more importantly, also served to highlight the universality of the messages. The framework of 'separate spheres' in gender relations was further complicated by an insistence on the importance of the role of the father within the family, not merely as a distant provider, but as the moral centre of the family. Manliness was thus linked, not to physical prowess, but to morality and domesticity.

The recitation's encouragement of children to do whatever they could – by their comportment and their actions – to make their homes a more welcoming place for fathers who might otherwise be tempted to stray away from home was repeated by many authors. For example, in one Band of Hope article, working-class girls were encouraged to gather flowers for their homes. 'If Band of Hope children would try to make their home prettier, and sweeter, and brighter, perhaps they could sometimes tempt their fathers to remain in them instead of seeking the false pleasures of the public-house.'[11] In fact, children were themselves described as little flowers who gave pleasure to all who knew them.[12] This association of childhood with good, innocent things, as beacons of purity to adults around them, will be discussed in greater depth in Chapter 4.

In other texts, girls and women were encouraged to feel that, by their own example, they could influence men to behave responsibly. In an 1883 temperance story, 'Don't Marry a Drunkard', Susie's aunt recommends that she not encourage a young man who is courting her, because he drinks moderately and is reported to swear while out of the presence of women. Susie thinks that her aunt is exaggerating and marries the man anyway. Eight children later, he is a drunkard and the entire family has dropped drastically in social status and is destitute. The narrator then asks rhetorically, 'Is this not a wretched picture?' A lament follows: 'hundreds of maidens are preparing for themselves a future as bad. There can be placed no dependence on the *manliness* of the man who drinks, or on his kindness and good nature.'[13] By this sort of cautionary text, both women and men were instructed on what was required of them in marriage. Men who wanted the chance to attract a good woman were to display manliness by being temperate and good, to understand before marriage what it meant to be manly; women were to make sure that they were shrewd enough before marriage not to fall for the wrong sort of man, one who would be untrustworthy and irresponsible.

In another story, 'A Deliberate Choice',[14] this one in the 1893 *Leisure Hour*, author Anne Fellowes presents a young woman who must choose between a model of a 'good' man and that of a 'bad' man. The good is learned, kind and honest, but poor; the bad, whom she marries, is rich and well-born, but transpires to have a vile temper. The good in this case counsels the young woman to do her duty and remain with her husband, despite her misery. The moral, the importance of character over wealth, of the delayed gratification of domestic happiness over a compulsive 'love of pleasure', is archetypical.[15]

Another classic device of the story is its demonstration of manliness as outwardly apparent, comparing the physiques of the two suitors. The bad 'had a handsome face, with strongly marked features', but 'was short and ill-made. Despite his good looks, his appearance was unprepossessing. There was a look of evil temper in the heavy eyebrows and in the clear-cut thin lips.' The good man, however, 'was tall and spare, his features irregular but refined. The whole

charm of the face lay in the deep-set, melancholy blue eyes, and in the smile
that but rarely lit up and transfigured his countenance.'[16] Lives of inward virtue
were worn on the exterior. The good, though perhaps not handsome, would be
refined. Sincerity would be apparent in the face. Talk and artifice were not manly.
Stoic silence, however, was more likely to be.[17]

Women had responsibilities in addition to judging the character of their
future husbands. Papers for girls, like the RTS' the *GOP*, argued that though
women were gaining greater educational and professional advantages outside
the home, they were to remember what were their core duties. The following
exchange between father and daughter makes this clear:

> Daughter (home from school): 'Now, father, are you satisfied? Just look at my
> testimonial. Political economy, satisfactory; fine art and music, very good; logic,
> excellent!'
>
> Father: 'Very much so, my dear, especially as regards your future. If your husband
> should understand anything of housekeeping, cooking, mending and the use of
> a sewing machine, your married life will indeed be happy.'[18]

Women were certainly instructed that their proper place was in the home. They
read in great detail about how to take care of their households, but the emphasis
lay on the physical care required of a manager of servants, rather than on the
emotional care of their families. That said, women were taught that they must be
responsible for their husbands' happiness and well-being. A socialist paper, the
*Yorkshire Factory Times*, gave the following advice to wives:

> Unless a man is really depraved and heartless, any woman of tact can keep her
> husband at home if she wishes to do so. Make him feel each time he enters
> the home that his presence is really desired, and show him that his comfort
> and happiness are the business of your life. Make the home itself as bright
> and attractive as possible, and pay particular attention to your own personal
> appearance. Don't worry your husband with domestic troubles if you can help it;
> but if this is absolutely necessary, keep them till he has had his meal.[19]

Women were by no means always seen as positive forces in the home, taking on
the moral roles their husbands could not or would not perform. In some texts
women were held directly responsible for husbands' failings, their unhappiness
and their straying from home:

> Women are often so capricious, so exacting, so tactless in their treatment of
> the man they have married that they drive him into ways and habits which,
> although in themselves wrong, are in reality the outcome of the wife's conduct.

Thus things gradually go from bad to worse, and the happiness of two lives is ruined, all perhaps for want of a little tact in the first place on the part of the woman.[20]

In articles such as this one, from the RTS' paper for girls, wives are to blame for their husbands' misdeeds. The author goes on to sum up why this is so: 'He is the master, the head of his household; his word is, or should be law, and the wife's duty is to submit and carry out his will'.[21] This sort of advice for wives is not a great revelation to scholars; more surprising were the lessons for boys and men concerning their domestic roles. The 'good husband', despite the focus of the 'Temperance Wives' recitation, implied far more than the simple avoidance of alcohol. In this understanding of gender relations, husbands and fathers were not only to be the final authority, but also the strongest moral influence, and therefore the emotional foundation for family life. Mothers, on the other hand, were increasingly displaced in this period from this moral centre.[22]

## The moral man is the family man

One of the most well-known images of Evangelical fatherhood is the grim tale of a stern and strictly religious father and his stifled son recounted by Edmund Gosse in his *Father and Son* (1907). But this does not provide us with the complete image of evangelical parenting that historians usually, and misleadingly, draw from this kind of source. RTS writings provide us with a different, richer picture. For RTS authors, tenderness and familial love were within the reach of the late Victorian male. John Gillis' phrase, 'a worldly stranger to domestic life', encapsulates the assumed marginality of the father, with the increasing distinction between home and work.[23] Yet, discursively, manhood and fatherhood were still inseparable constructions. In fact, domesticity could be the principal test of character for men, as one author declared: 'When a married man, a husband, or a father, is fond of spending his evenings abroad, it implies something bad, and it predicts something worse. . . . Home is the test of character.'[24] According to popular advice writer, Sylvanus Stall, 'if the husband has the true father-spirit, the privilege of frequently remaining at home to spend the evening with his children will afford more pleasure and more profit than could be secured elsewhere.'[25] Domesticity and fatherhood were thought to be the greatest goal for men. They were also their greatest responsibility: 'What his home is, what his children are to become, will depend as much, and possibly more, upon what he is and does',

Stall thought, rather than what his wife is and does.[26] In an era acutely concerned with the generation to follow, the idea that a man's children's future depended on his actions would have seemed serious indeed. His actions would of course also determine his own happiness.

According to one 1882 article in *Onward*, the Manchester Band of Hope paper, 'a young man's highest ambition should be the establishment and maintenance of such a home, which shall be the reservoir of his best life, and a perennial fountain of joy' and therefore this young man should 'scorn to bring to his [future] wife, a heart that has flirted with a dozen girls, or a body impure from evil thoughts and practices'.[27] The advice was echoed by Alfred Dyer, who thought that parents should encourage their sons to begin courtship at a reasonable young age (e.g. 20 years old) and to expect fewer material comforts in the first few years of marriage. Among other things, this would prevent self-abuse and the devastating moral and physical consequences that Dyer thought went along with it.[28] Once married, this advice still applied. In 1904, the *Sunday at Home* published counsel along similar lines from the Archdeacon of London, William Macdonald Sinclair: 'Do not let your own affections wander and stray in a series of vain sentimentalisms. The wife who is neglected, slighted, or coldly treated, is just as unhappy as if the law permitted her rival to be installed in the family circle.'[29] Young men were to prepare themselves for their future roles as husbands and fathers by leading chaste and temperate lives while still young. The key to future domestic joy was the reining in of untrammelled passions and sentiments. The idea that a young man's wife was somewhere out there to be found was to be a stimulus for him to eschew temptation and 'to attain all that is worthy and complete in a perfect manhood'.[30] For many, marriage was seen as the culmination of youthful efforts to succeed in life, financially and morally.

This view of the importance of domesticated men was typical. Charles Darwin had produced statistics in his *Descent of Man* to prove that unmarried men over the age of 20 were far more likely to die than married men. It was not that marriage per se safeguarded life so much as it tended to be 'that the intemperate, profligate, and criminal classes, whose duration of life is low, do not commonly marry'. Moreover, men of a 'weak constitution, ill health, or any great infirmity of body or mind, will not wish to marry, or will be rejected'. Marriage, in the Darwinian view, ensured the selection and survival of the finer moral qualities, and was therefore to be recommended for the moral individual. To be sure, 'sound and good men who out of prudence remain for a time unmarried, do not suffer a high rate of mortality', but bachelorhood could not be recommended for the course of life. And once married, the moral man had a role to play.[31] J. W. Kirton, for example, in his *Happy Homes and How to Make Them*, appeals to young husbands to make themselves useful at home and if there are any children, to play with them, 'for without any loss of dignity you can now and then rock the cradle or nurse the baby, and in this way share the burden of the house with your wife.'[32] Another commentator opined that 'It is not only the privilege, but the honor of the father to be found enjoying the pleasure and satisfaction of holding and caring for his children.'[33] Yet, far more important than taking care of the physical needs of the children, the father was supposed to instruct his children in their moral and spiritual lives. Family reading was a widely promoted method of centring the moral education of the family around the paternal voice (Figure 3.1).

Family reading taught men and boys that though providing for their future family's material needs was an essential role, it was not by itself sufficient. They also learned of the necessity of being morally good, in order to provide a positive example for their families. For example, one article condemned the modern trend of seeing wealth as a main life goal. Young men 'toil on the belief that no one can be fairly said to have "risen" unless his pockets are well filled.'[34] Monetary wealth was certainly secondary to moral health. Belief in God was the 'real' way to 'rise' and become a man. Men who were deceived into worldly pursuits only might rise in wealth, but would most certainly 'fall' when judged in substantial, moral ways.

Readers (and listeners) were shown that fathers must be especially Christ-like with their progeny. In 'A Search for a Wayward Son', one evening a young man came home very late and very drunk. His father, disgusted by his son's behaviour, threw him out of the house, but then repented and blamed himself for his son's unmanly conduct. The father then went out searching for his wayward son, and said to him 'My dear boy, I want you to forgive me; I've never prayed for you; I've never lifted my heart to God for you; I've been the means of leading you astray, and I want your forgiveness.'[35] Patience and love in the home were paramount.

Some fathers were portrayed as being on the road to failing the principal test of domestic character. In 'Bob Hilmore's Escape', the main character is a working-class father and a drunkard.[36] His two children, Jenny and Hal, go to find their father in the pub. 'For a moment the father's heart went out in love towards the pale face [Hal], and he longed to clasp the child to his breast.' He is, however, embarrassed in front of his drinking partners and instead yells at Hal, who staggers back and falls. The father's fatherly instincts, the reader is led to think, are impaired because of his drinking habit and because of the bad associates this brought as a consequence. The father is sorry and no longer afraid

**Figure 3.1** *Onward* (1878) cover page.

of his companions, and carries his son home. Then comes the real moment of crisis, of moral and emotional awakening, which drives Bob to change his life. As he sits intensely thinking, in a drunken state, he accidentally drags off the table cloth and with it the paraffin lamp. This starts a mighty blaze. Bob, 'sobered at last by the terrible danger to which his little ones were exposed', saves them and his wife from the fire. He later recalls 'how his drinking had nearly robbed him of those he held most dear'. The end of the story is a happy one for Bob and his family as he becomes a total abstainer, and succeeds in leading many men like him to follow his example. The story appeared in the CETS's family publication, which provided models for 'flawed' fathers and would-be fathers to follow. Though the road for Bob was not smooth, in the end, he becomes a good model for his children.

The importance of fathers was made most clear in the role they were exhorted to play in their sons' moral development, amid fears that mothers' dominance in the home would have disastrous consequences on their sons' manhood. The recitation called 'Following Father' in the CETS's *Young Crusader* illustrates this point. A 6-year-old boy follows his father's footsteps in deep snow in order to tend the sheep with him. When the pair come home, tired but happy, the moral import of this kind of father–son activity becomes apparent. The father realizes the importance of the influence he has by the example he sets for his son. The recitation concludes:

> Oh, fathers leading in life's hard road,
>
> Be sure of the steps you take,
>
> That the sons you have when grey-haired men
>
> Will tread in them still for your sake.
>
> And with loving words to *their* sons will say,
>
> 'We tread in our father's steps to-day'.[37]

The father was to be careful not to develop vices, while remaining religious, thoughtful of his wife and a good provider for his family. The belief that sons would follow in a father's footsteps placed a special responsibility on the father. Mothers, by contrast, were loving and supporting, but morally peripheral. There is a strong sense of the continuity of generations in recitations such as these. Not only is it assumed that this son will marry and have children of his own, thereby passing on his father's name, but he will also pass on his father's traits as well. This was the nub of the matter for many such authors and what made these lessons so important.

The *Young Crusader* targeted middle-class boys, but often with working-class themes, perhaps to demonstrate the universality of the lessons and to encourage a broader readership.[38] As this was directed at youth, it would have served to emphasize a message of paternal moral responsibility to readers without children, to stress future thought and action. This went along with a prevalent belief that it was better to educate boys to become conscientious before they became adults, rather than admonish men who were perhaps not taking their moral responsibilities to their children seriously enough.

The RTS's widespread publications, the *Leisure Hour* and the *Sunday at Home*, taught readers how to have a moral and religious home, one that would bring harmony and create a fitting environment for the raising of children. They continually emphasized the central spiritual role the father should have in the family. The wife had to replace the husband when needed, but she was not the preferred moral centre of the home. From its inception in 1799, the RTS' view of the father's central role within the family remained constant, yet in its early period, the RTS' portrayal of fatherhood took for granted that fathers would impart moral and religious teachings to their children and undertake their spiritual guidance. Examples of such publications are *A Present for the Young* (1828), the *Boy's Week-day Book* (1836) and the periodical *Child's Companion or Sunday Scholar's Reward*, in addition to early issues of the *Leisure Hour* and the *Sunday at Home*. In the late nineteenth and early twentieth centuries, this fatherly role could no longer be taken for granted.

In RTS stories, the traditional evangelical connection between the father and the Father is made clear. The father receives his authority over his family from God, but God is the ultimate Father, ready to fill in for the earthly father when he fails to meet his moral responsibilities to his family. When adequately performing his role, the earthly father is, however, held to be a direct and essential moral force in the family, whose influence over his children is significant. Other stories show the negative effects on children of a father who does not live up to the evangelical ideal and is not an adequate moral guide for his children. As many of these stories mirrored the lives of the (mainly middle-class) readers and of their social superiors and reflected men's changing roles, stories of fathers who always took the moral lead in the family were less common towards the end of the century, making apparent RTS authors' worry that late nineteenth-century fathers were not living up to their duties. The RTS continued to emphasize the importance for young men to have a strong role model and guide in their fathers. The young man in each story is led away from the family by immoral and worldly influences, only to return to the family in the end, redemptively, through the memory of the father's influence.

By the 1880s, members of the Society perceived a need to reinforce traditional evangelical values and began more actively to defend paternal authority both explicitly and implicitly within the content of its publications. In RTS family stories, young men return from abroad to be with family or to start their own. They do not usually neglect their interactions with women and children by engaging in long-term homosocial activities. On the first page of almost every story in which the central character is a boy, the formula followed is to describe the child, then the father and his occupation. Thus the father invariably figures prominently in these stories. Yet his central importance is not always ascribed to the positive effects of his presence within the family. It is often his physical or emotional absence that marks his relationship with his son and the rest of his family.

In the absence of the real father, God, the heavenly Father, is ever present in the RTS' the *Leisure Hour*, the *Sunday at Home* and the *BOP*. The term, 'The Fatherhood of God',[39] often repeated in RTS publications, is an important signifier of the close ties between God and the earthly father. In many RTS stories, this tie is so strong that Father and father are used interchangeably. One stanza of the poem, 'The Little Boy's Faith in God', is telling:

'Our Father', sir, the prayer begins,

Which makes me think that he,

As we have no kind father here,

Would our kind father be.[40]

This poem, from a paper with a mainly middle-class readership, describes the unconditional faith of a poor 6-year-old boy, one of four children of a widow who could not find her family enough bread to eat. The boy says the Lord's Prayer with complete faith that God will provide their daily bread, when their mother could not, in the absence of an earthly father to provide for all of them. In this case, not only does the Father replace the father as moral and educational head of the family, but, by the end of the poem, the author also indicates that the boy rightly expects Him, at least figuratively, to take on the breadwinner role of the family.

There are many other examples of stories in which the heavenly Father substitutes for the earthly father. 'A Discontented Boy'[41] is one of many stories in which the father is physically absent. Herber Letter had been close to his father before his death. They had shared a love of books. His mother could not have become his moral and educational centre because, too weak to sustain herself and her son, she died shortly after his father. Herber is not fortunate enough to find an adequate surrogate father, and he is portrayed as a sad, 'discontented boy' because of it. He is adopted by his uncle, a man who does not share Herber's intellectual interests or his spirituality.

Although Herber's new home takes care of his physical needs, his spiritual and emotional needs are unmet. His direct relationship with God fills his spiritual void, as the Father replaces the father. Though persecuted by his uncle's family, Herber perseveres in his intellectual and spiritual pursuits and finally develops a true relationship with God. He is no longer a 'discontented boy' and declares, 'I feel as if I could hunger no more, nor thirst any more, because I have found Jesus.'[42] Father and father may not be entirely interchangeable concepts, but God becomes a more than adequate fatherly figure for Herber when no earthly substitute for his father is available.

The connection is more closely related in 'A Lost Son', a typical RTS story of a young man who temporarily forsakes his family and is led astray by many nefarious temptations in the city. In the end, this tale represents the triumph of the older values of middle-class domesticity, as represented by the values of the father, over the fast life of the fin de siècle. Julian Serlcote, the son, takes no interest in his father's shop, and is a 'weak, pleasure-loving, self-indulgent young man'.[43] Yet, his father Joshua, 'stiff, prim old martinet that he was, had a secret pride in this son of his'.[44] When he first talks to Agnes, Julian's fiancée, of Julian, the old man shows his fatherly emotional connection and

> betrayed with touching simplicity the pride and delight he had in his son. No detail seemed to have been too minute for his notice. 'I never saw the gentleman who could hand a teacup with more grace than that which is natural to my boy', he said one day.[45]

Joshua's pride, however, has its human limits. As Julian drifts increasingly away from his family, Joshua speaks about Julian in an apologetic tone. Embarrassed by his own behaviour and unable to face Joshua, Julian flees his father's house after stealing a large sum of his money, to continue his downward spiral of vice in the city. Julian's mother is saddened, yet she remains peripheral to the plot. It is his father's 'hardening' grief that is thoroughly explored.[46] Religious themes are emphasized to uphold and strengthen the position of the father in the family, and consequently, of the family itself. When news that Julian is dying alone in the city reaches Agnes she exclaims pleads with his father:

> He is alone, penniless, dying, and pleads that he may not die unforgiven. Is it possible that you can refuse to forgive him? Think of that other father – the father of the prodigal son in the Bible! When the prodigal was yet a great way off, his father saw him, and had compassion, and ran and fell on his neck and kissed him.[47]

The Parable of the Prodigal Son in Luke's Gospel is the familiar story of a rebellious son who rejects his father's upbringing. Prideful and strong, the son, like Julian

Serlcote and many other characters in this moral tales, leaves his father for a wild life of adventure, and squanders everything of value (literally and symbolically). The son returns home when confronted with failure and despair, repentant and willing to do anything to win back his father's favour. Agnes wishes that Joshua would emulate the father in the parable who forgives his son and welcomes him back lovingly. The wish to have the earthly father emulate the heavenly Father in forgiveness is quite apparent in this story, as it is in many others. The father was also to provide a good moral example for his children, especially for his sons, thus ensuring that his sons eventually follow the moral path and embrace evangelical domestic values, even if temporarily led astray by worldly temptations.

Joshua does indeed regret that he is not more forgiving, more God-like, towards his son. Angry with Julian for neglecting his responsibilities towards his family and his fiancée, he does not open his letter asking for assistance for eight days. As a result, he comes to believe that his son has died because of his stubbornness and inaction. Conjuring with another biblical tale, Joshua laments his 'Absolom'.[48] Absalom (II Kings, iii, 2, 3) is an Old Testament example of a wayward son. He is alienated from his father King David and eventually banished for plotting against him. David forgives his son once and allows him to return to the city. Absalom does not repent, however, and yet again plots against his father. In the end, the son is killed, and David mourns his loss. Likewise, Joshua fears that his feelings of anger towards his son have contributed to his death.

The ending for Joshua and his son is a happy one. Julian sees the error of his ways, remembers Joshua's moral teachings and returns to his father's house. Joshua finds his son lying on the ground and subsequently collapses as he believes him to be dead. Both father and son recover together and Julian goes on to assume all the duties of a domesticated evangelical man. Predictably, with the usual evangelical emphasis on the New Testament rather than the Old, in the end, his and his father's fate resemble the parable of the prodigal son, rather than that of Absalom and King David. As the narrator explains, the men settle into lives of happy domesticity: 'Joshua Serlcote lived to see his son an honoured man and trusted; lived to see his niece [Agnes] a happy woman much loved and much loving; lived to find joy in the affection of his little grandchildren, who grew up about his knee; and lived to thank God.'[49] God's role is essential, as it is his example that ultimately shapes the conduct and influences the feelings of father and son. Yet without a strong earthly father as a model, it is clear that Julian would have lacked the deeply moral conscience that eventually led him back to the family.

The secular AP serial stories also provided boys with (surreptitious) lessons on fatherhood for its mainly working-class readership, which were reinforced by the popular editorial sections. Hamilton Edwards stressed the relevance of serial stories in the *Boys' Herald* for the lives of his boy readers:

> No one can be ignorant of the great influence exerted upon a boy's future by the early teachings of his father. If that father is too mild towards his son, the result is ofttimes deplorable, on the other hand, if the father is too harsh and strict, the result is every bit as bad – sometimes worse.[50]

Readers were encouraged to think that fathers' influence on their sons was great. They could be a positive example that their progeny could imitate, both as children and later as men. This example extended into all facets of life, both in the home and in the wider world. One typical *Boys' Herald* story from 1904 is about 'Two Drummer Boys', both about 16 years old.[51] Dick Wild is a good boy who tries to do the right thing. Jack Tillett steals from Captain Robinson and is generally morally reprehensible. Since Wild's father is supposed to have been a thief in his army days, his son was blamed for the crime against the Captain and goes to jail. Tillett continues to steal when Wild gets out of jail. Good confronts evil and both boys almost die. Thinking he is dying, Tillett finally confesses to the crimes, and also has an even more serious revelation for Wild. It was actually Wild's father who had been a hero in the army, and Tillett's was the thief. 'The stain' on Wild's father's name was lifted, and thus by extension, his son's as well. Tillett confesses to Wild that, 'I've been a bad lot. I was cruelly unjust to you always, and you behaved like a Briton. Will you forgive me?' One of the morally good character traits associated with being a 'Briton' is clearly forgiveness, for in a rather lofty way, Wild replies, 'I do, with all my heart', as he gives the boy his hand. 'But go the straight road in future, Tillett', he adds. The message here is clouded in sensationalist writing and unrealistic plot lines, as was the way with most serial stories in the AP papers for boys. A reading beyond the surface of the action reveals a twofold message to its young, mainly male and working-class, readers. First, having a morally strong character would serve them well in the end. What this entailed could be gleaned from Hamilton Edwards' editorial sections. Second, fatherly conduct (whether sons were cognizant of it or not) was a hereditary stain, impacting the moral development of his sons.

The fear that vice, criminality and immorality were heritable qualities activated the literature and activities of all groups concerned with fatherly responsibilities, but not least the NSPCC, at a time when physical and emotional abuse by fathers was less tolerated than before. In a 1910 book designed to highlight the *Wilful Waste* and the consequences of bad parenting, Robert Parr, the Society's director, demonstrated that 'the sins of the fathers are visited upon the children unto the third and fourth generation.' Whereas the damage done to future generations was clear, the abuse often remained hidden. His aim, in common with all the others considered in this book, was to make manifest this concealed immorality. Parr gives an example of a man who appeared to be a good father, since he was a hard worker and earned good wages. In reality he was cruel and ruined the lives of his children. His oldest son was in an infirmary, said to be the result of the epilepsy brought on by his father's mistreatment. His daughter was in a workhouse with two illegitimate children. He also had two boys in the workhouse, and yet another at home, who though 14, was dirty, neglected and illiterate.[52] Parr also featured on a temperance lantern slide, succinctly stating the consequences of alcohol at the level of the heart, where, through the drink habit, 'cruelty replaces love', marking a 'decline in proper parental instinct'. 'It may be difficult to believe that anyone will raise a hand to strike a child', the Parr slide said, but 'DRINK MAKES PARENTS DO THIS'.[53] Physical and emotional scars were the result of abuse; moral, social and physical degeneracy were their legacy (see Chapter 6). This fear, a popularization of late nineteenth-century evolutionary science, was repeated in advice literature:

> No one can doubt the law of hereditary transmission. Our inherited and acquired characteristics are sure to be transmitted to our descendants. Indeed, so thoroughly does character permeate one's entire being that it might be said of each drop of blood that in its characteristics is a miniature of the person in whose body it was secreted. Eminent characters do not emanate from degenerate parents.[54]

The antidote was provided by reaching boys before they had tried alcohol and other vices. To the Band of Hope question, 'How long must I keep my [total abstinence] pledge', a little boy answers 'I think I shall never break my pledge; I mean to keep it as long as my father, and he says he shall keep it as long as he lives.' The little boy sensibly asks, 'What's the use keeping it just while we are children, and then go and drink when we get to be men?'[55] In one article in *Onward*, the lesson on temperance is given added weight as it is framed as a discussion between father and son concerning the chemical properties of alcohol. The father instructs his young son that it is useful outside of the body, but never within it. The boy concludes that when he becomes a man he will try his best 'to get people never to allow a drop of this stuff to go into their mouths'.[56] The fatherly lesson emphasizes the importance of knowledge (formal or self-taught) and would impact not only the life of his own son, but by extension the lives of his son's family as well.

## The new woman and the ideal husband and father

According to Elaine Showalter, 'what was most alarming to the *fin de siècle* was that sexuality and sex roles might no longer be contained in the neat and permanent borderlines of gender categories.'[57] As women's roles expanded, the role of men became a source of anxiety. In one 1893 article in the *Leisure Hour*, women were pressed to regain their 'womanliness', despite the allure of a 'manly' education.[58] The author was not wholly unsympathetic to women's plight, and explained that it was partly as the result of 'long and unjust intellectual disabilities that the sex so long debarred from knowledge should be prone to exaggerate its value, and regard it as an aim, rather than one means to the attainment of a much better thing, wisdom'.[59] It was thought that young women needed to be coerced into accepting their domestic roles and to excel at them, for their own good. They had to 'break [themselves] in (or be broken in) to do pleasantly these thousand and one small things', while 'still young and pliant'.[60] They were to start perfecting the necessary domestic skills, or else their lives would end in misery, from which their advanced education could not protect them. Put another way: 'Or else, as a *woman*, she is a failure.'[61] Another article insisted that the 'Ideal Husband' must accompany the new woman.

> The new woman has determined that she will share the man's life in every sense of the word, and that men are to lead lives surrounded with the safeguards and self-restraint that have hitherto protected women. The standard of life is to be reversed. Women are to know all, and men are not to be permitted greater liberty and indulgence than women. Thus we have the advent of the new man and the ideal husband, both the creation of the new woman and the feminine spirit of the time.[62]

We might think of this as a modern appeal for men to engage to a fuller extent in their families and in household affairs, yet this is not so. The author goes on to point out that it is tiresome if men seek control over the minutiae of the running of the home and that this should generally be left to wives. The husband was, however, usually to be master of the house, as he was the breadwinner. The article concludes that the best way to ensure an 'ideal husband' was to be an ideal wife.[63]

At the end of the Victorian era, one humorous piece by George Scarr Hall on 'The New Woman', intended for recitation at temperance and Band of Hope meetings, declared: 'You must not suppose for one moment that the "New Woman" is a head without a heart. She has a head and can think, and she has a heart and can love, but note, please, it must be a man, not a beer barrel on a pair of legs.' It goes on to describe the various bad habits and incompetencies of men in the home. 'Fancy any woman called on to love, honour and obey a thing like that. The "New Woman" never will, it is one of the most impossible of impossibilities.'[64] The 'New Man' needed to be able to have as complete a grasp of the world as his female counterpart: he needed to be able to operate equally well in the home and in the wider world. An accomplished woman who could do anything she wanted required a man who would excel at professional and domestic duties and be emotionally sympathetic.

The fin de siècle certainly witnessed the complication of gender relations in the home. While some men doubtless took domesticity seriously – 'meddling in the minutiae of home life' – others were eschewing the responsibilities of marriage for the freedom of bachelorhood. Contemporary commentators perceived this as a crisis, as it would exacerbate the 'problem' of spinster women.[65] There was also a fear that modern ideas were destroying the view of the home as a sanctuary. According to Phyllis Browne, writing in the 1895 *Leisure Hour*, 'The influence of home has done much good in the past, but there is reason to fear that it is losing its power.' To her mind, 'the cause of this mischief [was] the devotion exhibited by the young people to outside interests – interests, that is, that are apart from the home.'[66] Historians too have seen men's rejection of domesticity as a positive choice in favour of a more homosocial life.[67]

One CETS story, however, 'Why Bob Was a Bachelor: A Story for Mothers and Daughters',[68] puts the blame on intemperate women. Bob comes from a good, temperate family. He could provide for his future family with his income as a porter. His sweetheart, however, comes from an intemperate family, and although she seems sound, she slips into an intemperate life after her mother dies from alcoholism. Bob cannot marry an intemperate woman, and though he remains patient in trying to guide her towards temperance, he never marries. In a time when there was a shortage of eligible young men, this was seen as a waste. Though this story was clearly a cautionary tale directed at women, whose life goal was assumed to be their own marriage or the marriage of their daughters, it also contained a message for men. Men should choose their wives carefully, but if good, temperate women were available, marriage should be the natural choice for men.

In 'A House Beautiful', the author gives advice to readers in the form of a dialogue with her husband, thereby providing advice on how to have a meaningful and comfortable home on a limited budget, from a feminine and a masculine viewpoint. Though the author acknowledges that it might be difficult for a young man to get married and set up a home with limited means, she decries the modern trend for young men to put off marriage indefinitely because they would have to give up luxuries. 'His income is insufficient for marriage because it will not support these luxuries *and* a wife', she scoffs, 'And he prefers the club, the first-class carriage, the cigar, and the lemon kids. So he gives up the wife!'[69] For the author, the RTS journal editors and other important writers on marriage, these are clearly wrong-headed priorities – far better to have a good home life, than to enjoy luxuries outside the home. In the view of Charles F. Goss, the author of *Husband, Wife and Home*, it was the responsibility of all healthy men to marry and to have children, since nothing could be 'more irrational than to be afraid to perform the functions of nature – to be afraid to live, to labor, to marry, to bear children, to found a home, to suffer, to die'.[70] Domesticity was seen as a major and 'natural' part of the lifecycle of men. To have a happy home, however, required some effort, in the view of popular advice writer, Sylvanus Stall:

> If you wish to preserve and perpetuate that which is noblest and best in your wife and your children, you can only do so by making your home the centre of your thought, and by making your loved ones the sharers of your purse and your pleasures. If you wish them to live for your comfort and happiness, they have equal right to expect you to live and sacrifice for their comfort and happiness. Almost any promising bride may soon be made an ill-tempered wife, a discontented homekeeper and an indifferent mother by an improvident, extravagant, selfish and neglectful husband. In most instances ruined homes come principally from drink, idleness, bad temper, shiftlessness, and thriftless habits, brutal husbands, slatternly wives and Christless living. Do your duty faithfully to your wife and your children, and then, if home and happiness are wrecked, the responsibility will not rest upon you.[71]

Home and happiness are the key words here. This kind of summary of husbandly and fatherly duty and the causes of its failure was widely supported and promoted by the male and female authors of the juvenile and family-oriented publishing industry at the fin de siècle, as well as by the organizations that backed them. The new woman had given the periodical press pause for thought. Novel educational, recreational and employment opportunities for girls and women were represented in the periodical press, but they often sat on the same pages as more traditional representations, co-opting the new woman into a domestic ideal that was remarkable for the consistency with which it was presented.[72]

# Conclusion

Domestic bliss was to be the culmination of a young man's efforts to build for himself a good career and a good character. Boys' (and girls') moral education in the periodical press had fatherhood as a focus. The absolute moral authority of motherhood was in question and provided reasons for men not to stray from the home.[73] Women's influence on their children and their husbands was cast into doubt, usually implicitly, but sometimes explicitly, by the focus on the father as moral centre and the focus on children to act as beacons of moral goodness from whom fathers might learn. Furthermore, emphasis on the importance of the father was supposed to leave young male readers with no doubt that they had a crucial role to fill once they had reached their professional and personal goals in manhood. In the late nineteenth century, manliness was still equated with domesticity for many ubiquitous and influential elements in popular culture. It is important to stress the continuity of message among boys and men of all classes. Cultivating good (and abstaining from bad) habits, adherence to religious faith and attention to (formal and informal) education were the means to achieve these goals. The future citizen's (informal) education stressed well-rehearsed prescriptions on what made 'good husbands and good wives'.

# 4

# The Child: Father to the Man?

Amid attempts to encourage the positive development of fathers and boys was the perception that, to some degree, the current generation of fathers was failing the future of the country. The combined advice of religious and social groups and the periodical press played the role of social surrogate father – a safeguard in case actual fathers were failing or absent. Often their messages incorporated a distinctly unromantic corruption of Wordsworth's 'child as father of the man'. Teaching the correct values in the boy would hard-wire them in the man. The boy's future self would accord with how he was as a child. But there was also a more literal interpretation of this aphorism, in which it was thought that boys could act as 'moral beacons' to their own errant fathers. The correct moral behaviour and emotional responses of the informally educated boy would in turn, it was hoped, rescue the drunkard, the gambler and the abuser who had himself chosen the wrong path on the road to manhood. The 'good' boy was envisaged, quite literally, to be a fatherly example to his own father. As essential preparation for this role, the boy first and foremost had to learn when, and how, to practice denial of his emotional gratification. But this in turn depended on boys having a positive idea of why such a denial was desirable in the first place. At the core of the juvenile press' combined message was the recipe for ensuring that manly citizens emerged from the nation's boys. Manliness, therefore, was given a positive image. This chapter begins with the periodical press' strategies of teaching manliness to boys, thereafter the installation of the capacity, central to good character, of denial, leading in turn to the image of the child as father of the man. The chapter then returns to the question of the home, and the intergenerational emotional dynamics of domestic life.

## Teaching strategies and reception

Diverse strategies were utilized by the periodical press in order effectively to teach manliness in tandem with direct social interventions. The *Church Friendly*, for example, was the magazine of the Church of England Temperance Benefit Society. Founded in 1878, this Friendly Society insured men, women, boys and girls against sickness, accident and death and was advertised in this magazine and in others for family and youth readership. In 1903, there were over 180 lodges in England and Wales, with a membership of over 9,000, with claims paid exceeding £49,000. The *Church Friendly* published fiction and non-fiction about total abstinence from alcohol, smoking and gambling. The magazine and the Friendly Society it promoted brought forward mutually sympathetic and affirming messages of morality and purity. In a 1901 serial story in the *Church Friendly*, 'A Nonentity',[1] Sir Thomas Quartermayne is a plain non-entity compared with his handsome and charismatic brother Edward, who had been loaded with University honours, was a rising Member of Parliament and a universal favourite. Sir Thomas is cautious and quiet, but responsible and virtuous. He notices that Edward drinks a lot of brandy, and warns him that he will develop the same bad habit as their father. Edward asks 'If I'm in such danger, why not you? We're both his sons', but his condition deteriorates in dramatic form, until he wakes up to find himself weak, sick and robbed of everything in a back room in a close, narrow street in Glasgow.[2] He despairs, wants to jump off a bridge and the narrator recounts:

> As he looked back to the first remonstrance of his brother, he could see clearly how each step downwards had followed, and he wished, with a very passion of longing, that he had taken warning at first, that he had conquered the craving before it conquered him, and he told himself that it was too late now.[3]

Edward admits that he is beaten by his father's curse, and begs his brother to let him go abroad in order that he might be out of the way.[4] In the meantime, there is a fierce rumour that Sir Thomas is the drunk. He sacrifices his chance at love with Carrie (whom he thinks is in love with his brother anyway) to take his brother on a three-year sea voyage on a temperance ship in order to get Edward to overcome his drinking problem. When they return there is a (false) rumour that Carrie is about to marry someone else.[5]

In the end, all is well. Edward is cured of his problem with alcohol, and he explains everything to Carrie who happily marries Sir Thomas. The conclusion that 'Tommy's not quite such a nonentity as we used to think', provides the reader with a clear contrast between different masculinities.[6] Sir Thomas's stoic and virtuous manliness turns out to be vastly superior and more successful than his brother's more ambitious, outgoing and hard-drinking masculinity.

Papers with edifying messages were often coupled with other, sometimes more practical incentives for readers and followers. The links between story, periodical and society serve as an entry point into some of the pedagogical techniques used by the writers of boys' papers in order to get their messages across to their readership. I want to demonstrate that stories were not unconnected to the 'real' world, and were central components of varied strategies to inculcate appropriate forms of boyish, and thereafter manly, behaviour. The many references to various organizations for boys across the periodical press all address ubiquitous concerns about young men and their place in a changing modern world. Publications and youth groups cooperated with each other. The CETS publications and other temperance papers encouraged participation in the Band of Hope, the Church Lads' Brigade, and many other thrift and purity societies. The AP encouraged participation in its own 'League of Boy Friends', and also the Boy's Brigade and the Boy Scouts. Other organizations promoted in the papers include Harmsworth's 'The League of Health and Strength', 'The League of Health and Manliness', the Boy's Life Brigade, the National Association for the Suppression of Bad Language (all advertised in the *BOP*) and of course the mass Band of Hope movement. All of these groups had pledge forms for boys to sign and a code of conduct to uphold. They must have also engendered a sense of belonging in their youthful members.

The formation of two of the most influential groups for boys, the Boy Scouts (1908) and the Boys' Brigade (1883), is usually associated with increasing militarism and physical training for boys, but this was by no means the whole story.[7] The Scouts' leader, Major-General Baden-Powell, was also elected patron of the 'League of Health and Manliness', formed in connection with a parish church, and directed against smoking for boys under the age of 21.[8] In addition, Baden-Powell's *Rovering to Success: A Guide for Young Manhood* (1922) later repeated much of the advice given in earlier boys' periodicals, with a focus on avoiding the 'rocks' of women, wine, horses and irreligion, among others, and on building up character and the positive values associated with it.[9] In 1908, the same year as Baden-Powell published his *Scouting for Boys* and shortly after his movement began, he wrote to Hamilton Edwards, the editor of the *Boys' Herald*, congratulating him on 'The Wolf Patrol', a serial story about the Scouts.[10] In fact, Hamilton Edwards promoted the Scouts, saying that 'the manly principles, the self-reliance, the discipline, and the open-air life it encourages should make fathers regard the movement favourably', and started many schemes in his boys' papers to promote the Scouts, including 'Our Boy Scouts' Corner', in which boys who wanted to join patrols, or patrols wanting new members, could have free advertising space.[11] In 1909, The *Boys' Herald* even started 'The League of Scouts' to encourage 'boys to become alert, vigorous men and loyal citizens'.[12] In a private letter to Harmsworth, Hamilton Edwards expressed his intention of giving away 10,000 free scout uniforms to readers of the *Boys' Friend*; this seems not to have materialized, but six uniforms were offered as prizes in the *Boys' Herald*.[13]

'The League of Boy Friends', advertised in the *Boys' Friend* and the *Boys' Herald*, was one of the best promoted of the AP's organizations for boys and claimed to have a membership of over 35,000 in 1904. The rules of 'The League of Boy Friends' bear repeating, as they are a common refrain in writings directed at youth:

> 1. To endeavour to lead a manly, honest life. 2. To be polite to all seniors and to girls. 3. To protect the weak as far as lies in the member's power. 4. To abstain from bad language. 5. To be kind to dumb animals. 6. To abstain from smoking until twenty-one years of age. 7. To strive to be a bright British boy – always a patriot and lover of his country. 8. To assist fellow-members under all rightful circumstances.[14]

A similar club in these papers, 'The League of Health and Strength', also included abstention from alcohol, gambling and 'evil habits' (masturbation, among others).[15] The leagues had secret passwords, badges, certificates and pledges. As with the Boy Scout promotions, the AP surely wanted to boost sales of its juvenile papers by creating these clubs, but the league rules also reflect a pervasive view of boyhood and male adolescence, one which demanded constant repetition for its growing youthful readership.

Some of these rules are quite transparent, others much less so. What, for example, would it mean 'to lead a manly, honest life?' Or 'to be a bright British boy?' The correspondence sections of the AP boys' papers, especially the *Boys' Friend* and the *Boys' Herald* provide part of the answer. Boys and young men were to be respectful of their parents, work hard, prepare for a good career, be self-controlled, refrain from close friendships with women until they were self-sufficient enough to marry, and generally be gentlemen. To be a gentleman (a title perhaps now available to men of any class) was quite simple, according to one major Band of Hope periodical: 'By being true, manly, and honourable. By keeping himself neat and respectable. By being civil and courteous. By respecting himself and others. By doing the best he knows how. And finally, and above all, by fearing God and keeping His commandments.'[16] Even the 'secular' press for youth, like those controlled by Harmsworth, would have agreed.

One organization advertised in the *BOP* was 'The Boys' Life Brigade'. Boys in uniform, but without arms, were instructed in military drill. They were taught how to save life from fire, drowning and accident. There were also classes in hygiene, ambulance and first aid. But its goals were broader and, like the Boys' Brigade, it promoted 'the advancement of Christ's Kingdom amongst boys', and the 'habits of obedience, reverence, discipline, and self-respect, and all that tends towards a true Christian manliness'.[17] This focus on the values associated with the movement rather than with its apparent militarism was also promoted by local Boys' Brigades, who needed to appeal to adults to drum up support and money in order to buy the boys' uniforms and musical instruments.[18] As with the Scouts and the other groups already mentioned, militaristic trappings served to entice boys to join these movements, but the emphasis for the leaders was really on the values and good habits taught within them. 'Manliness' denoted the kinds of characteristics required of these future men, and that in turn typically depended on a regime of emotional control that would foster the qualities of obedience, reverence, self-control and discipline.

In one article by a scientific lecturer to the Lancashire and Cheshire Band of Hope and Temperance Union, the link between various pedagogical tactics and child nature is made explicit. Negative teaching would encourage the child to think about and consequently to do whatever is disapproved of by the teacher. Positive teaching, conversely, would lead by example, as young children would want to emulate whatever the teachers put before them. In the case of drink, as in this article, an example of negative teaching was: 'do not abuse your body and mind with drink', whereas the positive exhortation was: 'try to make mind and body as wise and as strong as you can; take care of them as God's good gift held in trust.'[19] This pedagogical method was employed by much of the late nineteenth- and early twentieth-century literature for boys. Instead of demonstrating how far from the ideal the prevalent contemporary situation was, these authors stressed the ideal itself. Instead of presenting overwhelming, negative emotions, positive emotions like happiness and love were stressed. Since children were considered 'unmoral rather than immoral',[20] their learning both at school and church, and in their reading matter, had to play an important part in forming their moral characters. According to one Band of Hope leader, the Band of Hope provided

[A] semi-religious platform upon which our scholars may meet and mingle on week evenings without fear of contamination, and in large centres of industry, especially, this feature has been found of great value as a Sunday School auxiliary. It inculcates early habits of restraint, and supplements the lessons of true religion and holiness with those of *kindness* and *forbearance* to one another.[21]

'Kindness and forethought' were also the characteristics that described Band of Hope teachers.[22] Training the emotions, especially those associated with Christian faith, went part and parcel in this period with character building, and therefore with manliness.

Boys characterized in the boys' papers are often temperate, well mannered, kind, caring, who will turn into model husbands and fathers. When negative examples are provided of boys and men who have succumbed to vice and immorality, the authors leave no potential space for the young readers to glamorize or fantasize about these 'bad' boys' and men's lives. As in 'A Nonentity' and in numerous other examples, boys are not provided with any leeway in which to interpret what real manliness meant.

An important goal for the boys' papers in order to encourage growth in readership was to ensure that their publications were deemed wholesome by parents, clergymen, schoolmasters and others in authority over boys. Some papers had an easier time in convincing the public than others. The *Band of Hope Review* could boast enthusiastic support from Northern English newspapers: 'As an assistant in the proper training of the youthful mind, THE BAND OF HOPE REVIEW is the best publication we have seen,'[23] and 'The price is so ridiculously small that we feel almost afraid to say that the serial is filled with good engravings and well-written articles, and everything to make it valuable and acceptable to the juvenile population.'[24] Other temperance journals felt the need to explain their existence. In the first issue of the *Abstainer: An Illustrated Temperance Monthly*, the editor, James Fletcher of Uxbridge, explained that his paper was to meet the needs of temperance workers in all parts of the kingdom and intended to provide a 'family journal that will be read with interest and profit by all classes of the community'.[25] Whether they succeeded or not, it was a general claim of all these papers that their content appealed to all social classes and all ages. Fletcher also repeated another common refrain: that (perhaps with the exception of some socialist papers) the papers were conducted on Christian principles. Most also claimed to be non-denominational and non-partisan.

The *Boy's Own*, backed by the formidable evangelical RTS, had an easy time taking the moral high ground, while attacking other publications for boys that were judged to have negative influence as 'penny dreadfuls'.[26] Unlike penny dreadfuls, the *BOP* was advertised as entirely free from the lurid light of crime, the taint of vulgar bravado, and the vapid but only too seductive sensationalism of the day; but it will at the same time possess the life and 'go', the stirring and rousing action, the spirit and enterprise, that the genuine boy rightly desires. If it sparkles with fun, however, its mirth will leave no bitterness, and its laughter no regret.[27]

Temperance publications did the same. The *Young Standard Bearer* boasted that the first issue of the paper had a larger than anticipated circulation. Providing 'something pure, bright, and attractive' was thought the best way to counteract 'wicked, poisonous literature' for young people.[28]

Hamilton Edwards also promoted the AP boys' papers by comparing them to the religious papers, which were known for their positive moral influence on readers. As he wrote in the editorial section of the *Boys' Friend* in 1898:

I defy anyone to prove that the moral tone of the BOYS' FRIEND is one whit less than the moral tone of the most religious journal published. As a matter of fact, I have seen things in so-called religious journals which I would not permit of publication in my own paper. I feel very strongly upon this point of the morality and healthiness of the literature which goes into the BOYS' FRIEND, because I am thoroughly convinced that the welfare of the rising generation depends largely upon the literature which it reads; and if this literature is good and healthy in tone it will re-act upon the boy, and help him in his conduct towards his fellow-creatures. If he reads sensible, healthy literature it will induce his mind into sensible and healthy channels, and afterwards make of him a useful citizen.[29]

As with the religious and temperance juvenile publications, the AP papers made the connection between uplifting literature and good traits in manhood and citizenship. On the other side of the same issue, the AP boys' papers also warned their readers against the evil influence of penny dreadfuls, and even had a recurring column to that effect, detailing the stories of boys who had committed real crimes after having read nefarious literature. The real punishment for these crimes was shown to be much more severe than the stories indicated.[30] Hamilton Edwards defined these stories as 'absurdly sensational and improbable [. . . with] more improbable pictures'.[31] Yet, unlike the RTS, CETS and Band of Hope publications, AP editors could not assume that potential readers and authority figures viewed their papers as wholesome, since they lacked religious affiliation and contained sensationalistic adventure and crime serial stories. Hamilton Edwards admitted that the AP boys' papers were viewed with suspicion by parents and teachers and they were attacked as a new form of penny dreadful by some of the other organizations. He denounced 'A Prejudiced [Sunday School] Teacher', who thought that the AP papers were unwholesome compared to the religious boys' papers.[32] In his editorial sections, he frequently repeated that reading the *Boys' Friend* and the *Boys' Herald* was morally beneficial for boys, as well as being educational and entertaining: 'every paragraph in the BOYS' FRIEND is published with due consideration to its moral teaching, as well as to its interesting nature.'[33] In his editorial section five years later he restated that AP papers were fit for Christian boys to read: 'it has always been my endeavour, in publishing stories to publish nothing which would give offence to the most earnest or thoughtful Christian.'[34]

Not only did Hamilton Edwards assert that his publications were wholesome and parent-approved, he also made clear that he was a knowledgeable advisor, a sound counsellor and even a good friend to his boyish readers. 'I want all my boys to look upon me as their firm friend and adviser. There are few men who know boys as well as I do, and there are no little trials and troubles, perplexities and anxieties, in which I cannot help and assist my readers.'[35] He advised boys on everything from detailed 'Hints on Shaving'[36] to future careers, to personal relationships with family, friends and possible love interests. In his Christmas greeting of 1894, he encouraged his readers to write to him regularly and he would, as their friend, 'sympathise with them in their sorrow' and 'rejoice with them in their happiness.'[37] This perceived personal, emotional bond with his young male readers was seen as an important selling point for the AP papers. The *Boy's Own* similarly promoted itself as understanding boyhood. 'The principle of this Journal is, in one word, Sympathy. Its writers understand boyhood well, and enter heartily into its pursuits and pleasures.'[38]

Boys were to be attracted by the entertaining content of the papers, but the real goals of the publishers were far more lofty, striving to 'show that true courage is ever something vastly different from the swagger of foolhardiness and self-assertion, and that the noblest manliness and Christian honour are very closely akin'. This was to be accomplished 'not so much by precept as by example – by providing really entertaining reading that shall prove food, and not poison – the stimulant to high endeavour, and not the allurement to ribaldry and vice.'[39]

As this advertisement in the RTS workers' paper for the first issue of *BOP* indicates, one of the clear ways for publishers to make their papers appealing to boys and to their parents was to declare them manly, or manly making. This was the strategy of the RTS, CETS and Band of Hope papers, providing this manliness training in a securely Christian context. The AP boys' papers took a similar position. Hamilton Edwards called the *Boys' Herald* 'The Manly Paper', noting that 'every feature in it is a thoroughly man-making one'.[40] He assured potential readers that his papers contained 'sound, healthy stories, conveying no bad lesson, but teaching boys rather to be *manly*, and to fight adversity, and to struggle against any obstacle which may come in their path'.[41] The seventh Earl of Shaftesbury, a promoter of the CETS and many evangelical causes, and particularly that of children's education, was quoted extolling the gentlemanliness of the *BOP*.[42] This was one of the many links between the content of boys' papers and the movement to ameliorate social problems, in which he so actively participated. Shaftesbury, according to John Wolffe, 'was held up to late Victorian and Edwardian manhood as a role model of noble Christian endeavour'.[43] This was certainly true of the periodicals, as Shaftesbury's name was used to promote manliness and success.

Shaftesbury was an exemplar of the attempt to attract readership through what could be termed celebrity endorsements. Diverse figures like Eugen Sandow, the famous strongman,[44] and Robert Baden-Powell supported the messages of the papers by writing on the dangers of smoking and liquor.[45] Earlier, the famous cricketer W. G. Grace was featured in the *BOP*. All of the papers utilized this tactic to get their messages across, as well as to attract increased readership drawn in by the desire to learn about famous or great men. In the tradition of the important voluntary organizations of the age, some papers also obtained the support of leading political and religious men. The *BOP*, through the existing RTS networks, was supported by archbishops, bishops, the chairman of the London School Board, the president of Trinity College, Oxford, the president of the Royal Society, the president of the Royal College of Physicians, and the leaders of the YMCA and charitable homes for boys.[46]

Apart from the major organizations like the Band of Hope, the Boys' Brigade and later the Boy Scouts, the publishers also tactically created lesser-known organizations (such as the AP's League of Boy Friends), examinations and competitions to encourage 'boys to grow up into strong men physically and morally – true specimens of the great race and Empire to which they belong'.[47] To promote loyalty to the groups, they had conditions of membership, secret passwords, 'handsome' certificates and 'beautifully-designed' badges.[48] Hamilton Edwards made it seem as if these leagues were exclusive, not only in terms of their membership requirements, but because members, if they were 'honourable lads', were shown to resign from the group if, for example, they started smoking, or broke another one of the rules. Hamilton Edwards wrote that while he felt like he were parting with friends, he would rather that 'every member of the league resigned rather than one should remain a member whilst being false to

his pledge.'[49] A major motivation in creating these supplementary offshoots of
their papers was clearly to increase readership and thereby to increase the reach
of the papers, the organizations backing them, and their messages.

For its part, the RTS conducted religious instruction and examinations. In
1881–2, for example, a total of 5,380 children and pupil teachers participated
and 1,139 prizes were awarded.[50] The CETS also had annual examinations and
inter-diocesan competitions, associated with its Bands of Hope. In 1914–15,
for example, the theme of the associated handbook was 'My duty, to God, to
my country, to my home, to myself' by Rev. C. F. Tonks. In the section, 'Love at
Home', students were to learn that '**Drunkenness destroys love in the home**',
and that the '**home may be happier and more prosperous without strong
drink, while intemperance brings poverty and unhappiness into the homes
of England.**'[51] These handbooks were widely distributed. Every member
of the Band of Hope was supposed to have a copy. Competitions served to
increase juvenile interest in religious affiliation and in moral rectitude.
They also provide us with a clearer understanding of the links between the
discursive messages of the organizations' publications and the wider goals
of the organizations themselves in reaching out to individual children. By
understanding the periodicals and the organizations' other activities as part
of the same project, we can better understand the vast impact of the 'manly'
messages of the publications. Though it remains difficult to assess how readers
absorbed particular messages in the texts they read, involvement in the
organizations' activities is a good indicator of the reach of these messages, as
the periodicals and the organizations' other activities were mutually promoting
and perpetuating.

## Teaching boys to say 'no'

Boys were not expected to find the right path independently of any authority
or moral guidance, but it was clear, at least to the juvenile press, that families,
especially fathers, were failing in this regard. Several publications for boys directly
took on this fatherly role. The RTS established the *BOP* in order to provide
a moral paternal voice in a perceived void in the juvenile periodical market.
Hamilton Edwards also took on the paternal role in the papers he edited.

The AP papers may have been more sensationalistic than their religious
counterparts, but they did promote similar moral goals for boys. It was in the
editor's replies to letters that this moral message was made most clear. It was all

the more important because of the perception that moral and manly instruction was inadequate both in homes and in schools:

> It seems to me a pity that boys are not taught at school the admirable quality of moral courage; are not taught to admire the lad who can deny himself some foolish pleasure because it is wrong; are not taught the manliness of being able to say 'No' at the right moment. But they are not; and their parents also neglect this side of their teaching, with the result that many a lad finds himself in evil paths simply because he is unable to say 'No'.[52]

Manliness by such a definition was intrinsically tied to the greater satisfaction of having avoided the immediacy of an immoral sense of gratification. Manliness *felt* moral, and was designed by the negation of wilful sensations. Temptation, then, was a test of manliness. The capacity to say 'No' marked out a boy as of a high stamp of character. His own self-mastery would enable him to reform others.

One of the main concerns was the temptation of smoking, which was denounced vociferously as detrimental to boys themselves and to society.[53] As with temperance appeals, anti-smoking articles employed men of influence to speak to the dangers of tobacco. Baden-Powell addressed a large gathering of boys at the Central Hall in Liverpool in 1907, under the auspices of the Anti-Cigarette League. He reminded boys that some of the best men in sports and the professions were non-smokers.[54] Eugen Sandow, originator of modern body-building, was quoted in the *Young Crusader* as saying to boys that 'By smoking you are slowly but surely poisoning the system, and sapping the energy which you should reserve for the duties of life. Do not abuse the body which God has given. But that is what you will do if you smoke.'[55] Physical degeneration from smoking was a real fear during this period.[56] If men who were so physically strong believed that boys should be God-fearing and abstain from tobacco, then these choices would be more appealing to readers than if they were told in an overtly didactic way. The passing of the Children Act of 1908, which banned smoking for those under 16 years of age, vindicated the approach. In the temperance periodicals, smoking was linked to drinking as a secondary vice.

The process of moral enculturation, of practicing denial, was intended to be accomplished through subtle negotiations among the publishers, the parents and the boys themselves. The RTS publications, in particular, were not bound by rigid distinctions between juvenile and adult reading matter, but rather were intended for family reading. This served to encourage family cohesion and moral transferral from parents to son (Figure 4.1).[57]

**Figure 4.1** Frontispiece, *The Leisure Hour* (1852). From its inception, the *Leisure Hour* emphasized reading's importance for family cohesion, centred around the Paterfamilias.

In contrast, the AP publications were intended for boys' reading alone, yet parental approval was sought and even published to ensure the papers' wholesome content, thus obviating the charge that they were penny dreadfuls. One mother wrote to the *Boys' Herald* to say that she approved of its antidrinking and anti-smoking stance, but believed it should also take a position against boxing, which the paper continued to advocate as a manly pursuit.[58] But even occasional specific differences did not alter the fact that the papers worked in partnership with parents, as the same mother exhorted: 'Let us teach them to be peaceful, law-abiding, God-fearing citizens.'[59] The papers sought to entertain, but more importantly, to shape boys in a period of rapid change. According to one commentator, most parents tried to hand over their responsibilities to others, 'not because we shrink from trouble but because we feel painfully unfit for our infinitely difficult fourfold work of turning out healthy, educated, moral and religious children'.[60]

Instilling the capacity to say 'no' was seemingly all the more difficult among the temptations of urban life. One city clergyman in the *BOP*, warned that many a young man found himself 'lost and lonesome' in a big city, where 'no one seems to see him, and his loss of individuality disheartens him and leaves him open to temptation.' This is contrasted with the individuality felt by youths in their native towns, where the 'wholesome scrutiny' of the community prevents young men from vice. This sort of environment was to be actively re-created by young men in cities by finding a church or social organization, where, as the clergyman advised, they could surround themselves with 'a little group of friends who will applaud . . . success and encourage . . . after failure.'[61] Indeed, coupons could be found for 'The Boys' Herald Hobby Club'[62] in that Harmsworth paper, as an attempt to keep boys off the streets and engaged in hobbies that might prove useful to their future careers.

The Band of Hope was the most extensive example of this ideal. Its goals remained unchanged throughout the organization's history, and are demonstrated by the following from the manual for Band of Hope workers, written in the 1940s, but indicative of the movement's premise from its beginnings: 'If you teach a child to say "No" when offered intoxicants, you are doing more than making him a total abstainer; you are teaching him to resist other evils; you are teaching a way of life.'[63] This 'way of life' was not just made up of negative exhortations; it promoted a positive moral and emotional model for youth, founded on 'purity, honesty, uprightness, manliness, sincerity, conscience'.[64] This was similar to that promoted by so-called secular organizations such as the 'The League of Boy Friends' and in many poems and recitations, like this one in the CETS's *Young Crusader* in 1892:

Boys are wanted whose strength can lead,

The weaker on them leaning;

Boys whose 'No' is a 'no' indeed,

And whose 'Yes' has an equal meaning.

Who are strong not only when life decrees

Its bitter and heavy trials,

But can practice its small economies,

And its every-day self-denials.[65]

Teaching boys to have the moral and emotional fortitude to say 'no' to bad habits and 'yes' to doing the right thing in the face of peer pressure was important. It was crucial, however, for boys to remember these lessons as men, because temperance organizations often found it much easier to attract juvenile members than to retain adults.

In 1913, for example, there were 400,477 juvenile members of the CETS, compared with 109,968 adult members.[66] As early as the 1850s Joseph Livesey, an influential temperance reformer, worried about the tendency to concentrate on educating children in temperance principles rather than reforming their drunken parents: 'to retreat from the great world of known drinkers in order to teach boys and girls merely, is, to my mind, an indication of weakness, and rather a symptom of despair.'[67] Yet the core of the Band of Hope's teachings was its insistence on the dangers of alcohol, especially to boys and young men, in the hopes that they would come to have a positive influence on their peers and on their own fathers. According to one Band of Hope instructors' guide, 'Not only does alcohol deprive the youth of his self-control, but perverts his thoughts and ideas, and excites his passions. The youth who is under the influence of strong drink is at the mercy of his passions and has no resistance to temptation.'[68] A man at the mercy of his passions could not be manly, but nor could he extol manliness. As with anti-smoking campaigns, prominent men were appealed to in order to give the cause more weight. For example, the *Workers' Onward* printed a strong message of temperance and good character for young men from the Lord Mayor of Leeds, J. Hepworth:

I have been a total abstainer all my life, and have found it a good thing in every way. Young men who begin with temperance principles, must be prepared to fight hard against the many temptations open to them, and if they do their part well, they are bound to become worthy and respected citizens. We like young men with determined force of character to conquer the many difficulties of life which they have to meet, and there is only one way of doing it, and that is, by fighting against temptation. At no time in English History has there been a greater demand for sterling men than there is at the present.[69]

Resistance to temptation was the surest way to become a real man, with all the domestic and civic duties that entailed. While the sense of urgency in ensuring the next generation's temperate and dutiful men and citizens was widely shared, it was hoped that the moral fortitude of disciplined youth might yet set an example to their own parents.

## Showing the way: Boys as fathers to their fathers

The Band of Hope publication for Greenwich and West Kent, as with many others of its kind, featured a Children's page, in which was printed a two-part story, 'The Two Homes: A Story Founded on Fact'. The first image is of a happy home in a little Kentish village, with a neat wife and mother keeping this home clean and respectable. The children exclaim, 'Father's coming', and compete with each other to be the first to meet their parent returning from work. The man feels 'as happy as a king!'[70] because he has this wonderful home, a loving family and no real cares, for although they are poor, they are happy. The second instalment of this story is in stark contrast to the first. It shows the destructiveness of the metropolis and the ruin of the family because of the father's drunkenness. The entire family is dead, save for the father and one last daughter dying of consumption. Their home is cramped, filthy and demoralizing. The father grabs his daughter's one comfort, her Bible, and pawns it to buy drink. The narrator describes how the father feels remorse at this most despicable act, but the reader is led to understand that he did not have a real choice in the matter, for he was already consumed by his vice: 'Yes, the way of transgressors is hard.'[71] The author claimed that this was not merely a fictional account, but one that was 'founded on fact', to lend it much weight and seriousness. It was a cautionary tale about the dangers to the entire family of fatherly irresponsibility and irreligion.

Many husbands and fathers, like the father of the second home, did not live up to moral ideals. But aside from the decisive factor of geography in these scenes, the attitude of the children themselves in their interaction with the father figure seems to have some implicit importance. The father's kingly joy is directly related to his children's demeanour towards him. In many stories, it is clear that children of all classes are seen as moral beacons, able to exert a strong moral influence on parents who are themselves deficient. Temperance supporters encouraged children to feel that they could have a positive impact on their parents. In the words of one clergyman, more parents 'were reclaimed from intemperance and added to my church through the zeal of these little ones than from any other agency. Surely, "A little child shall lead them!"'[72] The NSPCC's founding director Benjamin Waugh also represented the widespread opinion that children were naturally moral and could influence their parents to lead more wholesome lives. It was the 'mystic power of a child' that could lead to positive change in his parents.[73] This idealized vision of children dictated that they were all to be regarded as holy, innocent and Christ-like. Boys, especially, could act as a father to their own fathers, showing them the right way.[74]

In many stories, boys are shown to be more intelligent and responsible than their own intemperate fathers. In 'The Boy Who Beat His Father', Mark Halliday is a widower with one son, who is liked by his fellow workers but not respected by them because he is the 'slave of drink'. Halliday looks to his young son Paul 'as if he were a sort of moral prodigy', as the youth not only abstains from alcohol but tries to encourage his father to become steadier and to drink less. The roles of the father and son became increasingly reversed as the youth 'leap[s] prematurely into manhood' and begins admonishing his father for his drinking and swearing. As the narrator explains, 'Paul was deliberately taking in hand the moral education of his father', and told his father on several occasions that he would beat him if he misbehaved.[75] At the end of this story, Paul saves his father from a dangerous work-related accident and rejoices that he has 'conquered' his father.[76]

The significance of this story, and many others like it, is twofold. Lacking moral virtue, the contemporary generation of parents was seen to have failed. Boys, so this line of reasoning went, required a better moral education in order to be better men and fathers of the future. Moralizing juvenile literature was seen to benefit both boys and parents. The child could thus act as a moral beacon for his family, encouraging good behaviour in his parents and even disciplining them when they strayed. Stories were also meant to teach boys how proper fathers behaved, with the aim of influencing their later lives. When properly directed, the kind of literature was thought to be a powerful proselytizing force.

Many Band of Hope stories were written for the organization's main base, working-class children, including some from very disadvantaged backgrounds. Here too, children show their parents the way. In one sad story, a very poor boy named Willie joins the Band of Hope. Both his parents are drunkards and provide their son a poor moral example. Willie keeps his pledge but is mortally wounded at work in the shipyard. He speaks to his father on his deathbed about giving up drink and turning to God. The author remarks how good it is that God has made little children so useful:

> Willie's life was clouded by a dark sinful home; but he carried sunshine everywhere, and at the last even led his parents up to the light, for his father became an active worker for good in the town in which he dwelt. Thus live for the truth, dear children, and witness for it by shining actions, and a pure clear faith in God.[77]

In this the Band of Hope was consistent. Two lines of a song introduced at the first Band of Hope meeting in Leeds in 1847 make clear children's responsibility towards making their homes and their country happy: 'We'll ask our fathers, too, to come and join our happy band; True temperance makes a happy home, and makes a happy land.'[78]

Children were taught how to do this by the positive example of boys who resisted temptation. 'A Brave Boy',[79] for example, is the story of Arthur Mason. Unlike his father, who had been jailed for drunkenness and violence, Arthur joins the Band of Hope and vows never to go into a pub. He receives shouts and mocking laughter from a group of boys standing at the corner of the street, who want Arthur to go into the pub to fill a jug with beer.[80] 'Well, here's a go! Arthur Mason setting up to be a saint, and his father a gaol bird', the boys taunt.[81] Arthur tells them with emotion that though his father has always been good to him, it was true that his father had been tempted by some bad men into the pub, and in a fit of rage, had struck one and had gotten into trouble for it. He tells the boys that he has given his word at the Band of Hope that he will never enter a pub.[82] Arthur wants to fight the boys who are taunting him but he resists. The narrator explains that Arthur is not a coward for not fighting, but in fact strong. Then Arthur's father, who witnesses the incident, speaks up, confirming that his son's 'resolution and pluck' are the keys to his salvation, and bids to aid Arthur in any fight.[83] The narrator concludes that the boys on the street are the real cowards, now seemingly disinclined to fight, though Arthur and his father return home and continue to 'FIGHT THE GOOD FIGHT'.[84]

Insofar as this fight – for morality, character and ultimately citizenship – was centred in the domestic realm, it was led, at least in part, by children themselves, and especially by boys. This entailed the cultivation of both the right kind of homes and the right kind of boys.

## Emotional conditioning and emotional control

The earthly home, in fact, was seen as a proxy for the heavenly home. One CETS temperance talk aimed at a wealthier audience entreated children to 'let our home be as sweet as it can and as much like heaven' and drew an analogy between building up the comforts of the home with the emotional constitution required to keep the temperance pledge. The pledge 'builds a character house', preparing the child emotionally for his/her life and interactions with others. According to the address, in a 'perfect home', consisting of 'loving parents' and 'obedient children' 'there should be love and joy and kindness and sympathy in the hearts of all.' The home was used as a positive and a negative example, with the 'good' and 'bad' emotions associated with virtue or vice starkly highlighted.[85] These two stanzas, from a much longer Band of Hope poem to be recited in meetings, makes clear the connection between moral rectitude, good character and associated emotions in the home:

> Our home is bright and happy now,
>
> Contended mother reigns;
>
> The frown, once seen on father's brow,
>
> No longer there remains;
>
> In peacefulness the days go by,
>
> No care nor want are known;
>
> Gone are the silent tear and sigh,
>
> The heart-pain and the groan.
>
> How different are these happy days
>
> To those a year ago!
>
> Then father followed drunken ways,
>
> And we were filled with woe!
>
> The rooms were comfortless and bare,
>
> The things we had were mean;
>
> No carpets, pictures, books, or chair,
>
> As we have now, were seen.[86]

Not only was temperance supposed to determine physical comfort in the home, but also to bring emotional fulfilment. Here again, happiness and its lack are stressed as well as feelings from the heart. In an annual competition, older children within the movement were examined on the consequences to the home and the family if the father or mother was intemperate. The model answers stated that it brings 'unhappiness into the homes of England' and that it destroys 'love in the home'.[87] Thus, in a very direct way, 'good' feelings were associated with restraint and 'bad' feelings with succumbing to temptation. This was perhaps a difficult sell for children who might associate acting on passing urges with immediate 'good' feelings, but within the religious idiom of the love of God and true emotional reward in Heaven, this schema becomes clear.

In the *Band of Hope Chronicle*, the paper for its workers, the 'The Influence of Example' was made clear.[88] 'Dissipated' fathers would raise dissipated sons, even if the fathers thought that they were hiding their bad habits from their children. Profane language, drinking and spending too much time away from home, in homosocial environments, were the targets here. A certain Dr Talmage described what he thought to be a typical scene across the country. The morally laudable image of family 'seated at the tea-table' is shattered when 'the father shoves back his chair, says he has an engagement, lights a cigar – goes out, comes back after midnight.' The author then rhetorically questions whether any man would want 'to stultify himself' by justifying this as right, or honourable. He then describes the son's role in this lethal chain, whereby the moral laxity of the father is passed on to the subsequent generation. 'Time will pass on', he says, 'and the son will be sixteen or seventeen years of age, and you will be at the tea-table, and he will shove back *his* chair, and have an engagement, and he will light *his* cigar, and he will go out to the club-house, and you will hear nothing of *him* until you hear the night key in the door after midnight.' However, this is not merely a repetitive chain, but one of degeneration. The son's 'physical constitution is not quite so strong' as the father's. The forecast is for the son to catch up with the father 'on the road to death', despite the father's head start.[89] Physical degeneration was crucially linked to moral degeneration, the son imitating the father's bad habits, following his immediate bodily and emotional desires. This would lead to moral laxity which in turn was linked to physical danger. This sort of story was intended to stimulate fear and a sense of duty in both father and son.

The Band of Hope's weekly meetings were designed to be entertaining as well as morally and emotionally instructional, featuring recitations, songs and magic lantern shows, in order to encourage shared feelings among its young members. Songs were especially stressed, as they created a feeling of familial unity and emotional togetherness. As the movement's chronicler says, 'When there is joy in the heart, it is usually expressed in a song.'[90] Magic lantern shows were prized as an exciting novelty for the young, and a good instructive tool for leaders. Pictorial teaching was a specialty of the Band of Hope.[91] In addition, 'model making and exhibiting, physical training, Brains trusts and Spelling Bees are a few of the methods employed by enterprising teachers who realize the value of variety and plan their evenings accordingly.'[92] The bands also offered children and young people summer trips to the seaside, teas with sweets and other incentives to be faithful to the movement. In its early days, the Band of Hope allowed young members to 'express themselves audibly and often volubly', which seemed 'scandalous to professional teachers' of the day.[93] These educational innovations attracted children to the groups, serving as a showcase for new didactic methods, both for other youth groups and for the formal education system, and acting as a model of intergenerational cohesion, or familial unity writ large.

In the words of one Band of Hope recitation, the 'boys that are wanted' were the ones who placed the love of home and family above all else:

'Wanted – boys', this want I find

As the city's wants I read of,

And that is so – there's a certain kind

Of boys that the world has need of.

The boys that are wanted are sober boys,

Unselfish, true and tender;

Holding more dear the sweet home joys,

Than the club or the ball-room's splendour.[94]

The message here is unambiguous: duty to home and family was to take priority over homosocial or individual pleasures. Not only the positive actions of sobriety and the negative action of staying away from bad influences were required, but also the 'right' kinds of emotions, of being 'Unselfish, true and tender' and of mustering up the 'right' emotions at the 'right' times, which most importantly involved the appreciation of the joys of home life. Joy was not brought about by indulging in vices or by obeying immediate impulses, but rather by being thoughtful and good towards others:

He reaps reward in doing good,

Finds joy in giving joy,

And earns the right to bear the name:

'A gentlemanly boy'.[95]

In linking positive emotions to good character and manliness or gentlemanliness, the Band of Hope clearly identified one means of shaping future citizens. While the direct impact on children of this strategy is difficult directly to measure, the continual repetition of similar messages, as well as the popularity of the movement among the young doubtless affected perceived standards of emotional and moral propriety. Informal emotional and moral education was not just about correct emotional exploration, but also about teaching boys emotional control. And this circles us back to the central importance of the capacity to say 'No' in the face of temptation. 'The Boy Who Dared to Say No' (1897) is a poem about the correct choices a young boy makes and his emotional moderation. He refuses to smoke any form of tobacco, to drink wine, to tell lies and to seek amusements on the Sabbath. Though merely a boy, he also clearly knows what it truly means to be a man:

'Would you not strike an angry blow

To show your pluck and manhood?' 'No!

Our preacher says who dares do right

Is the true hero of the fight.'[96]

'Heroes', then, were boys whose budding manliness was defined by the acts of being kind and gentle. No matter what his social class, a 'noble boy', though perhaps 'hidden amid hard conditions and under unattractive garbs, will work out and show his manhood. He may not always find friends to appreciate; but, determined, virtuous, and willing to endure, he will in due time conquer.'[97] This advice was repeated in numerous contemporary advice manuals for boys and young men. The boys who were 'wanted' were ones whose hearts and brains would 'ever be true', who were 'honest, faithful, earnest, kind', who were blind to 'evil' and whose hearts were 'gold'; in short, those who had the right emotions at the right times.[98] The heart, poetic seat of the emotions, was also considered to be the location of 'true' religious feelings and love for God. The emotions were thus tied, fundamentally, to expressions of morality and religiosity.

Fears of degeneracy fit into the context of a pervasive concern with national efficiency and the corresponding imperative to produce fit, healthy young men as future fathers of a strong nation. The perceived sins of this age, the state of immorality in the domestic realm, cast a threatening shadow over not only individual homes, but also the whole future of the nation. If bad parenting led to a permanent downward spiral of degeneracy, then what hope was there for the nation and its empire? Such a vision placed domesticity, paradoxically, at the very centre of the imperial project.

# Recasting Imperial Masculinity: Informal Education and the Empire of Domesticity

The Empire was sometimes viewed figuratively by its leaders, builders and settlers as one big (ideally harmonious and happy) family. The shared sense of duty, civilization, patriotism and morality defined, as we have seen, in the context of the home, was writ large to encompass Britain's whole Imperial domain. Of course, this view glosses over many important tensions and different views, even for the settler colonies. Yet this chapter will test to what extent this notion of Empire as family can be extended even further, to colonies far more religiously and culturally diverse. In particular, it discusses the extent to which the ideals of informal education, defined by domesticated manliness, were exported to the heterogeneous colonial context of the Raj. Could the primacy of home life in the British sense have been transported with the imperial man, his institutions and his family? Moreover, to what extent was the colonial subject – commonly portrayed as a 'childlike' figure, docile but also corruptible –used as a fitting analogue for the British boy who must choose the right path?

Transnational flows of communication and advice were vibrant in this period. The RTS distributed its papers for boys and girls throughout the settler colonies. The AP was a huge international concern, and even published papers like the *Harmsworth Self-Educator* in Dominions like Canada. The Band of Hope and its papers reached as far as the Antipodes. Though content was in some cases altered for local markets, there was presumed to be a shared understanding of the concept of childhood and youth, and the informal educational modes and media desired to influence children and youth along those lines. Indeed, in Angelique Richardson's view, the family functioned as 'the basic building block of society' and as 'a microcosm of empire, fulfilling its duties of citizenship through reproduction'.[1] How successful was the British attempt to export the consensus about the correct path to civic manhood, to educate and build a moral empire?

## Imperial men

India had long been a cause for moral concern for British missionaries and colonial administrators. In the late nineteenth century, similar language to that used to understand boyhood 'problems' at home was used to describe the 'problems' of Indian boys, and similar tactics were used in their informal moral and emotional education. Yet important differences remained between their education and that of their counterparts in the metropole. Whereas class was increasingly downplayed in Britain, caste was acknowledged as an important factor in the Indian context. Cultural transfer is evident in the ways in which tactics developed with British boys in mind were changed and adapted in an Indian context, and sometimes these tactics were imported, in their changed form, back to the metropole. Significantly, the export of boyhood ideals to India stopped short of encouraging a juvenile Indian citizenry; imperial subjecthood was stressed; representations of the superiority of British ideals of morality and education remained constant.

The colonial man was perceived as a child, and, additionally, the colonial child was seen as plastic and therefore malleable. Yet childhood in India was not entirely defined by age, and could also be constructed with reference to a nature that could be hard and irredeemable.[2] If properly trained, this child could, in manhood, overcome the childish state of his adult predecessors. As Elizabeth Buettner has put it, 'Indians could be depicted as analogous to children and Britons seen as parental – yet in a political and cultural as distinct from a biological sense.'[3] This notion was captured in a speech by Samuel Wilberforce in 1880, on the Civil Service of India. He noted the British 'vocation' to 'leave as the impress of their intercourse with inferior nations, marks of moral teaching and religious training, to have made a nation of children see what it was to be men'.[4] Worried that Indian conversions to Christianity were largely among the poor, and for less than pure motives, many British educators focused their efforts on wealthy or high-born Indians, who, it was thought, by their own moral example, would influence their inferiors. Just as it was hoped that emerging British men would lead the way for the future of the race, so the Imperial man, both British, British-educated, and Christian Indian, would serve as moral messengers in what was seen as an empire of emotional, moral and character control.

Historians have generally agreed that there was a refashioning of what it meant to be a man in the period from 1880 to1914. This has been a remarkably consistent idea, marking a shift from domesticated, spiritual and intellectual manliness, to imperial, secular, bodily 'muscularity'. The thesis was developed by David Newsome and the idea propagated chiefly by J. A. Mangan.[5] For many late Victorian men, the lure of the Empire or the club became stronger than that of leading their own families. John Tosh, in his *A Man's Place*, provides us with the most comprehensive study of male middle-class domesticity in nineteenth-century Britain.[6] He points to a 'flight from domesticity' for middle-class men in the 1880s. He refines this argument in a later article, showing that with the 'New Imperialism' beginning in the 1880s, a complex relationship developed between the imperial and the masculine whereby British men were being moulded to fit the demands of the Empire and in turn the Empire would 'make' men.[7] Thus, according to this argument, the Empire along with the public schools would fashion men who preferred to eschew or to delay the choice of starting a home with a wife and children.

Though the 'flight from domesticity', even among middle-class men, has been exaggerated (as Tosh himself acknowledges), many contemporaries were apprehensive about such a shift. Historians widely agree that marriage and fatherhood were the benchmarks of manliness for much of the late eighteenth and early to mid-nineteenth centuries.[8] Was it not still true then, as it had been throughout the century, that a man only obtained full manhood in marrying and in becoming a father? By concentrating on the mother, a more prominent historiographical category than that of the father[9] and on imperial masculinity, we are left with the impression that the late nineteenth-century father is mainly absent, if not physically then at least emotionally or figuratively. Many late nineteenth-century commentators would have agreed that men were shirking their familial duties and that mothers' dominance in the home would have disastrous consequences for their sons' manhood.

The idea that there was a general rhetorical shift towards imperial masculinity in this period has been influential.[10] Tosh himself is clear that though he points to a general 'flight from domesticity' for middle-class men in this era, the situation of individual men varied greatly and that many still embraced domesticity. In fact, as Martin Francis has pointed out, men could simultaneously embrace and reject domestic manliness.[11] Men could have all the trappings of a traditional family life, while maintaining an escape in the homosocial environment of the club or even in an adventurous imperial fantasy life through reading. A. J. Hammerton has added nuance to the argument, shifting 'the key site of discussion of lower-middle-class masculinity away from imperial enthusiasms, which originated with other classes, toward men's own preoccupations centered in the domestic sphere.'[12] He points to a lower-middle-class commitment to marital partnership, meaning that these men did not participate in the 'flight from domesticity'.[13] This book has so far demonstrated that, at least rhetorically, the shift away from domesticity was in no way complete. In fact, influential organizations continued to promote domesticated masculinity and men's spiritual primacy in the home. Historians of the colonies have shown how British domesticity and adequate manliness have been contrasted with the effeminacy of imperial subjects, and how a 'superior' British model of domesticity justified violent rule over 'aboriginal peoples' in the white settler empire.[14] In these studies, the dynamic relationship between imperial masculinity and male domesticity has been successfully explored. I shall pick up the interconnectedness of Imperial and domesticated masculinities here.

India, the brightest jewel in the British crown and in many ways a testing ground for British policies in the wider empire as well as at home, is the crucial object of study. It served as a significant site of contestation and negotiation, defining questions of morality, gender and class (caste) norms, and who was allowed to define them in religiously, socially and ethnically diverse locations, far from the metropole. This was especially true after the Rebellion of 1857, which provoked a rethinking of British social and religious policies in India to prevent further civilian disquiet and to change moral codes, in addition to the more concrete institutional and formal consequences, such as the termination of the East India Company's charter and the imposition of direct government of India from London under the Raj (1858–1947).[15]

The more informal and indirect responses to the fallout from the Rebellion have remained rather neglected in comparison. These changes had a direct role to play in increasing efforts to educate, with moral education at the centre. Growing nationalist sentiment among Indians also encouraged the British to emphasize moral education to keep the threat at bay. This chapter shows how British youth experts and some within the Indian context perceived the Indian boy in similar ways to his British counterpart, campaigning similarly for his moral development, yet with important differences, defined by difficult linguistic, cultural, religious and social (caste) obstacles. The sources used include the literature of evangelical and other religious societies in Britain and their missions in India; advice literature written by British authors specifically for Indian boys; and school and university commissions.

As we have seen with the British boy, special attention to childhood and youth was clearly associated with ideals of individual character and morality. In Britain, those qualities were a means to the end of citizenship. In India, that end was, for the most part, loyal subjecthood, although as Carey Watt has pointed out, Indian Social Service organizations in this period encouraged 'Indians, especially young, upper-caste Hindu males, . . . to become manly, dynamic and patriotic citizens serving the motherland.'[16] 'Active citizenship' as a form of 'nation building' (ideas sometimes predating colonial influences) were the goals here.[17] But whatever the role, it still necessitated a moral education specific to boys. The colonial child, and in particular the boy, was expected to play a major role in safeguarding civilization, and its pinnacle, the British Empire, in the present and in the future, through loyalty. As with his metropolitan equivalent, he was not only instructed on the moral path that would lead to the ideal of domesticated Christian fatherhood, but he was expected to shine, beacon-like, so as to influence his own parents for the better.[18] By such instruction the good subject was made or lost. By the early twentieth century, Watt argues, the definition of character was the same as that for Britain – 'physical health, manliness, self-sacrifice, self-control, obedience, patriotism and loyalty' – but attempts were also made to embed it within indigenous traditions.[19] Still, the association between character building and citizenship was strong, and alternatively could serve to benefit either the Raj or the Indian nationalist cause. There was, according to Watt, 'a fervent desire to restrain youth by emphasizing duties and responsibilities, and this is where religion and generalized Brahminical notions of morality and *dharma* became important'.[20]

The methods devised to educate boys and young men in colonial India represent, ultimately, an example of how Indian middle-class children 'became, under the growing cultural impact of British rule, the arena in which the battle for the minds of men was fought between East and West, the old and the new, and the intrinsic and the imposed'.[21] The British not only fought for young Indian minds, but for their hearts as well.

## Loose adaptations

Even if the metropolitan ideals of informal education, exported to various colonial contexts, were pursued in British India with special vigour, the near consensus in contemporaneous British boys' publications and organizations on how boys were to be morally educated was lacking. A great diversity of languages, beliefs and practices in India existed confusedly alongside British norms that were themselves adopted, rejected or adapted. Certainly, British reactions to male youth and potential delinquency took on new dimensions in the context of the Raj.[22] British ideas were informed by understanding and by prejudice, transplanted to, but also transformed in, India.

In India, potential youth trouble was coupled with the threat of political and social unrest and the problem of an increasingly educated and dissatisfied Anglicized Indian elite. British writers on juvenile moral conduct imported their understandings of the importance of the distinct categorization of childhood and youth, while making significant gestures towards the differences in the social and religious contexts between India and the metropole. While it was easy rhetorically to draw lines between the efforts to educate the urban poor with efforts to inculcate morality in the colonial 'other' in India, these parallels fell apart in British efforts on the ground because of the social and gendered stratification of Indian communities.[23] The language of difference, both in positive and negative terms, was used to a far greater extent in India than it was in Britain, where the ideal of universal boyhood moral conduct was promoted. Yet an increasingly stark generational differentiation in Britain, largely brought about by urbanization and industrialization, was not shared in India, where 'childhood' institutions, like schools or recreational groups, were still nascent, and where 'adult' institutions, like work and marriage, were still commonplace among the young. Nevertheless, among British missionary societies, their associates in colonial government and education, and their Indian supporters, the problems related to male youth were posed in a Christian idiom and as a religious struggle.[24] Their moral teachings for boys, and the ways they attempted to form the next generation of effective heads of families and good subjects, were largely conceived of in relation to male youth, no matter what their social class, in the metropole. Under the Raj new educational opportunities, especially for the privileged, meant that the concept of adolescence, as a period between childhood and adulthood, developed in India.[25] This idea was by no means universal, however, and was not as pronounced or developed as it had become in Britain by the early twentieth century. And with this more equivocal age definition came less exaggerated fears associated with this particular age group. Whereas in Britain the liminal period of adolescence became a 'problem' and one of potential emotional and physical danger, these fears were less tied to this specific category in

India, where there was a different, weaker and more ambiguous adult–child differentiation.

The many British religious and missionary organizations, literary societies, purity and temperance organizations attempted to exert their influence over young men through their work on the ground and through their publications.[26] There was a range of approaches, political divergences and potential for cultural feedback. Hannah Catherine Mullens' novel, *Faith and Victory: A Story of the Progress of Christianity in Bengal* (1865), for example, was written in English by this Calcutta missionary and subsequently loosely adapted for publication in Bengali, with many changes apparently to make it more palatable for the local population. It was then retranslated from Bengali back into English as *Prasanna and Kamini: The story of a Young Hindu* (1885), adapted for the RTS by J. H. Budden of Almorah, North India, with further amendments for an English-speaking audience.

Meanwhile, Alfred Dyer, whose involvement with the purity movement for British young men has already been noted, shifted his attention to India in the mid-1880s. He moved to Bombay (Mumbai), where he published his *Slavery under the British Flag: The Iniquities of British Rule in India and in Our Crown Colonies and Dependencies, to the Friends of Social Purity* in 1887, and became editor of an evangelical newspaper. Increasing his efforts to promote purity among British soldiers in India, he published *British Soldiers in India in Regard to Their Morals and Health* (1897) and gave lectures to the Young Men's Christian Association on chastity, published as *The Knight of the White Cross* in 1899.[27]

The Anglo-Indian Temperance Association, begun by British politicians and temperance advocates, had strong support from the nascent Indian National Congress and the missionaries, especially those connected with education.[28] On the first temperance tour, at least 300,000 Indians, all of whom were educated in English, heard the plea and initially 40 native temperance associations were formed and 100 groups in the first three years.[29] The main temperance enthusiasts, organizers and new lecturers were Indian students, with many associations forming in schools and colleges and becoming the 'backbone' of the Indian movement.[30] As Lucy Carroll argues, students and Hindu reformers saw the movement as an opportunity 'to make a contribution to the regeneration of India by taking the message of sobriety, economy and education to the poor of the city and the village' and also to learn efficient political agitation, thus becoming a target of official suspicion.[31] The movement was seen as all the more necessary in light of the contemporaneous import to India of a competing construction of manliness and the corresponding mistaken 'proof of advance in civilisation' that hinged on the capacity to consume large amounts of alcohol.[32]

Other British and local efforts in India to build 'character' and 'good citizenship' also met with resistance. The Boy Scout movement, first introduced to India by missionaries in 1908, and soon embraced by Indian organizations as a good way to promote the qualities encompassed in the term character: 'physical strength and fitness, endurance, self-control, courage, honesty, obedience, duty, sociability, manliness, altruism, self-sacrifice, loyalty and patriotism', provoked contradictory, sometimes hostile reactions among government officials and even by Baden-Powell himself, and led to fears that Indian boys would become politically militant.[33] The exact same moral and emotional qualities strongly encouraged for British boys as future citizens became potentially dangerous for young, male Indian subjects.

The main focus here, however, lies with just one component of the mosaic: the late nineteenth-century British RTS's efforts in India, and those of its Honorary Agent, Scottish Missionary Dr John Murdoch (1819–1904) and Murdoch's own organization, the Christian Literature Society for India, which had linked societies in every region of India.[34] The RTS, with its many missionary activities throughout the world, trod a fine line between seeking to strengthen traditional family values at home, while encouraging activities in the Empire. Its attempts to export and adapt the boyhood and manly ideals of the metropole are particularly indicative of the extent to which the conception of boyhood universality could be maintained and applied, and indeed, where it failed.

## Murdoch's mission

There was an explosion of periodicals and books in India, in English as well as in vernacular languages, between 1890 and 1912.[35] Vast numbers of books, periodicals and newspapers were imported into India from Britain, making it the second most important market for British publications after Australia.[36] In the nineteenth and early twentieth centuries, the RTS published in 44 languages in India and 22 languages in Bengal alone. It was dismayed by the educational policy of 'our' Government in India and saw it as their 'imperative duty to provide some clean, wholesome, interesting and profitable reading for the boys and young men of the great dependency'.[37] It supported many endeavours to promote and distribute Christian literature in India, like that of the Lieutenant Governor of Bengal, Charles Elliott and the Director of Education Department of Bombay, who formed a pure literature society in the 1890s to counteract 'the evils which were found to exist in the supply of books to the different school boys and college boys of Calcutta'. They feared that enemies of the Raj and of Christianity were supplying boys with 'publications of the lowest class, both immoral and depraved literature, and seditious and anti-social literature'. All varieties of behaviour that could be classed as the problems of youth – that might lead to crime, murder, political upheaval – could be blamed on the supply of morally impure literature and on education. This impure reading matter also accounted for the tightening of sedition laws.[38] Not all of the impure influences on youth were seen to have Indian cultural or religious roots. British and imperial culture, through its profusion of 'obscene' publications, was sometimes seen as a 'threat to the strength and purity of the Indian "race" and "nation"'.[39]

Much of the RTS advice for Indian boys of the period was in a similar vein to the British literature. An example is John Murdoch's *The Training of Children for Indian Parents*, which was already in its third edition in 1897, with a total of 8,000 copies printed.[40] The training of children depended on the training of parents (especially fathers, as mothers were thought still too ignorant). For example, rule number one of Murdoch's basic rules for parents cautioned that 'If children turn out badly, it does not arise from fate [implying this is what Hindu parents thought]; but, in nearly every case, from neglect or mismanagement on the part of the parents'. The work dwelt on traditional British precepts like self-help, temperance, honesty and the exhortation to 'always do what is right'. It echoed advice that could be found in the *BOP* or any number of other publications for British boys. Also, Murdoch made clear that parental responsibility followed from responsibility to God; the successful training of parents (especially fathers) depended on their own obedience to the heavenly Father.[41]

Murdoch's *The Indian Student's Manual*, first printed in 1875, went through several editions. His book for a similar audience, *The Indian Young Man in the Battle of Life* (1903), was also reprinted in several versions.[42] *The Indian Student's Manual* reveals many of the lessons on character, responsibility and morality that the British, missionary and non-missionary alike, wanted to impart. It borrows its assumption that the years immediately before manhood are crucial in a lifelong path of right or wrong, or as Murdoch put it, that 'the whole career of every person is greatly modified by the habits he formed in his youth.'[43] Most of these lessons are identical to those produced for British youth of all classes in this era (and presumably the author mainly had them in mind). In fact, much of the book, Murdoch admits himself, is merely a compilation from British sources.[44] In order to mitigate the potential for future religious strife, the British government in India had developed a policy of religious neutrality for its colleges and a large part of this book, on 'Religious Duties', was intended to be used by students to counteract the 'deficiency' in the curriculum. There are even Christian prayers at the end, intended for daily use. The book includes many chapters that would have been familiar to British boys. There are prohibitions on smoking and drinking, for the good of the body and for force of character.[45] Gambling is also similarly prohibited.[46] The section on 'Moral Conduct' is predictably the biggest and most important.[47] But there are also chapters on caste, on the women of India, and in addition to a chapter on duty to country (ideas about mutual assistance between classes or castes, which one might easily find in a similar British book) there is a chapter on duty to government (obedience to the Raj). Murdoch developed what he meant by this type of obedience in a chapter called 'Patriotism, False and True' in his 1903 book for Indian boys.[48]

Murdoch believed in the possibility of universal moral attributes and a universal boyhood. Yet, as Deana Heath points out, English texts in India were also 'characterized by ambivalence, since while colonial educators were forced to treat [them] as culturally ambiguous (in order to disavow their goal of inculcating Christian morality, or for missionaries the more explicit goal of conversion), they at the same time actively resisted such an approach', thereby denying the universality of morality that they were in fact trying to teach.[49] Murdoch acknowledged that these universals were nevertheless inflected by distinctions of race and class. As he states: 'Right and wrong, duty, and country, benevolence towards men and responsibility towards the unseen Power by which human action is guided and controlled – these are not ideal phrases. In all countries and ages they have retained their meaning'.[50] Most of his advice could have been found in any British boy's manual, though he peppered his text with Indian and Hindu examples. Integrity, frugality, purity (of thought, deed and reading material), avoiding bad companions, temperance, industry, modesty and good manners, moral courage and virtue were all stressed, as was truthfulness (which he said was a particular challenge for Indians).[51] Murdoch was most concerned with boys aged 16–20 – the 'most critical period of life' – but in general his advice pertained to the stage a boy had attained irrespective of age, where the responsibilities of study, marriage and family could all come at an age much younger than in Britain.[52]

Also borrowed from the British model was the importance of home. Home duties, filial piety and fatherly responsibilities were to be cultivated in Indian young men. But in contrast to British books of this kind, there was also a section on 'Duties to Wife'. Unlike young British men, many Indian students were presumed to be married, but the 'educated native is nowhere so miserable and crestfallen as in his home', torn between his educated public life and his 'unquestioning submission to the requisitions of a superstitious family'.[53] This goal as the young head of this family was to slowly educate its members, including his wife, and to show moral courage.[54] There is also a particularly condescending section on 'The Hindu Family System', in which Murdoch states that 'one great difference between Hindus and Englishmen is the marked spirit of independence possessed by the latter. Hindus are like a flock of sheep, moving in one body; Englishmen are more like lions which live alone or in couples.' Needless to say, Murdoch's texts had a perceived civilizing role. He thought the British family superior and worthy of emulation.[55]

The main goal of the Christian Literature Society, of which John Murdoch was an agent, was to provide cheap and edifying Christian literature for the newly literate. In the 50 years after its creation in 1858, the Society published almost 4,000 publications and almost 39 million copies in 21 languages, including many schoolbooks. Murdoch's various guides for boys were repeatedly reprinted well into the 1920s. The purpose was to get the moral messages across, in whatever language (vernacular or English) possible. For British men like Murdoch, good character and morality were intertwined with Christian faith and the English language. English and Christianity were to be the vehicles through which Indian boys would improve themselves and their colony and the British Empire as a whole. For Gauri Viswanathan, 'The equation between the English nation and the Christian God is rewritten as (but emphatically not supplanted by) an equation between the English nation and *new forms of knowledge* produced by historical development and material progress.'[56] For men like Murdoch, progress involved the physical, spiritual and emotional development of the individual boy, in order to bring about positive change to the family, to the community and to the colony and, in turn, to the metropole. Murdoch and many others devoted their lives to furthering Christianity in India, with boys especially in mind, as they would be the ones to encourage further conversions in their own communities. In his mission, Murdoch received support and advice from such luminaries as Florence Nightingale, who prompted him to make new tracts for Hindu children on Botany and Zoology, using birds to teach about God. She also praised him on his 'fruitful' work in India and prayed that he would continue 'to enlighten her [India], her men and her women in the first principles of morality, education and hygiene.'[57]

Educators were concerned that young Indian men with good English educations, the target audience of manuals like Murdoch's, and generally a desirable group, could also prove dangerous because of frustrations that they were not receiving the work and stature that their education should have afforded them, and that in such cases they would be 'animated by hopes and stirred by emotions, to which they were previously strangers'.[58] These emotions were to be controlled. It was absolutely clear to writers like Murdoch that education, moral teaching in particular, concerned the cultivation and control of the emotions in general, although the perception was activated by a painful awareness of the lack of any such concern, and made more acute by the prospect of what would fill its place:

> As to any influence of the teachers over the pupils – any attempt to form the sentiments and habits, and to control and guide the passions and emotions, – such a notion never enters into their conceptions, and the formation of the moral character of the young is consequently wholly left to the influence of the Casual associations amidst which they are placed, without any endeavour to modify or direct them.[59]

Until the education system could be improved, Murdoch maintained that reading material was to fill the gap in emotional training. He was also critical of religions other than Christianity in this regard. Emotional control through Christianity was what was required for Indian boys. Murdoch viewed native Indian religions as allowing 'the passions and affections . . . to grow up wild without any thought of pruning their luxuriances or directing their exercise to good purposes'. It was this, Murdoch identified, that accounted for deficiencies in 'moral and social obligation' and the 'radical defect of the native character', defined by its 'narrow and contracted selfishness'. Murdoch proposed that the young mind be 'taught to look for the means of its own happiness and improvement in the indulgence of benevolent feelings', the path to which, and subsequently to a moral existence, could only be found through Christianity.[60]

The Calcutta University Commission called the elite, educated Indian youth a 'menace to good government', especially in Bengal where 'the small educated class is alone vocal'.[61] Though the government adopted a policy of religious neutrality,[62] it encouraged religious organizations to set up their own colleges. In government colleges, though no religious training was allowed, they recommended the implementation of moral training (already present in the colleges supported by Missionary Societies) through a moral textbook[63] and through a series of lectures, every session on 'the duties of a man and a citizen'.[64] This sort of moral education had been implemented in British elementary schools in this period, with mixed results and with a continuing debate on whether moral education should be religious or secular in nature.[65] On an informal level, the missionary interventions of men like Murdoch were already filling in the details for the educated Indian youth in his 'Battle of Life', guiding his 'moral duties', 'truthfulness', 'purity', 'temperance', 'Modesty [and] good manners'.[66]

## Education and political order

For educators and missionaries, distributing the right sort of literature to the 'right sort' of boys and young men was thought to be crucial.[67] In an article titled 'How India Must Be Saved', Rev. F. B. Meyer asked rhetorically: 'Do you realise that in Madras scarcely a student leaves the University without receiving a packet of infidel literature?' He concluded that 'this widespread dissemination of anti-Christian literature is one of the standing menaces of the English rule in India.'[68] The Calcutta Christian Tract and Book Society, for example, promoted books like *Exposure of Hinduism*, which it judged 'should be of real worth to all who are engaged in the training of young men in schools and colleges, and we would commend them to their notice'.[69] Though literacy rates were increasing among Indian boys overall, only a small number of Indian boys could read English and an even smaller number were Christian. Whereas in Britain the widespread dissemination of immoral literature was a cause for concern, the solution to which was improving literature, in India immoral influences could not easily be reduced to 'dreadful' literature and the major problem was getting a reforming message across at all to any but a few of the most educated boys.

Missionary schools were popular in India in this period, both in urban and rural settings. Families and students understood this education 'to be a form of welfare and social advancement which the colonial state had largely failed to provide'.[70] The schools reproduced Indian values as well as British and Christian ones, emphasizing a system of morality and discipline (imagined to be universal), and traditional caste hierarchies. In Vidarbha, for example, influencing students' morality was a concern in school, but 'the scholars were more influenced by their home surroundings, customs and social ethics than by their teachers'. The solution was the creation of a 'School Boy League of Honour', similar to many such leagues in Britain, with the goal of reforming the bodies and morals of boys and, in the process, society as a whole.[71] Traditional customs related, for example, to sexuality, early marriage, or to the care of the body, combined with traditional spiritual and religious beliefs, remained in opposition to attempts at developing British and Christian understandings of the moral and physical self. Perhaps more fundamentally, traditional ideas of the collective nature of the family and the community conflicted with British notions of self-cultivation in the individual.

The RTS published many books for boys intended either for an Indian market, usually inspired by the British writers' missionary experiences in India, or for a young British readership. As we have seen, books originally written in English for a British audience could be adapted into Hindi or Urdu, then adapted again in India, back into English.[72] There was even a Bengali version of the famous British *BOP*, issued by the Calcutta Christian Tract and Book Society, with RTS material, and founded with similar aims to the original *BOP* of 1879. After its first year of publication, the Calcutta Society was printing 10,000 copies per month, with reprints of around 20,000 copies.[73] Clearly, the books written about India for British children were intended to impart moral lessons, but probably more importantly, they were intended to muster support and money in Britain for the missionary cause. The object of one story about Hindu life in South India, written by an itinerant missionary, was for 'young readers, to understand clearly the difficulties which Hindu children and young people have to surmount in order to become Christians'.[74] Another was promoted as making 'a capital present to a boy whom it was desired to interest in his coloured brothers'.[75]

One story, *Seed-Time and Harvest. A Tale of the Punjab*, published in several editions by the Christian Literature Society for India, is a good example of the often misguided ideals of the British Christian literature societies in India and of their fears for the future if young men failed to adopt their standards of morality.[76] The story's main character is Narain Das, a boy from a rich and influential Hindu family, who converts to Christianity. The chapter 'The Light of Home'[77] is the most important for its moral message, both in its illustration of an evangelical personal awakening and because of its emphasis, as in Britain, on family life. Often in British stories of this type, the son will guide the father, through his good example, to change his ways. In this story, Narain Das's father's conversion to Christianity takes place thanks to his son, but only after the crisis point of near death from depression over the loss of his son and from losing some of his riches.[78]

The character of Amrit Lal, Narain Das's friend and an educated university man belonging to the same high caste, provides the author with an opportunity to bring forward some of the arguments of the Hindu majority of that social group. 'It is the manner of life I object to', he says. 'I mean both the religious and social manner of life of the West. It is a rigid growth which can never take root in Indian soil.' 'Friend', Das replies, 'I scarcely need remind you that the Lord Jesus was an Eastern; His teaching is suited to the allegorical mind of the East.' The Indian 'cry for civilization . . . is the secular name for Christianity . . .

India is hungering, not for bread, but for the Word of God.' In the Bible, the Eastern mind is to find all it needs. It would supply the wants, according to Das, of 'the greatest intellect and the simplest child', in 'both East and West'. In the end, Narain Das's friend also converts.[79] Just as Christianity is shown to be universal for a young Indian and British readership, so are the ways to upright boyhood and manhood.

True religion was to bring about political order, but also individual morality and strong families, combating the potential for delinquency at its roots. The most obvious similarity between efforts to educate and reform boys in Britain and India was the belief that Christian values would save boys from delinquency. The most obvious difference, of course, was that British boys in this period were raised within a broadly Christian culture. The religious training of Indian boys could not be taken for granted. Thus there was a vigorous campaign to demonstrate to Indians the benefits of Christianity. Christian texts tried to combat the widespread idea that Christianity only appealed to the most down-and-out in Indian society, those most interested in food for their bodies rather than for their souls. Samuel Satyanatha, in his book for the Christian Literature Society for India, *Sketches of Indian Christians*, explains that the idea that Christianity was only successful among 'the very lowest classes of Indian society' is simply false, and he gives examples of high-born Christian conversions.[80] Work done by foreigners and paid agents of the Missions would have been better were it done by high-born Native converts. The message might have been more readily accepted too. Indeed, he argues, it was the high caste convert who had 'a great mission to fulfil' in demonstrating to his countrymen the change Christ had wrought in him:

> If by his life and conversation he can make it clear that conversion does not mean merely a change in dress, in food, in language and style of living, but a radical change of life, a thorough readjustment in standards of judgments, in motives and in conduct; if he can show what he has gained in self-control, in self-reverence, in charity, in meekness and in power to help others.[81]

There was much debate among the English, even those promoting Christianity, as to whether English or vernacular languages should be the medium of moral instruction. One British minister, recently returned from a tour of Mission inspection in India, said:

> I should like to plead for one moment the cause of educated young men in India, the English-reading, the English-speaking young men. . . . I think I should like to read to you the words of a young student. . . . He was one of those who shrink from giving a definite answer to the question, 'Are you a Christian?' He writes: 'I

consider Hinduism to be a bundle of lies, superstitions, and abominations.' Then
he goes on to speak of Christ, and tells of a book that was given to him at college,
and a copy of the New Testament, and how carefully he read those books over,
and read others. . . . Then he closes by saying: 'There is no religion in the world
to be compared with Christianity and its divine Saviour.' That is the condition of
these young men.[82]

Books were believed to be powerful tools of conversion and morality, but also
of potential danger. A 'Bengali Gentleman', and not a Christian one is quoted as
saying that: 'If the world and infidelity have their literature in such abundance
for our young people, religion and faith ought to have theirs also.'[83] Missionary
literature societies used such 'support' to increase their printing and fund-raising
activities in India and in Britain.

Though British writers often attempted to adapt their messages to their
Indian audiences, they were not wholly successful, due to a lack of cultural
sensitivity or a wilful disregard of it. This affected boys' learning. As part of
the Indian Universities Commission of 1902, Justice Gooroo Dass [Gurudas]
Banerjee, the first Indian Vice-Chancellor of the University of Calcutta, pointed
to unsuitable textbooks and courses of study as reasons why Indian boys had
imperfect command of English: 'One reason why our boys learn English so
badly', he said, 'and why they mechanically commit to memory many things
without understanding them, is, because we often use reading books in English
which are only imperfectly intelligible to them, by reason of their relating to
scenes and incidents wholly foreign to the Indian student, and we often prescribe
subjects and text books involving ideas which cannot be clearly comprehended
and realised by boys of tender age.'[84] A few decades before, the Indian Education
Commission recommended that many boys were better served by learning in the
vernacular, not in English, but that it was better for boys to learn both languages
so that they could proceed with their own education.[85]

The British did not pursue a policy of systematic mass education in India,
unlike in Britain, where a process towards universal education, starting with
the Elementary Education Act of 1870, was increasingly taken for granted. In
India, therefore, the moral suasion of the educated elite was seen as paramount,
as this would eventually lead to the moral education of the masses.[86] Some
suggested that the British were better friends of the poor and uneducated than
they were of the Indian elite, going so far as to recommend the 'optional use of
Roman, or Romanic, letters for Indian languages or dialects, so that, besides
other advantages arising from their use, the many millions of poor, unlettered,
unleisured peasants of that land . . . may have the opportunity of receiving the

benefits we ourselves have derived from our Alphabet, our Bible and our Saviour.'[87] Since they were ignored by the general education system, the argument was that poor people should be taught to read the vernacular in Roman letters because they were being held down by rich and educated Indians. This view was in direct opposition to the more prevalent idea of the trickle-down effect of morality from higher caste to lower. Education which led to low-caste social mobility, however, was criticized by newspapers in both Hindi and Urdu.[88] As for the elites, some British commentators believed that teaching them only in English and denying them access to their own canonical works would be a disastrous attempt to 'denationalize the people of India.'[89] Other British commentators would certainly have approved of attempts to dampen Indian boys' national feelings.

For all that the British wished to dampen national feelings, the passions in general remained a cause for concern. Mission narratives made it quite clear that Christianity not only set the moral compass, but that no other religion could adequately prime the emotions to accept and absorb moral instruction. Scottish missionary John Murray Mitchell (1815–1904) warned in his oft republished *Letters to Indian Youth* that 'the chief danger' for the 'educated youth of Bombay' was to forget religion. Without Christianity, the human nature laid bare would be subject to the 'exceedingly strong' and 'corrupt passions of human nature'. Left unguided, the 'tumultuous violence' of the passions 'drowns the voice of reason and conscience'.[90] Without an appropriate religious framework, 'the heart deceives the head – the feelings mislead the judgment'.[91] Murdoch would surely have agreed. The missionary effort, much like the metropolitan campaigns to train the child, ultimately rested on the same central assumption: the Christian path was the moral path, open only to those with sufficiently controlled emotions. To that extent, moral qualities in both countries were thought to be the same, 'fixed and immutable' in Mitchell's words; but 'moral character' – the degree to which an individual truly embodied, or felt, moral qualities – could only be derived from Christianity.[92]

## Conclusion

In the words of the Madras Native Christian Association on the occasion of Murdoch's 50-year anniversary of service:

> This long period he [Murdoch] has spent in fostering Christian education by means of useful training institutions; in preparing an excellent series of educational text-books, permeated with the spirit of Christianity; in helping

to purify the vernacular texts prescribed by the local University; in travelling through the length and breadth of this vast country with a view to promote the cause of healthy Christian literature; in producing in marvelous succession a long series of readable and compact treatises on religious, moral, economic and social subjects of great practical importance.[93]

Yet, after around 50 years of efforts, the Christian Literature Society did not have a glowing report of its progress, nor of the Indian population it was trying to 'educate'. Circulation of its publications was a real problem, which they blamed, especially in South India, on the 'entire absence of any desire for self-culture' and they acknowledged that they had not found a type of 'Christian literature which will "take on"'.[94] This lack of desire for self-culture would have been especially odious for Murdoch and his peers, given the emphasis on self-help in his books and the long tradition of this form of education for young men in Britain.[95] Even without mass conversions, Murdoch could still claim success by pointing out the ways that 'Hindu public opinion [was] being Christianised'. Especially for those Christians concerned with the moral upbringing of boys, Murdoch thought the establishment of a *Hindu* Young Men's Association in conjunction with the Christianizing of Indian opinion, ought to have provided some comfort.[96] But, for men like Murdoch, a thorough moral education for boys was still thought only to be found within Christianity.

The RTS, the Christian Literature Society and others like it recognized a problem with youth in India and tried to remedy it in the same way as they did in Britain: through Christianity and reading material. Through their many periodicals, these organizations argued that the potential for delinquency not only put the family and the colony in peril, as it did in the metropole, but it also created the possibility for political instability as well. The long shadow of the Rebellion (1857), and growing nationalist sentiment, served as excuses to double their efforts at education and conversion in India and at fund-raising at home and in the settler colonies. It seems fair to conclude, therefore, in agreement with Ashis Nandy that 'children bore the brunt of conflicts precipitated by colonial politics, Westernized education and exogenous social institutions'.[97] In Britain and in India the stakes of youth concerned the efficient maintenance of a paternal system. In Britain this included the citizen father as a central component of the paternal State. The British boy was to be saved through appropriate reading matter and fashioned into a fair citizen; the Indian boy, by a similar means, was to become politically inert: a dutiful and loyal subject. While it could be argued that this was not too far removed from the formal education working-class children were receiving in the same period in

Britain, the potential for active citizenship and the franchise remained elusive for Indian children, making their subjecthood more complete.[98]

Cultural transfer, however, works both ways. If Indian notions of childhood (which remained ill-defined in this period) presented a striking contrast to the British, the influx of ideas was nevertheless employed by Indians, and to Indian ends. Nita Kumar's suggestion that 'no narrative of the child exists in modern India, perhaps because the child as a category has not been discovered or invented yet', can be challenged.[99] Kumar herself acknowledges a 'specific experience called "childhood"' related to the 'politics of age domination'.[100] The process of lifecycle differentiation in India may have been slower, but a clearer notion of childhood did emerge as an important concern that was tied to a process of modernity, both for Indian nationalists as well as for the Raj.[101] Some scholars see an idea of childhood in India as beginning in the colonial period, along with the creation of an influential British-educated Indian middle class. I would tentatively suggest that it coexisted alongside and sometimes merged with an idea of childhood that was rooted in indigenous traditions.[102] As Swapna Banerjee has shown, this concern for shaping the minds and hearts of future citizens through reading material was not limited to the British in India. Indian authors expressed similar ideas about childhood, good character and links to the nation in Indian languages, with different ends in mind than those of the British. The Bengali elite, for example, made concerted efforts to produce literature and periodicals for children and youth, realizing the potential value to the nation that cultivating youth would make.[103] As Pradip Bose has noted, nineteenth- and early twentieth-century Bengalis began to stress the importance of character building in children, that they could be 'moulded in accordance with the future needs of the nation so that they could bring glory to it'.[104] In Urdu, the word 'sharif', meaning 'noble', shifted its meaning, in the opinion of Gail Minault, from something indicating a 'sense of birthright to position or wealth' to a 'sense of good character: honourable, upright, cultured, and respectable'. A 'sharif gentleman was pious without being wasteful, educated without being pedantic, and restrained in his expression of emotion.'[105] Around the same time, childhood began to be defined as a distinct period in the lifecycle and children were defined as innocents in need of protection, but conversely, more pressure and guilt was placed on them, and parents were encouraged to apply discipline and reason in raising their children.[106] Dipesh Chakrabarty also sees nationalism at the heart of the redefinition of childhood in British Bengal, with Bengali authors, inspired by their British counterparts, linking morality to the idea of the strong family and nation.[107] The 'National Efficiency' movement and eugenic concerns, so pronounced in Britain at this time, infused the ideas and language of Indians by 1910, grafting them onto native 'living traditions' and feeding the growing nationalist movement.[108] At least partially blaming themselves, Murdoch and many others judged that Indian nationalism stemmed from a 'failure of the educational system to foster ethical, moral, and religious training'.[109] The failure was that this training was not a British-orientated one. The British therefore lost control, at least partially, of their attempts to modify citizen-building strategies at home into loyalty-inducing strategies in India. What served as good reading matter for the 'problem' stage of youth was as good for the colony as it was for the metropole. If the nation and the citizen lay at the heart of metropolitan strategy, we should not be surprised to see the nation and the citizen also emerging as the ends of Indian moral guidance for the Indian youth.

# Storm and Stress: The 'Invention' of Adolescence

Chapter 6 explores the ways in which an increasingly professionalized body of youth educators, psychologists and social workers appropriated the work of religious and social youth workers of the preceding decades and adapted their focus on the development of character, understood as a specific set of moral and emotional qualities, for a scientifically engaged adult audience. The cultural consensus explored in earlier chapters is shown to have influenced the new field of child psychology, informing educational and social theories, as well as providing impetus for legislative intervention into child welfare. The study and observation of childhood emotion, increasingly developed into a science (or at least framed by scientific rhetoric), was an important component of this new development. But in studying and presenting scientific guides to childhood emotion, its control, and how to steer it towards maturity, direct appeals to the child on an emotional level were substituted for schematic guides for parents and educators. This chapter therefore traces the connections between the partial scientification of childhood feelings and the de-emotionalization of approaches to childhood development.

At the same time as social institutions relating to childhood slowly replaced those with more overtly religious motivations, there was increasing political intervention in domesticity. The State, supported by the rigor of scientific analysis, and encouraged by the social pressure brought to bear by the highly public activities of the NSPCC, essentially took on the role that had been fashioned by the informal educators of the fin de siècle. Fathers were no longer seen as having sole, or even dominant, authority over their children. The State took on new powers to intervene in the interests of the child, overriding fathers' authority. This child-centred approach to the governance of what were traditionally 'family affairs' was morally induced and influenced by the thinking of older child activists, but was also motivated by the eugenics movement and notions of maintaining the integrity of the race. Children who were both morally and physically robust would produce future generations of good citizens. In sum, the scientification of, and State intervention in, childhood, brought to fruition the aims and ideals of those groups and publishers who had seen it as a moral mission to ensure the next generation of moral and emotionally sound male citizens.

The child was increasingly understood in his/her own terms, not merely as property of the father. Thomas Barnardo (1845–1905), philanthropist and founder of Dr Barnardo's Homes, referred to the great progress in children's rights at the end of the nineteenth century: 'Sixty years ago the child was a mere chattel. Enlightened popular sentiment is now on the side of those who affirm that childhood has a right to innocence and decency, and kindly care and education.'[1] This new vision of the child occurred in the context of increased fears of physical deterioration, especially in urban settings. Discomfort regarding Britain's position in relation to strong economic and imperial rivals turned into alarm during the South African War of 1899–1902, when high numbers of young recruits were deemed physically unfit for military service. The near defeat of the British army also encouraged fears about the future of the 'British race'. An Inter-Departmental Committee on Physical Deterioration gathered to investigate the issue and, reporting its findings in 1904, pushed the discussion on adolescence further.[2] It found that young people were lacking the education necessary to prevent physical deterioration. Parental guidance was absent and little other supervision on physical and moral development was available.[3] For the poor, material improvement was necessary before any moral or religious development could occur. The committee concluded that these results were in danger of being lost by the premature provision of religious teachings.[4] Urbanization was understood to be a great potential threat to young men. This continued a wide social debate in the 1880s and 1890s about the morbidity and degeneracy of the urban populace in general.[5] The Committee was also concerned with what they termed a 'depletion of rural districts by the exodus of the best type'.[6] The associated fear was that once the move to the city was made, the young would succumb to the problems of urban life.

The augmentation of legislation and the increase in professionalization in the treatment of children's issues were related in this period, and depended upon a novel understanding of childhood, of its development into adulthood and of parental responsibility. First, increasing inquiries and legislation related to childhood and youth required a repositioning of parental rights and responsibilities. Second, these inquiries into child life also began increasingly to be fashioned by professionals dedicated to the scientific study of children, whether in the fields of child rescue or child improvement. Where professionals were absent, the language used to discuss childhood issues and advice was still intended to convey a sense of professionalism. Third, this increasingly scientific or pseudo-scientific study of children required a more specific categorization of the different phases of childhood. The most problematic of these phases, adolescence, thus became a period of acute concern, and the focus of much writing for boys. The Inter-Departmental Committee on Physical Deterioration was impressed with the conviction that 'the period of adolescence is responsible for much waste of human material and for the entrance upon maturity of permanently damaged and ineffective persons of both sexes.'[7] Guiding this transitional phase from childhood to adulthood focused the attention of reformers, parents, professionals and youth groups alike on the physical, mental and emotional well-being of future citizens.

Boys of a certain age were singled out as problematic. Conventionally, girls, it was assumed, had to be prepared for marriage, whereas male youth had to be instructed for their roles, considered more complex and more important. Boys between (very roughly) the ages of 8 and 18 (or even older), were of more concern than younger boys or girls of any other age. This 'queer sort of creature' was increasingly called an adolescent.[8] The American psychologist, G. Stanley Hall, cautioned that increasingly urban environments put male adolescents at risk. This observation, though present even at the start of our period, was popularized by Hall and encouraged campaigns against drinking, smoking, dancing, gambling and 'pernicious' literature.

## Legislation for children and parental authority

In addition to all the Education Acts, beginning with the 1870 Act, there were many inquiries into child life and consequently much legislation was enacted throughout our period. There was therefore an increasing codification of childhood as a distinct and crucial time of life. The concept of state responsibility was fairly new. As late as 1881 Lord Shaftesbury, a champion of children's causes, had declared the evils of child abuse 'enormous and indisputable' but that it was 'of so private, internal and domestic a character as to be beyond the reach of legislation.'[9] In 1889 the first Act of Parliament for the Prevention of Cruelty to Children, 'The Children's Charter', was passed. It enabled English law to intervene, for the first time, in the domestic relationship between parents and children. The police could now arrest anyone found ill-treating a child and obtain a warrant to enter a home if a child was thought to be in danger. The Act also included guidelines on the employment of children and outlawed begging. After five years' implementation it was evaluated and in 1894 was amended and extended. Children were to be allowed to give evidence in court; mental cruelty was recognized; it became an offence to deny a sick child medical attention.[10] The Prevention of Cruelty to Children Act (PCCA), 1904, amended the law relating to the Prevention of Cruelty to Children by enlarging the category of child to include boys under the age of 16.

These new child-centred laws had important consequences for parental rights and obligations. For example, the Youthful Offenders Act of 1901 made it possible for a summons to be issued against the parent or guardian of the child or young person charging him or her with contributing to the commission of the offence if he or she had 'conduced to the commission of the alleged offence by wilful default or by habitually neglecting to exercise due care' of the child.[11] The Children Act of 1908 strengthened this law, whereby parents could be punished for their children's crimes. The Bill's framer, Liberal MP Herbert Samuel, stated that 'penalising the parent, in proper cases, for the misconduct of the child, would strengthen the sense of parental responsibility, and conduce to a more careful and effective exercise of parental control.'[12] In 1907 the Probation Offenders Act was passed, enabling petty offenders to serve probation rather than imprisonment. The Act aimed to prevent the economic deprivation of dependents following the imprisonment of a family's wage-earner and encouraged parental responsibility.

The Children Act of 1908 (also named the 'Children's Charter') extended state responsibility to all children, ended child imprisonment, restricted corporal punishment and instituted the first national system of juvenile courts. The Children Act began nominally as a consolidation bill. It repealed 21 whole Acts and part of 17 others, besides codifying, consolidating, extending and amending legislation generally concerning children. Children working under the Factory and Workshop Act, however, were untouched, and street vendors and those employed between school hours were also omitted. As a late addition from a failed Licensing Bill,[13] children were excluded from Public House Bars (Sec. 120). The Act was more important for what it represented than for establishing novel laws. It came into force on 1 April 1909 (Sec. 134), with the exception of the restriction of imprisonment (Secs 108: 10 and 112) – providing 'places of detention' – which did not become obligatory until the following year. There were six main parts to the act: Infant Life Protection; Prevention of Cruelty to Children and Young Persons; Juvenile Smoking; Reformatory and Industrial Schools; Juvenile Offenders; and Miscellaneous and General.[14]

The Children Act was attacked as a usurpation of parental rights, tending to weaken home life and the independence of the individual and increasing 'officialism' and the use of Government Inspectors.[15] The Liberal MP for Sleaford, Lincolnshire, Arnold Lupton, thought the Children Bill 'simply absurd'. His objections are worthy of study, since they demonstrate much of the resistance in popular opinion to governmental and other 'professional' interference in what were considered parental rights.

> Already children had been taught by law to think that there were other people in the country superior to their parents. The father might think it a good thing for his son to smoke, and why should the boy not say he was smoking because his father thought he should? The law in future would forbid a boy to smoke a cigarette, but it would permit him to drink a glass of rum, and the boy would say the law did not forbid him to drink a glass of rum, but only his father, and that if the Government thought it wrong to drink rum they would have passed a law to that effect.[16]

Apart from the quite predictable resistance to State interference in what were considered private, familial concerns, Lupton's objections reflect wider assumptions about the relationship between father and son. It is also interesting to note the ridicule that boyhood drinking of strong liquor provoked at this time. This widespread recognition that childhood drinking was unacceptable was still novel to some. Despite objections, the origins of the Children's Bill were seen by H. J. Tennant, Scottish Liberal MP for Berwickshire and brother-in-law to Asquith, to be a change in opinion: 'the livening and quickening sense of responsibility which has been gradually growing toward the potential citizens of this country'.[17]

Potential citizens required even more protection than adults. Liberal MP Sir Donald Maclean judged that this widely reflected popular opinion: 'The people of the country at least appreciated the fact that the protection of the State was due to the child from the day of its birth as well as to adult citizens.'[18] Herbert Samuel, the Bill's framer, who was influenced by Fabian socialism,[19] insisted that children's rights did *not* lessen parental authority. Instead, the Bill served to 'strengthen and guide parental authority, only to punish it where evil, where possible to reform and conserve the child's home even when temporary removal is advisable, and instead of increased officialism, to rely upon the aid of voluntary men and women'. To its supporters, the Children Act was merely 'a splendid guide, with the power of the law behind it'.[20] The real work was to come from citizens, parents and guardians of the citizens of the future.

There was clear tension in this era between ideas of state intervention and parental rights. One female author and social worker, M. Inglis, who campaigned for the Children Act, still accorded parents primary God-given rights over their children: 'Family and household rights do not arise from the existence of the State, but are antecedent to it. They belong to the law of nature, a law that no nation can overthrow or annul with impunity; that great immutable pre-existent law by which we are connected in the eternal flame of the universe.'[21] Inglis insisted that the Act reinforced the truth that '*the* great factor in the training of a child is *home and parent*' and asserted that the State still recognizes that 'the Trinity of *Home, Parent, and Child* is the only safe and lasting foundation on which to build up the future greatness of a nation.'[22]

In his memoirs Samuel credited Inglis, whom he described as a Scottish lady 'keenly interested in social work', with the inspiration to create the Children's Bill.[23] Inglis herself wrote a book after the Act was passed, directed towards the growing field of social work. It demonstrates that professionalization of children's advocates had become crucial by this period. It was directed at social workers, who 'can aid in carrying out its provisions, and how all may co-operate to rescue the children, guide the parents, and conserve and reform, if possible, the homes'.[24] These new professionals had detailed knowledge of the Act and could aid most effectively in its implementation, where previous voluntary interventions had failed.

Sometimes legislation that was intended to promote children's rights had unfortunate and ironic consequences, demonstrating the problems associated with the novelty of these kinds of law and the difficulty in interpreting their intended goals.[25] For many years the Derby and Derbyshire Band of Hope Union had held a festival called 'Crowning the May Queen'. The local police informed the organizing committee that in consequence of the Prevention of Cruelty to Children Act it would be necessary to obtain a magistrate's license to allow the children to take part in the festival. This was done under protest, although it meant that around 50 children under 10 years of age were excluded. The Committee of the UK Band of Hope Union, at the request of their Derbyshire associates approached the Home Secretary who stated that he thought that the children would be exempted from the operation of Section 2 of the PCCA, 1904, by proviso 1 of that Section; and that they would not be held to be engaged in employment within the meaning of the Employment of Children Act, 1903 and that he forwarded this to the Derby magistrates. The UK Band of Hope Union provided the following assessment: 'friends generally throughout the country will rejoice to know that the innocent gaiety and helpful service of the children is now not likely to be frustrated by the hostile interpretation of an Act which was meant not to restrict, but to add to the happiness and well-being of the children of the land.'[26] Publishing this incident in the annual report would have been of use to local societies, who were encountering similar difficulties in local interpretations of the new laws designed to protect children.

## The National Society for the Prevention of Cruelty to Children

State intervention, by safeguarding homes as physically and morally secure, was designed to reinforce the notion that homes (and schools) were the only proper locations in which to provide children with the right foundations for life. The greater goal of this intervention was to create future generations of citizens who were modern and competitive on an international stage. Thus, as Hugh Cunningham notes, 'Child-saving aimed both to provide the child with what was thought of as a childhood, and to ensure the future of society. The two aims were thought to be entirely consonant with one another.'[27] The future of society depended on saving the current generation of children. The NSPCC was a prime location for these endeavours.

The founding of the NSPCC and its methods typify the ideas about children and the strategies used by the other organizations and publishers discussed here. In 1910 Sir Robert Parr (1862–1931), the second director of the NSPCC, wrote of the centrality of children to religion, to the home and to the nation:

> As the child is the central figure in religion, the moving force in the home, so it should be the main hope of the nation, and when the national mind is concentrated on this ideal, the nation's responsibility will begin to be fulfilled.[28]

By this time Society was already on solid ground. It had weathered investigations into its financial management; it had become incorporated; its early supporters had largely been responsible for the first child cruelty legislation in the United Kingdom; and it had been granted 'authorized status', enabling its inspectors to remove children from abusive or neglectful homes without police involvement.[29] Under the 1907 Probation Offenders Act, NSPCC Inspectors were responsible for supervising probations relating to child abuse or neglect. Yet all of these successes mask slower changes in public opinion, which Parr tried to address. Regarding the child as a future citizen, with all the rights and protection of the State associated with that status, was novel. The NSPCC was founded in 1889 and incorporated by Royal Charter in 1895. Its objectives were clear yet formidable:

1. To prevent the public and private wrongs of children and the corruption of their morals.
2. To take action for the enforcement of the laws for their protection.
3. To provide and maintain an organisation for the above objects.
4. To do all other such lawful things as are incidental or conducive to the attainment of the above objects.[30]

Benjamin Waugh (1839–1908) the society's founder and director, was devoted to his cause. During the ten years building up the society he took no pay except a small annual sum for editing the *Child's Guardian*.[31] Robert Parr, in his tribute to Waugh, explained Waugh's devotion to protecting children's rights in the form of a story: in a cottage on the estate of a well-known countess who took an active interest in social reform 'lived two people whose children were terribly neglected; the parents were abstainers, and there was no poverty. Warnings had failed to secure proper treatment for the children.' The countess ignored this deplorable situation, but Waugh could not and proceedings were started on the parents and they were convicted. The woman withdrew her ten guinea subscription to the Society.[32] This story is typical of the message the NSPCC laboured to convey. The dedication of its director and its workers, the universal potential for abuse, even without such external causes as poverty or intemperance, are highlighted here and repeated regularly in Waugh's writings, in the NSPCC's official paper, the *Child's Guardian* (launched in 1887), and in the texts of other supporters of the Society. Waugh made clear that 'the NSPCC is not just another children's charity. It is an organisation which will fight to obtain the citizenship of every child and justice for all children.'[33] According to M. J. D. Roberts, it was 'a distinct advantage for the NSPCC that, in dealing with the "best interests" of potential, rather than actual, adult citizens, it was generally able to avoid the tensions about the moral responsibility of the individual which so irritated relations between state policy-making elites and voluntary society leaders in adjacent areas of social policy debate.'[34]

Inspired by the New York Society for the Prevention of Cruelty to Children (1875), the first British Society was founded in Liverpool in 1883. The London

Society was formed a year later, with Lord Shaftesbury as President, and Waugh and Rev. Edward Rudolph as joint Honorary Secretaries. Patrons included Cardinal Manning (the interfaith nature of the Society was stressed), Baroness Burdett-Coutts, Dr Barnardo and Lord Aberdeen. By 1889, the London Society for the Prevention of Cruelty to Children had 32 branches, known as 'aid committees', throughout England, Scotland and Wales. In 1889, it revised its constitution and renamed itself the NSPCC with Queen Victoria as Royal Patron and Waugh as Director. At this time the NSPCC employed 29 Inspectors, and dealt with 3,947 cases of child abuse and neglect.[35] The NSPCC was widely promoted and supported, as in the RTS magazine, the *Leisure Hour*.[36] In 1891 Princess Mary of Teck (later to be Queen Mary) took out a subscription to the Society for herself and her younger brothers, which inspired the formation of the Children's League of Pity, whose newsletter started in 1893. The League and its newsletter enabled children (mostly of the middle classes) to learn about the NSPCC's work and to become involved in fund-raising activities.[37]

According to Christine Sherrington, Benjamin Waugh's idea of citizenship of the child was a 'genuinely forward-looking concept' and the basis of his campaign.[38] 'For the first time in English history', Waugh wrote, after the passage of the 1889 Children Act, 'a new year has dawned on English children with civil rights, as real and as vital as the civil rights of grown people.'[39] In Sherrington's view, Waugh 'saw child cruelty as resulting from the child's powerlessness, a denial of its natural rights of citizenship and personhood, calling for "a courageous assertion and honest enforcement of the principle that every child is a member of the State and subject of the Crown".'[40] In the words of a supporter, because of the NSPCC and the 'Children's Charter' (1889), 'the *child* has as sacred rights as the *parent*'; children had become '"citizens of the State" instead of, as formerly, mere "goods and chattels" of their parents'.[41]

As with the Band of Hope, the NSPCC was careful wherever possible to avoid treading on parental rights and authority. Regarding school medical inspections, the vice-chairman of the Society, Harold Agnew made it clear that parents had the right to prevent inspections of their children. Furthermore, he stated that the NSPCC 'must not be used to harass these parents. Independence may become a rare virtue. Easy facilities are being given to overthrow it. Whatever may be done by others, the Society's duty still remains, to induce all parents to do their duty, and, if necessary, to help them in its performance.'[42]

The NSPCC directors and workers were sincere in their desire to preserve the family intact. As the *Child's Guardian* explained in 1914:

> It would be very easy to sweep a thousand children off the streets and to place the responsibility on the ratepayers. The easy way is not always the best way, and though the task of reforming homes and of reforming parents is not always easy, it is always best. There is something in domestic association that no institution can give, and the noblest ideal for everyone engaged in work for children is that of making home a reality, and of making the names of father and mother a reality also.[43]

The NSPCC did not remove children from their parents' homes unless it was deemed a necessity. Less than 1 per cent of the children on whose behalf the Society intervened between mid-1889 and mid-1903 were removed from parental custody.[44] In the year ending 31 March 1909, for example, there were 49,792 cases reported to the Society, in which parents or others were neglectful or cruel towards children in their care; 2,399 cases were prosecuted. A more important duty than bringing offenders to justice was 'securing an improvement in the state of children by bringing about an alteration in the conduct of parents'. Of the 49,792 cases, 42,872 were effectively dealt with by warning.[45]

The role here of the NSPCC's inspectors as early social caseworkers is essential. They were the chief enforcers of protection laws until the early twentieth century. In 1900, there were 163 inspectors known as 'Cruelty Men'.[46] The 1904 Prevention of Cruelty to Children Act allowed them to remove children from abusive or neglectful homes without the involvement of the police, but with the consent of a Justice of the Peace. 'Cruelty men' were chosen for their moral uprightness and their positive example as family men, favourably judged by their own children's success in life.[47] 'Steadiness' and temperance signifiers of a sound character defined by emotional control were two of the most important attributes of the NSPCC inspector.[48] The NSPCC combined the efforts of the amateur and the professional into one organization. Inspectors were often aided by their wives. The NSPCC continued to operate during the First World War, with the wives of inspectors called up for military service taking on their husbands' duties at home.[49] Inspectors tried, by their visits and by their example, to encourage a sense of parental duty in the people they cautioned. The Society did punish parents who shirked their duty and often provided their stories as examples to others who might be in danger of abusing their children.

The NSPCC emphasized paternal responsibility. In neglect cases that were found to be due to the mother's indifference, inspectors were instructed to reinforce male responsibility by charging the husband as well. The excuse that the father was away at work was not admissible.[50] The *Child's Guardian* often featured articles about fathers who shirked their responsibilities towards their children. In part, this was to instruct NSPCC workers that they were to take fathers' neglect as seriously as mothers', indicating perhaps that public opinion by this time placed greater responsibility for the daily care of children on mothers. Often cases of abuse or neglect were tied to vice – drinking, gambling and laziness were often to blame. The *Child's Guardian* was careful to publish examples of negligent and abusive fathers from all classes, supporting Benjamin Waugh's insistence that child abuse happened at all social levels. In 1889, Waugh declared, 'cruelty is in no way related to i) education, or ii) material conditions and to dwelling or income or dress. These only affect the manner of it, not its existence.'[51] Morality, tied directly to the personality of the parents or guardians, was put forward as far more important determinants of cruelty than social class.

One article in 1914, for example, detailed the story of a 'lazy and indifferent' man who had stopped working and who drank constantly, while his wife had to take in washing to support their children. When the NSPCC inspector warned this man he answered, 'I have chucked up my job, and I am not going to work for 20s. a week for you or any other man. I don't care a _____ for you; do what you like.'[52] He was sent to prison for three months. In the NSPCC paper, this man is seen as reprehensible because he flouted his traditional duties as a husband and father. He did not provide for his family in monetary or in moral ways; the epitome of his depravity occurred when he forcibly removed the wedding band from his wife's finger and pawned it for drink. The paper also stressed the punitive impact on delinquent parents. For example, of a Barnsley father who badly neglected his children, it was stated in court that he had got rid of £900 in five years, mostly in drink and gambling. This father drew the 30s. maternity benefit on behalf of his wife, but paid nothing to the midwife who attended her. His wife had given him £169 to set himself up in business. On several occasions the inspector had advanced money to enable the children to be fed. The father was imprisoned for two months.[53]

Excessive parental drinking was often given as a reason for the neglect or abuse of children, though the NSPCC wanted to make clear that poverty and drinking were symptoms of a greater problem, not the cause of the abuse in themselves: 'Drink and poverty are, without doubt, answerable for such misery [cruelty to children], but the evils that affect children mainly come from sources behind these.'[54] Stories of callous fathers drinking away good wages while their starving wives and children were forced to beg indicated failures in the education of character and waywardness of emotional development, and were successful in creating the public outrage needed to fuel the temperance movement.[55] According to one author writing in 1899, 'The liquor party still try to raise the cry about the "rights of parents to send their children where they will"; "the interference with personal liberty," etc. But such high sounding phrases are no longer living arguments.'[56] That drinking was devastating to family life, and to children in particular, was an oft-repeated refrain in temperance circles. Each CETS Band of Hope member was supposed to be given a copy of a handbook which discussed the connections between drinking and unhappy homes. It bolstered its moralistic discussion of alcohol with the more 'scientific' findings of the NSPCC, quoting it as saying that 'ninety out of every hundred cases of cruelty are due to intemperance.'[57]

The NSPCC, from its inception, understood that the printed word was its most powerful tool in education and in changing or reinforcing perceptions of proper behaviour towards children, often achieved through an appeal to emotion, both positive and negative.[58] A table in the 1895–6 NSPCC report showed the direct correlation between increases in the amount of official literature the Society diffused and the number of children in need who were brought to its attention. In a section in this report called 'Our Literature and Children', the NSPCC argued for an acceleration of literature production, as it was convinced that in areas where it was received, children were much more likely to be protected than in areas where the literature was unavailable.[59]

The Society made full use of this medium to communicate its objectives, to gain support, to change public opinion and to prevent or uncover abuse or neglect. In 1902, for example, the Central Office issued 650,000 copies of the *Child's Guardian* and 54,000 copies of *The Discovery* (the 1901–2 National Report). 356,000 pamphlets and leaflets were also printed for use by 'Lady Collectors' and by promoters of meetings. 830,000 leaflets and show-cards were distributed, which outlined illegal practices regarding children and provided contact details for obtaining further information.[60]

Though novel in its child-centred approach, the NSPCC's mandate was to preserve and secure a conservative model of home and family. The interests of the child and of the State were one in desiring strong and stable homes, with fathers who not only provided for their families, but who were also positive moral and emotional models for their children. Waugh and the

NSPCC believed that children could in fact change their parents' vice-ridden lives for the better. Even more importantly, on a larger level, ensuring proper living environments for children, and especially for boys, would safeguard the next generation of capable heads of families and citizens. As Robert Parr put it: 'If the rightful place of the child is secured, and his interests properly safeguarded, the nation will breed a race of strong, independent, self-reliant men who will have no need of pensions in old age.'[61] The explicit attention paid to the production of men from boys placed the onus on adolescence as the key transitional period.

## Adolescence and professionalization

Though the first use of the term adolescence was around 1430, its modern use, to categorize a liminal, problematic time between childhood and adulthood, occurred in the early twentieth century.[62] Studies on the adolescent and what the category signified occurred simultaneously in several countries, most significantly in Britain, with legislation and governmental and voluntary reform programs for children and youth. Though working-class youth were targeted within wider Victorian and Edwardian projects as part of the attempt to clean up slums and to work against degeneration, all children and youth were touched in some way by these efforts. Concern over youth and the fate of the British nation reached a peak at the turn of the twentieth century. A number of social and intellectual currents converged to create a concentration on the category of adolescence, a much-used term after the publication of G. Stanley Hall's book, *Adolescence* (1904). The UK Band of Hope Union hosted a specific conference on the problem of 'Alcohol and Adolescence' with many high-profile participants in 1919. Though implied, it should be emphasized that the concern was focused on male adolescents, whose good condition was deemed essential for national strength, which rested on healthy manhood and families. It also rested on character and its constituent emotions. As one professor of education wrote in 1911: 'The deepening of the emotional life, including a higher evaluation of all social relationships, is the most important characteristic of the period [of adolescence].'[63] What follows is a brief account of what some writers in the nascent field of child and adolescent psychology pinpointed as some of the major risks and problems with this age group, how they defined adolescents, and how adolescence was tied to a particular understanding of the emotions. How did the concept of adolescence emerge? What was the dominant view of emotions in adolescence and how did this relate to the definition of adolescence itself? And, finally, what was to be done about these emotions?

Boyhood, youth, adolescence and young adulthood were still quite imprecise terms in this era, as they were often used interchangeably. In many cases, such as in the Children Act (1908), the category 'child' meant a person under the age of 14 years, and 'young person' a person between 14 and 16 years old. Often however the term 'child' was used to include both.[64] G. Stanley Hall's period under consideration in his *Adolescence* is between 14 and 24 years of age.[65] Sylvanus Stall, an American Lutheran minister and highly popular and prolific writer of advice manuals for boys and men clearly delineated the various age categories. In 1897, he published *What a Young Boy Ought to Know* (for boys 8 to 10 years old) and *What a Young Man Ought to Know* (for 16- to 18-year-old males and upwards). For Stall, adolescence for boys was defined as the years between the ages of 14 and 25. These years are 'fraught with perplexities, trials, and much danger. It is during these years that most boys make mistakes and go wrong; some physically, some intellectually, some morally, and some in all three of these respects.'[66]

Robert Hamilton Edwards saw the need for male adolescent education which surpassed what he could contribute in his boys' papers: 'There are some topics in connection with a boy's moral and physical welfare upon which it is difficult to dilate in the pages of a widely read magazine, such as the *Boys' Friend*', he said. 'Yet', he went on, 'these topics, relating as they do to the physical and mental well-being for the boy who is ultimately to become a responsible citizen of this Great Empire, and the possible father of future citizens, are of vital importance to him.'[67] He recommended that parents and their boys read Sylvanus Stall's *What a Young Boy Ought to Know*. Here the link between informal boyhood education, both physical and moral, good citizenship of nation and empire, and fatherhood is made explicit. Here too is the assumption that these sorts of life lessons could be taught through boyhood reading material, including formal advice manuals like Stall's, which would see them through the 'difficult' stage of adolescence. Robert Baden-Powell also advertised Stall's *What a Young Boy Ought to Know* in the first edition of his *Scouting for Boys*.[68]

Stall wrote many popular advice books, for males and females of all age groups, all published by his Vir Publishing Company, based in Philadelphia. He also had publishing offices in London where his British editions were produced. The name of his company, Vir (which means manly man, as in the stem of 'virtue'), typifies the kind of work Stall published, which consisted of conservative advice steeped in Christian morals, promoting traditional family structures (headed by husbands) and sexual restraint. Stall also published works by other authors, who had similar messages. He sometimes wrote the introductions to such texts, as in Charles Frederic Goss's *Husband, Wife and Home* (1905), along with Stall's *What a Young Husband Ought to Know.*[69] In a short work, *Parental Honesty*, Stall made clear to parents the importance and manner of safeguarding the purity of young children by the imparting of proper information about their bodies and about procreation.[70] Children, so he thought, would not remain innocent as they would be exposed to 'defilement' by other children in school. Only 'the truth' from a parent would allow a child to stay 'immune to deception and to much degrading vice, and it is the only thing that will.'[71] He suggested that fathers instruct their sons on such matters, as it was especially important for boys of a certain age.[72] The truth of how his mother got pregnant would awaken 'the true nobility of manhood' in a boy and prompt him to respect his mother and women and girls outside the home.[73] Stall then described a time of 'storm and stress' (i.e. adolescence) thus:

> The boy who was previously mild and teachable and tractable now becomes a perplexity to his parents and a mystery to himself. Nature is just unfolding; and he is emerging from the period of infancy into the period of early premonitions of prospective manhood. He is now passing from the nonentity of boyhood into the individuality of unfolding manhood by the acquisition of sex power. His nature is undergoing an entire revolution.

This age of perplexity required, according to Stall, an appropriate emotional example in order to guide the boy into manhood. Stall was critical of parents who effectively enhanced their adolescent sons' emotional ordeal, making 'his awkwardness . . . the occasion of remarks and jests which only bring humiliation and embarrassment'. Stall prescribed parental understanding and sympathy, bringing 'to the succor of their son that intelligent understanding of his nature which will enable him to comprehend himself and to forecast that future which his coming years are to unfold to him'. In addition, they were to make sure that the whole household likewise saved the adolescent from humiliation. In short, emotional maturity could not be achieved through emotional bullying.[74]

According to Stall, most young men were pure, but they were given the impression even by 'well-meaning' writers and public speakers that 'the large mass of young men are leading lives of impurity'. This gave pure young men an easy excuse to succumb to temptation. Stall advised that boys needed to have 'purity held up in its proper garb for their thoughtful contemplation and considerate adoption. They need to know that vice is always destructive of character, that sin always sacrifices self-respect and generally loses the respect of others, and that a life of vice is never safe from disease.'[75] Stall thought that the young needed to have proper knowledge of sexual topics and intelligence, but also to be 'guided by right precepts and religious principles'. This combination required good decisions and 'a pure life by an abiding moral character'.[76] It was essentially a prescription for emotional control. The emphasis fell not only on parents, but also on those organizations whose primary function, as they saw it, was to ensure the moral character of the next generation. H. F. Clarke, writing for the CETS in 1894, stressed the importance of gaining a personal knowledge of and influence over children in their Bands of Hope, so as to have 'a strong hold over them when the anxious period of youth begins'.[77] The tenor of this hold was not only moral but religious, diverting 'anxiety' into a balanced emotional state, and a spiritual life that would ensure the successful passage of boys through adolescence.

Nathan Roberts has rightly pointed to the interconnectedness of character, citizenship, education and psychology in this period.[78] Roberts recognized that in classroom education, character remained an important pedagogical goal, though the focus had shifted from religious or moral foundations to contemporary understandings of psychology or a 'science of character'.[79] Individual character remained an essential attribute as it had been earlier in the nineteenth century, since it was still understood to have implications for the health of the country and the Empire. It was considered especially important to encourage character formation in the young, who were to determine the future health of the nation. These ideas for an emotional education were repackaged in a 'scientific' language, stressing the crucial period of adolescence. Interestingly many of these ideas did not originate with scientists or youth professionals, but rather with religious organizations and publishers for boys. They were then picked up by the new child and adolescent psychologists, educational professionals and social workers, who claimed them as the province exclusively of the new sciences. These ideas, now 'scientified', were, in turn, repopularized. The link to religion (especially organized religion) became less easy to generalize, but the Church of England and non-conformist roots of these understandings largely remained. Many of these ideas were picked up in the emerging Eugenics movement, even before the war.

Eugenic concerns, prevalent in our period, reinforced the importance and the force of the messages to boys and their families. Influenced by Darwin's *Descent of Man*, Francis Galton coined the word eugenics in 1883.[80] Darwinian thought had become widely accepted in the scientific community, but more importantly for our purposes, in popular understandings of the human race and its place in the natural world. Importantly, this view of evolution retained the notion that it was possible for organisms to pass on characteristics acquired during their lifetime to their offspring, and to this extent Victorian understandings of the dangers of vice – both individual and societal – were enhanced by Darwin's ideas and their popular dissemination.[81] The press used the heritability of acquired characteristics as a strong warning to parents who morally or physically transgressed, or who suffered from alcohol or drug addictions. The message was that they should cease their reprehensible ways now, or else their children and their descendants would suffer the moral and physical consequences.[82] The other half of this pseudo-scientific equation was that parents who were morally upstanding and physically pure would surely produce children without hereditary 'stain', who would become strong Britons, capable of bolstering the race. Angelique Richardson has pursued the prevalence of this idea to account for eugenic feminists' insistence on rational love – on the redefinition of motherhood as essential to their own claims to civic value. But the wider implications of this view were encapsulated by Herbert Spencer's assertion that since society depended on the nature of its citizens, and the nature of the citizen depended on early training, therefore the condition of the family was of prime importance in ensuring that this early training was delivered. As Richardson points out, 'citizenship . . . *began* with the family', but in the context of late Victorian fears of moral degeneracy, this put the onus squarely on the father.[83] This was not only because of the greater fears attached to male immorality and degeneracy, but also because, in one of the great conceits of late nineteenth-century science, sexual selection in humans rested with the male of the species. Robert J. Richards appropriately retains this sexual bias of popular evolution in his assessment of the dangers of vice and immorality:

> Vice . . . was a disease, due to hereditary disposition, environment, and chance – influences to which anyone might fall victim. Yet the person persuaded of the transmutational view of morals would take care to select a healthy – morally healthy – mate, so that his children would be given the best chance to escape sin. Moreover, a man would see to the proper education of his children, since habits acquired during early life would become as instincts.[84]

Yet while Darwinian evolution did not preclude optimism about the human race, for many, according to Daniel Pick, 'There *was* sustained and growing pessimism in the 1870s and 1880s about the ramifications of evolution, the efficacy of liberalism, the life in and of the metropolis, the future of society in a perceived world of mass democracy and socialism.'[85] The 1880s represented an intensification of the discursive impact of degeneration, as the term was no longer simply of academic significance but was also related to perceived British social crises of the time.[86] These crises were manifold. Many of these have already been discussed: alcohol, tobacco, irreligion, imprudent early marriage, laziness, thriftlessness and the political demonstrations of the 1880s – all these were newly blamed on 'urban degeneration'. The fear that the human race, and specifically the British race, could degenerate, intensified after the first South African War and was examined by the Inter-Departmental Committee on Physical Deterioration. Though it refused to use the word 'degeneration' in the report's title, and did not support the idea that the entire race was 'unfit or degenerate', its recommendations were partly based on ideas surrounding degeneration.[87] This discursive tool was used until the First World War.[88] It is important to note that for at least some writers, degeneration did not begin with the poorest and work its way to the better classes, but rather could begin at the top and work its way downwards in society.[89]

## G.Stanley Hall and his impact on British thought

The professional conceptualization of adolescence made it possible to address the concerns highlighted in popular culture in new and effective ways. The periodicals discussed in this work provided a means to address issues related to boyhood in ways that were accessible to boys and to their parents and other responsible figures. The professional approach to the topic increasingly provided a means for the State and the voluntary sector to address these issues more thoroughly. These two levels of discourse did not happen in a vacuum. They occurred at the same time and mutually informed each other. As Roger Smith has put it, 'Psychology was first and foremost a discourse of lived experience, of religion, human relations, agency and responsibility, and such like. Only secondarily was it an academic subject area.' Psychology was 'shaped *in a public arena*, not through the specialization or differentiation of academic life' and 'periodicals played a major part in this.'[90]

Though this new treatment of adolescence was associated with the late nineteenth-century professionalization of the social sciences generally, the most important specific factor was the publication of G. Stanley Hall's *Adolescence: Its Psychology and Its Relations to Physiology, Anthropology, Sociology, Sex, Crime, Religion and Education* in 1904. Similar to Alexander Chamberlain's understanding of childhood in *The Child: A Study in the Evolution of Man* (1900), Hall maintained that the child represented the past and the future potential of humanity,[91] while arguing that the ages between 14 and 22 represented a period of dangerous imbalance and instability. Like Stall, he called this a time of 'storm and stress'.[92] Every step towards adulthood was 'strewn with wreckage of body, mind, and morals'.[93] Hall made adolescence the age of the emotions par excellence. '[W]e find', he said:

> that the period of youth is essentially the age of the emotions. Every ingoing nerve-fibre pours into the soul rich and glowing sensations, which sink in deeper at this period than at any other time. Nature makes a new and distinctively emotional appeal; the youth craves for adventure and excitement, and will strain every nerve to get it; . . . religion itself during early adolescence is in the main a matter of feeling rather than of reason. And the sex-feeling is responsible for emotions that seem to threaten the very integrity of the soul. All this renders the youth exceptionally unstable and vacillating – as is usual with natures in which the emotions are not subordinate to reason. And these emotions are so urgent that somehow or other they will have satisfaction, illegitimately, if not in natural fashion.[94]

Keeping these emotions in check, training them, would not only benefit the child, but would benefit society as a whole. Learning how to emote properly went hand-in-hand with the education of character, and was associated with religion and sexuality. Hall advocated legislation which he thought was urgently needed for the protection of youth, but he also encouraged far better education for adolescent males.[95] A great part of this education could come from reading material, but it was also supposed to come from parents. Also like Stall, Hall recommended that fathers talk honestly with their sons about sexual matters and their changing bodies, devoting a lengthy chapter to the topic.[96] As Hall and his colleague Ransom Mackie explained, education during adolescence should aim 'to train character, to suggest, to awaken, to graft interests, to give range and loftiness of sentiment of view'. It ought 'to develop mind, heart, will and Body, rather than attempt to distill a budget of prepared knowledge decreed by professors who know no more of the needs of this age than teachers of other grades'.[97] Hall was critical of clergymen, who professed to be 'spiritual and moral guides', but who ignored the topic of sexuality, falsely thinking that the omission promoted 'superior ethical purity and refinement', while in reality they were the embodiment of 'the sloth and cowardice that dreads to grapple with a repulsive and festering moral sore'.[98] He maintained that modernity presented difficult challenges for adolescents, which were not fully addressed by the institutions dedicated to teaching and guiding this age group: 'modern life is hard, and in many respects increasingly so, on youth. Home, school, church, fail to recognize its nature and needs and, perhaps most of all, its perils.'[99]

Hall was a pioneer in scientific psychology and in issues relating to childhood and adolescence. He was also interested in pedagogy and in reforming children's education based on new theories in psychology.[100] In 1904, Hall also published a shorter version of *Adolescence, Youth: Its Education, Regimen and Hygiene*, for use by parents and educators on how to approach young people.[101] His books sold widely in Britain and he had many followers. Hall's views on the topic were quickly adopted by British social scientists, psychology itself becoming established as an academic discipline in Britain at this time.[102]

J. W. Slaughter, Hall's 'pupil and disciple', was chairman of the Eugenics Education Society and secretary of the Sociological Society. These positions allowed him to broadcast Hall's already widely read ideas in his brief applied volume for youth workers, *The Adolescent* (1910). It was reprinted three times by 1919.[103] In it he maintained that 'civilization and a prolongation of adolescence are found together', and thus it was of utmost national importance to focus studied attention on this age group.[104]

Slaughter was critical of formal education, since its design did not consider adolescent-specific requirements. For Slaughter, the focus of education ought to have been on the 'human product' at this most crucial time of life.[105] 'The time occupied', he wrote, 'is undoubtedly the most precious of the whole lifetime for the growth of mind and character, yet it is thrown away in grind on materials of third-rate value – this for a stupid and scientifically obsolete tradition.'[106] Slaughter advocated reading for adolescents to satiate what had been identified as an age-specific passion for knowledge and new interests. This approach had also been advocated by various youth organizations, the Band of Hope being one of the most prominent since the 1840s, and by many publications since the publishing boom for boys in the 1880s.

A new approach was already well established by the time Slaughter wrote the *Adolescent*, precisely designed to address these failures in formal education. The scientific approach to adolescence and childhood impacted the juvenile organizations discussed in this work. The publishers were informed by this background of (pseudo-) scientific, professional and legislative activity, and formed their own consensus about boyhood development. They did so with remarkable consistency, transcending class, political and religious/secular lines.

They saw an essential need for an informal brand of education that might make up the shortfalls being acknowledged by the State, by voluntary societies and by the formal school system.

Some youth workers also tried to address the lack of direct education. Arnold Freeman quoted Hall extensively in his *Boy Life and Labour: The Manufacture of Inefficiency* (1914). Freeman was a leader in the University Settlement Movement (Sheffield), a writer, follower of Rudolf Steiner, adult educator, Fabian Socialist and Labour Party candidate. At the request of the Education Committee of the Birmingham City Council, he undertook an investigation into the conditions of boy labour in Birmingham. His task was 'to ascertain the causes of the deterioration in character and in earning capacity which has been observed in a great number of boys who fail to graduate to higher grades of labour'. He took a sample of 'such boys when they had reached early manhood and, by close individual inquiry into their experience and circumstances', determined what causes had led to their 'relative failure'.[107] Other supporters of the settlement movement also wrote about the adolescent boy problem, such as the volume on *Boy Life in Our Cities*, edited by Edward Urwick for the Toynbee Trust in 1904. As these authors observed, complicating this schema of adolescence was the problem of boy workers, who left school at the age of 14 and became breadwinners for their families. 'The result', wrote Urwick, 'is a species of man–child, in whom the natural instincts of boyhood are almost overwhelmed by the feverish anxiety to become a man.'[108] His character and his emotions were not fully developed, but he had the responsibilities and desires of a man. If emotional maturation was a gradual process of education and development, as promoted by psychologists of the day, then this sort of 'man–child' was to be avoided through a longer stage of education and training for all boys, including the working classes. Although Urwick's collection was published in the same year as Hall's, he shared similar ideas. Hall advocated protecting male adolescents because 'Reason and Will are not highly developed, whereas sense impressions and emotions are flooding the consciousness. It is this', he said, 'that enables us to see the urgency of protecting the youth during those early years, when his self-control is at the lowest point.'[109] Freeman read the new work on child and adolescent psychology and applied it widely.

C. W. Saleeby (1878–1940) also worked within the emerging idiom of psychology, drawing together prevailing concerns with new ways of describing them. A physician, he quickly turned to freelance writing and journalism in support of several important social issues. He wrote many popular psychology articles for the *Harmsworth Self-Educator*, including a series of articles on

'Emotions and Instincts', and wrote numerous books on temperance, manhood and womanhood, parenting, all under the ideological umbrella of eugenics.[110] Like Slaughter, he was involved with the Sociological Society and was a founding member of the Eugenics Education Society, but he quickly became at odds with the version of eugenics promoted by the society, affirming life rather than subscribing to the 'better dead' school, and revolting against the class bias inherent to the movement. Having trained as an obstetrician, Saleeby was unusual in connecting his scientific interest in heredity with that of nurture, incorporating the usual suspects of vice – sexually transmitted diseases, insanity and intemperance – into his vision of how to ensure the progress of the race.[111] He was on several national committees related to eugenics and children, including acting as chairman of the National Birth-rate Commission for the National Council on Public Morals, the object of which was the 'the spiritual, moral, and physical regeneration of the race'.[112] He is mentioned several times as an authority in Marie Stopes' *Married Love*. He was a staunch advocate of the juvenile temperance movement, writing for the CETS and giving many invited lectures for the Band of Hope, including the Lancashire and Cheshire Band of Hope Jubilee of 1913–14 and the UK Band of Hope Union Autumnal Conference of 1919.[113] He advocated eugenic education for the young, in order to make them 'into reasonable, moral, and fully human beings, to teach explicitly, without unworthy shame, that this thing exists for the highest of purposes, that nothing which the future holds for boy or girl can conceivably be higher or happier than worthy parenthood'.[114] He stressed the joy of life and 'vital instincts' and believed that 'The greater number of those who protest against this and that, who try to stop this and that, to frown on song and dance and feast, and the instincts of youth . . . – are really enemies of life.' But he also believed in adhering to strict eugenic principles, which for him included temperance and anti-smoking.[115]

At the root of Saleeby's ideas on nurture was the Darwinistic notion that a moral being would be moral instinctively, and that instincts were acted on according to the feelings they brought about. Morality, essentially, could be reduced to an emotional state that was encapsulated in the word 'character'. To this end, he directly addressed the shortcomings of formal education on the basis that 'we are ruled by our emotions', recapitulating in the language of science the informal educational strategies of religious groups who had preceded him:

> [M]en are not determined by their reason. The mainspring of action is the emotional nature, and it follows that, since the object of all education is to influence action, our efforts should first be devoted to the development and

training not of the reasoning but of the emotions and the will. It does not suffice to teach a boy that it is wrong to steal. . . . We should have turned our primary attention not to his reason, but to his emotions. . . . These psychological truths mean that the supreme end of education is character-making, since it is the character and not the reason that determines conduct.[116]

## Emotional education

As Thomas Dixon has recently reminded us, the merits of emotional education were debated long before recent interest in emotional intelligence and emotional literacy in the 1990s.[117] The debate centred not so much on whether young people ought to be subjected to emotional education, but rather where that education should originate: in the school, home or church. Categorizing adolescents, their distinct emotions and the potential dangers they faced, contributed to working out what sort of education they should have. A moral, emotional and even basic physiological education was deemed essential in avoiding the 'dangers' of adolescence and in creating the next generation of good husbands, fathers and citizens.

Just as distinct stages in the lifecycle were being delineated and theorized (and maybe even pathologized), some psychologists, like James Welton, Professor of Education at Leeds, and author of an applied psychology of education, categorized distinct emotions at distinct stages of the lifecycle. 'Every step in our enquiry', he said, 'when tested by our own remembered experience, shows us that many emotions are only possible to adult life, others to adolescence, others again to late boyhood and girlhood. Only the simplest and most direct are possible to early childhood.'[118] Other psychologists and educationalists argued that only the intensity, not the variety, of emotions changed in different phases of life.

James Sully, Professor of Philosophy of Mind at University College London (1892–1903), and half popularizer, half scientist, argued for a form of child psychology that was both respectably professional and scientific, and applicable to children's education in practice.[119] Sully's *Studies of Childhood* (1895) and his other work are full of the language of emotion in his definition of the young, thus demonstrating continuity with the work of Hall and others on the next life stage, adolescence. That emotions, their education and control, mattered, was made clear by Sully in his book, *Children's Ways*:

So far from saying that child-nature is utterly bad or beautifully perfect, we should say that it is a disorderly jumble of impulses, each pushing itself upwards in lively contest with the others, some towards what is bad, others towards what is good. It is on this motley group of tendencies that the hand of the moral cultivator has to work, selecting, arranging, organising into a beautiful whole.[120]

For Sully, emotional education had to start before adolescence, since, he said, 'all vivid imagination is charged with emotion' in children.[121] He was close to the views of Saleeby in maintaining that through child observation it could be determined that morals were emotional, that the growth of moral sentiment was achieved by feeling.[122] And what was needed, therefore, was a moral education to control the emotions and to focus morality.[123]

It would be misleading to make an absolute distinction between religious understandings of character and morality and newer, scientific approaches. With a background in divinity, Hall himself encouraged religious studies in school in order to train the character and will.[124] The link between the emotional instability of adolescence and religion was widely discussed. Freeman described the period as the 'golden age of morality and religion', and one 'most liable to vice', 'most susceptible to virtue'. As he states, 'At no other period have religion and education such an opportunity. The youth craves for moral grandeur, and if he is ever to be made a noble human being, it is now.'[125]

The Church of England Purity Society (which became the White Cross League in 1891) weighed in on the matters of religion, character education and the emotions.[126] The testimony of the Head Master of Harrow, Rev. H. Montagu Butler, describes the two competing voices of youth, the heart and the conscience:

The voice of the *conscience* says to all men alike, whatever their religious creed may be, 'Be pure; practise self-control; tread down the passions within you'.

The voice of the *heart* speaks somewhat differently. It says, 'Look on the weak and degraded who have none to help them and are beset by strong temptations. Let the feeling of pity and chivalry enter your hearts, to endeavour to save them from ruin.'[127]

These two voices were to combat the two giant evils of intemperance and impurity in the young.[128] Like the psychologists, Butler wanted an emotional education (but one that taught control) to assist in character building.

The National Council of Public Morals intervened in 1911, linking adolescence, emotions and character directly with citizenship as many other commentators had also done. Their report stated that:

[At the age of puberty] every child can be taught the elementary notions of justice and truthfulness, and honesty, and courtesy, his duties to himself and those duties towards others which are the natural results of living in relationship with others. In great urban centres, in which now the vast majority of children live, such moral instruction becomes both easy and necessary. It forms the basis of civic education, and, if made really effective, it becomes one of the factors in the regeneration of the race we are looking for.[129]

In contrast, the Council wrote that 'Religion is a grace and a privilege, an impulse of the heart which may be stifled by bad teaching, and cannot be generated by the best teaching if the inner impulse is lacking. But moral instruction stands on a totally different and much more prosaic level.'[130] Religion was driven by the emotions, but morality could be divested from religion and emotion. On this point various experts disagreed whether moral and religious instruction could be separated (and which was more emotional). Freeman acknowledged that there was a consensus among professionals working with adolescents that 'great masses of boys are growing up to manhood, inefficient for adult work, and incapable of performing the elementary duties of home-life and citizenship, but that there were no adequate solutions in place'.[131]

The Inter-Departmental Committee on Physical Deterioration that gathered in 1904 did not agree on everything, but they did agree that the time to start the process of regeneration was in adolescence (in addition to improving standards of physical health before, in babies and young children). What was thought to be equally important was to improve moral standards, through religion and civic education. The goal was twofold: to create future good parents who would pass on their positive physical and moral attributes to their own children, and to create good citizens. If the method was still vague, the hopes were nevertheless high. Freeman wrote:

> We cannot see what transformations the future will effect. What, however, we can see clearly is that safe and true progress will depend upon the character and intelligence of the oncoming generation. The generous training during adolescence of the workers of this country will go far towards building up that more competent race of men and women. It will secure in our own time a measure of happiness infinitely outweighing any sacrifice we are called upon to make; and it will enable our children to solve the problem of the future in a manner that will put our petty efforts to shame.[132]

## Conclusion

When the storm of adolescence broke, a thorough regimen of emotional conditioning was thought to be the safeguard of the future citizen. Most agreed that any such regime must centre on appropriately targeted reading material. The findings of the Inter-Departmental Committee on Physical Deterioration are striking in their endorsement of policies carried out consistently by the juvenile publishers considered in this book. It found that young people were lacking the education necessary to prevent physical deterioration; that parental guidance was largely absent and very little other supervision on physical and moral development was available.[133] For the poor, material improvement was necessary before any moral or religious development could occur. The committee concluded that these results were in danger of being lost by prematurely providing religious teachings.[134] But there was hope:

> The most significant stages are those which youth must pass through for themselves, and mostly alone, and which cannot be touched except harmfully by formal school methods; fortunately, the educative process proceeds on its own account in terms of spontaneous new interests, together with an eager desire for knowledge. This is the time of the reading passion and an ambition to master all knowledge.[135]

The solution to the problems of adolescence, therefore, could be found in appropriately constructed reading matter. The moral training of youth would thereby take care of itself, as if naturally. This would compensate for the shortfalls of formal education.

# The Legacy of Informal Education: Emotional Control, Emotional Outpouring, and the Duty of the Citizen

> My friend, Sir Robert Baden-Powell, has said to me that the real issue of the present war will be decided in 1940 by the quality of life then surviving at early manhood and womanhood in the now combatant nations. Clearly he is right. The real issues as to who shall rule and lead will be determined by the quality of the adult young citizens of 25 years hence, whatever military operations may occur to-day.[1]

C. W. Saleeby wrote this in 1917, worried about 'saving the future' while the war was still raging. After the war, efforts to train a new generation began in earnest, but they perhaps lacked the same naïve uniformity of message that had dominated before 1914.[2] In large part, this was a direct result of the war itself.

## Muted messages

When war broke out, the publishing industry as a whole slowed down due to shortages in supplies and personnel. There was still, however, an important place for periodicals during the war. The *Expository Times* suggested that 'Nowhere is the difference which the war has made more manifest than in the popular magazines. Some may not have risen to their opportunity; some have become great spiritual forces.'[3] The RTS papers, unswervingly published every month, struggled to maintain the same standard as before the war.[4] The Society was plagued by paper shortages, increased costs and a staff shortage.[5] The *BOP* had already been converted from a weekly to a monthly publication in 1913. The paper addressed the war directly (unlike its ambivalent treatment of the South African War) with, for example, Captain Charles Gibson's serial 'Submarine U 93', about naval battles in the North Sea, and with the regular monthly pages of 'War Notes and Pictures'. It also featured a series, 'Talks to Boys: By an Old One', in which the writer chatted with readers 'in a manly, straightforward manner, giving sound advice and pointing the road to a pure, Christian life'.[6] The *BOP* also created new diversions perhaps to distract from the difficulties of war. One such was the Boy's Own Field Club, for 'the young naturalist and pet lover'. According to the annual report, the field club was immensely popular, with large numbers of branch clubs both at home and abroad being formed.[7] The AP marketed the topical content of its boys' papers on the covers: 'In war time you should read – The Boys' Friend'.[8] The papers contained many war stories, and some letters about the war.

The war did not end temperance appeals, but the messages changed. The CETS suspended most of its periodicals for the duration of the war.[9] Special CETS publications were publicized, under the heading of 'The War and Temperance', with war pledge cards and patriotic pledge badges and books.[10] With the entreaty 'Sacrifice for England!', one CETS wartime pamphlet recommended that everyone stop drinking because drink had a deleterious effect on soldiers.[11]

Shortly before the war began, stories like the *Band of Hope Review*'s 'Eric's Resolve' were telling boys that 'whatever your future work may be, you will always faithfully do your duty. You may not wear a scarlet coat and have a medal on your breast, but if you overcome temptation and always do the right, you will be a hero indeed in the battle of life which all must fight'.[12] The message now changed to one of national sacrifice and patriotism. The RTS started publishing stories for young people like 'How I came to Enlist: How Ella, after all, Sent a Man to the Front', a story for girls on how men should be strong (not weak and intellectual) and go to war. It was the duty of good girls like Ella to encourage their men to enlist.[13]

The Band of Hope continued to have meetings whenever possible, although many groups were disrupted by the withdrawal for National Service of many male workers, who were not entirely replaced by women, as they were often needed for war service at home. Furthermore, unions and societies in air-raid districts found parents unwilling to let their children attend meetings. Some societies had to suspend operations when their meeting places were commandeered for war-related purposes. Railway and food restrictions prevented lecturers, speakers and others associated with the movement from meeting their commitments. In addition to these obstacles, the *Annual Report* noted 'the inevitable absorption of public attention by the great tragedy of the war and a corresponding diminution of interest in all social and philanthropic movements'.[14] The Band of Hope nevertheless managed to maintain a total estimated membership of over 3 million children immediately after the war.[15]

A full study of the war period and its aftermath in relation to the juvenile and family press, and the extent to which there was continuity of message, as well as change under new conditions, would be of enormous scholarly value and interest. Perhaps the war, which destroyed a generation of young men, prompted Britons to look to their children as future parents, and, even more than before 1914, as the hope of the nation.[16]

## Manly ideals and the meaning of duty

The period 1880–1914 is characterized by the interplay of legal, institutional, formal and informal forces in the lives of children, and particularly boys. Increasing professionalization (in education, sociology, psychology and social work), coupled with a heightened sense of responsibility on the part of the State, worked in dynamic ways with traditional forces of informal education. Importantly, it was through the informal education provided by the juvenile and family periodical press and their associated youth movements that the new morality of a professionalized society was transmitted. The periodical press remained an important provider of moral education and character training in a time of increasing institutional and professional interest in the child.

Despite contradictory currents of thought in society at large at this time, a central argument throughout this book is that juvenile and family literature, whether politically oriented (socialists/Christian socialists), religiously motivated (the CETS and the RTS) or profit motivated (the AP), demonstrated an extraordinary degree of consensus on moral matters for boys and male adolescents. They drew upon the new scientific, pseudo-scientific and legislative impulses, but also upon the traditional values of Christianity, and insisted on the virtues of domesticity, fatherhood and good character. It suggests that, although competing models of boyhood can be found, especially in the penny dreadfuls, the moral consensus of 'improving' media (arguably including the AP boys' papers) was enormously popular and highly influential. In an age in which religious participation was feared to be declining, the evidence of informal religiosity in these publications is profound. In constructing a detailed outline of what was meant by 'manliness', the wide applicability of this analytical concept is thereby demonstrated, and the richness of what contemporaries would have understood by it revealed. Manliness, and the no less elusive category of 'character', represented a cluster of carefully honed, controlled and directed emotions that were to ensure the embodiment, the emotional constitution, of morality. For British youth advocates, this was equally true in the context of Empire.

This process was thought to be essential because the child, and in particular the boy, whether in Britain or in India, was expected to play a major role in safeguarding civilization in the present and in the future. Not only was he instructed on the moral path that would lead to the ideal of domesticated (Christian) fatherhood, but he was expected to shine, beacon-like, so as to influence his own parents and community for the better. The emergence, as a distinct category, of the concept of adolescence as a transitional stage of life also threw into relief the concepts of the child and the adult. The passage from first to last through this newly recognized distinct phase was vital to those involved in informal education, for it was at this point that the good citizen (or subject) was made or lost. This in turn contributes to our understanding of how boys were raised to be future husbands and fathers. Male domesticity (fatherhood/husbandhood) was of paramount importance, even though home-ownership, marriage and procreation were, by the 1880s, no longer the only defining attributes of manhood.

The outbreak of war in 1914 saw two diverging trends. Between August 1914, when the Great War began for the British Empire, and December of that year, 1 million men volunteered to fight. By early 1915, new recruits were signing up to enlist at a much slower pace, and by the end of that year, the British government realized that conscription would be required to get the rest of the able-bodied male population to participate in the war. The prevailing explanation of the mass voluntarism of 1914 in Britain as an acute outpouring of the jingoistic and militaristic currents of the late Victorian and Edwardian eras, combined with an unrealistic optimism about the likely duration of the war, are simply not sufficient, nor do they explain why so many men chose to stay at home. Why did so many enlist, and conversely, why so few?

It is worth speculating that the effects of the preceding decades of the informal education of boys entering manhood offer an explanation that fits both of these trends. The process of citizen making ends with the internalization of duty, but the moral consensus that had attempted to build the ideal citizen ultimately failed to prescribe interpretations of the meaning of duty at the critical hour. Did the moral man volunteer for the sake of his family? The famous recruitment poster, 'Women of Britain say "Go"!' orchestrated the war effort around a notion of familial duty that implicitly begged the men not only to go, but also to come back.[17] This message, and others like it, played on the notion of the family as the basic unit of the nation, with the added assurance that 'the men of England will be better sons, better husbands, and better fathers, by having given some part of their manhood to the service of their country.'[18] Joanna Bourke has summed it up succinctly:

> The male body was nourished within the domestic sphere. . . . The declaration of war provided many men with an opportunity to probe the depth of their commitment to domesticity: quite literally, it was an ideal for which they might risk their lives. Married and unmarried men alike declared that they were fighting for their families.[19]

Paradoxically, this very notion explains the behaviour of (at least some of) the men who did not volunteer. To risk sacrificing the paterfamilias, when the home remained most important, was a risk too great for many.[20] The decision to stay or to go is rooted in an expression of emotion, or perhaps the lack thereof. I argue that emotional control in the face of war was the result of emotional training that placed duty before glory, but preferred courage to fear. The expression of this emotional control, either in the volunteer or the non-volunteer, can be interpreted as itself a felt emotion, the great outpouring of which defined the popular response to war. Thomas Hughes' forecast, from 1879, rang with a chilling truth in 1914: 'in testing manliness as distinguished from courage, we shall have to reckon sooner or later with the idea of duty . . . Tenacity of will, or wilfulness, lies at the root of all courage, but courage can only rise into true manliness when the will is surrendered; and the more absolute the surrender of the will the more perfect will be the temper of our courage and the strength of our manliness.'[21] To stay or to enlist – either may have been construed by the young man, eligible for duty, as bearing witness 'against those we love, against those whose judgment and opinions we respect, in defense or furtherance of that which approves itself as true to our inmost conscience'. Choosing the 'right' path, whichever path it may have been, must surely have felt like 'the last and abiding test of courage and of manliness.'[22]

## Contemporary resonances

On 4 August 2011, Mark Duggan was killed in Tottenham, London, after police stopped the car in which he was a passenger. A peaceful protest demanding justice for a man shot by police was the catalyst for violence that spread across England within a couple of days. Cars and shops were set on fire and for a while looters seemed to take what they wanted with impunity. At the end of this destructive orgy, nearly 3,000, mostly young, mostly male, people were arrested. The widespread incredulity at the reactions and emotions of young people was made more intense because this was the second round of mass, disorderly behaviour. Thousands of students and other, mostly young, people protested large increases in university tuition, with slogans like 'Education for the masses' a few months before. Some protesters became violent, creating what looked like a 'war zone' around Westminster.[23] After the riots, a poll commissioned by the children's charity, Barnardo's, found that nearly half the UK population agree that 'children today are beginning to behave like animals' and almost as many thought they were becoming 'feral'. The charity fears that 'many people are at risk of giving up on children altogether and that they are beyond help by the age of 10.[24] A BBC Radio 4 programme, 'Bringing Up Britain', focused on 'Feral Kids and Feckless Parents'.[25] Were children really lacking humanity and beyond repair at such an early age? Were parents really to blame?

Prime Minister David Cameron at first blamed gangs for the riots and for 'mindless' violence, but later acknowledged that these events might have been the results of more fundamental and complex problems. The society was in fact 'broken', and the concomitant 'moral collapse' needed to be addressed as a top priority. Cameron blamed 'children without fathers, schools without discipline and communities without control'.[26] Some young people caught up in the riots were suffering from 'a shortage of not just respect and boundaries but also love'.[27] In short, what was needed was more morality and the cultivation of the right kind of emotions in the young, through the means of education by the fundamental institutions of society: family, school, community and church. The Archbishop of Canterbury, Dr Rowan Williams, stated that England would face more riots if young people who think they have nothing to lose are not rescued, but questioned whether society was prepared to 'invest what's needed in family and neighbourhood and school' in order to do so.[28]

The Bishop of Manchester, the Right Reverend Nigel McCulloch, warned of a 'moral vacuum in private and public life', which had reached all social classes. He called on the church and schools 'to take a more robust approach, through intelligent nurture and clear guidance, to building up strength of character, encouraging a sense of purpose in life, and inculcating values that lead to a healthy society'. He also emphasized the 'importance of honesty'.[29] Character was to be cultivated to promote clear values and a healthy society. Love, honesty and pride were the emotions required of young people. Instead, as the Archbishop of Canterbury pointed out: 'We may well wince when some describe how the riots brought them a feeling of intense joy, liberation, power. But we have to ask what kind of life it is in which your emotional highs come from watching a shop being torched or a policeman being hit by a brick.'[30] How could emotions that 'feel good' be bad? What had made (mainly) young men and boys feel these inappropriate emotions? What was to be done to ensure they felt the right ones, instilling morality and character in the process? What is the relationship of youth to society and citizenship? How did governments, institutions and families fail young people? Labour MP Diane Abbott encouraged the government 'to address why many of these youngsters feel as though they have no stake in society'.[31]

The question of what it meant to have a stake in society, and the problem of how to nurture the nation's youth to uphold the values that constitute that society, are not new. What has been most striking about the reaction to the youth 'problem' of the 2010s is the paucity of historical reflection, and an overwhelming lack of awareness of the longue-durée continuity of the kinds of rhetoric about morals and emotions used to try to solve it. If we are to ask, 'what is wrong with the juvenile nation?' we would be well advised to enquire what answers historical actors came up with when faced with what sounded like similar problems. At the end of the nineteenth century, one of the most pressing questions concerned how to make a citizen of the 'right' stamp. Perhaps more importantly, how do you avoid making citizens of the 'wrong' sort? These questions, posed at the outset of the 'Century of the Child', are still being asked. They carry much the same acuteness of alarm and a similar perplexity – perhaps an even greater lack of understanding – about how to cultivate the feelings and behaviours of the young.

# Notes

## Introduction

1 John Tosh, *A Man's Place: Masculinity and the Middle-Class Home in Victorian England* (New Haven: Yale University Press, 1999).

2 Kelly Boyd, *Manliness and the Boys' Story Paper in Britain: A Cultural History, 1855–1940* (New York: Palgrave Macmillan, 2003). A commonly repeated observation by historians.

3 Allison James and Adrian James, *Constructing Childhood: Theory, Policy and Social Practice* (Houndmills: Palgrave Macmillan, 2004), 27.

4 James and James, *Constructing Childhood*, 26.

5 Ellen Key, *Barnets århundrade* [*The Century of the Child*] (Stockholm, 1900); R. Hercod, 'La protection de l'enfant dans la lutte contre l'alcoolisme', *The Proceedings of the Twelfth International Congress on Alcoholism* (London: National Temperance League, 1909), 130.

6 For the context of fears surrounding degeneracy see Thomas E. Jordan, *The Degeneracy Crisis and Victorian Youth* (Albany: State University of New York Press, 1993).

7 G. R. Searle, *The Quest for National Efficiency: A Study in British Politics and Thought, 1899–1914* (Oxford: Basil Blackwell, 1971).

8 M. J. D. Roberts, *Making English Morals: Voluntary Association and Moral Reform in England, 1787–1886* (Cambridge: Cambridge University Press, 2004), 282.

9 J. Tunnicliff, *The Band of Hope Annual* (London: Simpkin, Marshall and Co., 1865), 25.

10 Harry Hendrick, *Images of Youth: Age, Class and the Male Youth Problem, 1880–1920* (Oxford: Clarendon Press, 1990); John Springhall, 'Building Character in the British Boy: The Attempt to Extend Christian Manliness to Working-Class Adolescents, 1880–1914', in *Manliness and Morality: Middle-Class Masculinity in Britain and America, 1800–1940*, ed. J. A. Mangan and James Walvin (Manchester: Manchester University Press, 1987).

11 Roberts, *Making English Morals*; John Welshman, 'Images of Youth: The Issue of Juvenile Smoking, 1880–1914', *Addiction*, 91, no. 9 (1996): 1379–86; Lesley A. Hall, 'Birds, Bees and General Embarrassment: Sex Education in Britain, from Social

Purity to Section 28', in *Public or Private Education?: Lessons from History*, ed. Richard Aldrich (London: Woburn, 2004), 98–115.

12  Stephanie Olsen, 'Towards the Modern Man: Edwardian Boyhood in the Juvenile Periodical Press', in *Childhood in Edwardian Fiction: Worlds Enough and Time*, ed. Adrienne Gavin and Andrew Humphries (New York: Palgrave Macmillan, 2009); John Neubauer, *The Fin-de-Siècle Culture of Adolescence* (New Haven: Yale University Press, 1992); John Springhall, *Coming of Age: Adolescence in Britain, 1860–1960* (Dublin: Gill and MacMillan, 1986); John Gillis, *Youth and History* (New York: Academic Press, 1974), 13–17, 33–57. Adolescence studies were pioneered by G. Stanley Hall, *Adolescence: Its Psychology and Its Relations to Physiology, Anthropology, Sociology, Sex, Crime, Religion and Education* (2 vols, New York: D. Appleton, 1904).

13  Jenny Holt, 'The Textual Formations of Adolescence in Turn-of-the-Century Youth Periodicals: The *Boy's Own Paper* and Eton College Ephemeral Magazines', *Victorian Periodicals Review*, 35 (2002): 63–88 at 63.

14  W. Fielding, 'What Shall I Do with my Son?' *Nineteenth Century*, April (1883): 580.

15  Roland Barthes, *The Rustle of Language* (New York: Farrar Straus & Giroux, 1986), 336–7.

16  This term has as yet not been deployed to describe these varied forms. A rare counter-example is Yuval Dror, 'Zionist Cultural Transfer through Ties between Schools and Informal Education Frameworks in the British Mandate Period (1918–1948)', *History of Education Review*, 26 (1997): 56–71. Of course, there has been extensive work on voluntary education, which was gradually incorporated or excluded by the rise of state education in Britain. See the seminal work on the topic, Brian Simon, *The Two Nations and the Educational Structure, 1780–1870* (London: Lawrence & Wishart, 1960).

17  'Boys That Are Wanted', *Young Crusader* (June 1892): 63.

18  For example, H. S. Thompson, 'Home and the Choice of a Wife: To Young Men', *Onward*, 17 (1882): 127. This advice was repeated in numerous contemporary advice manuals for boys and young men.

19  Hugh Cunningham, *Children and Childhood in Western Society since 1500* (Harlow: Longman, 1995), 157; Stephen Heathorn, *For Home, Country and Race: Constructing Gender, Class and Englishness in the Elementary School, 1880–1914* (Toronto: Toronto University Press, 2000).

20  See, for example, J. A. Mangan, *Athleticism in the Victorian and Edwardian Public School: The Emergence and Consolidation of an Educational Ideology* (Cambridge: Cambridge University Press, 1981); J. A. Mangan, *The Games Ethic and Imperialism: Aspects of the Diffusion of an Ideal* (Harmondsworth: Viking, 1985);

J. R. de S. Honey, *Tom Brown's Universe: The Development of the Victorian Public School* (London: Millington, 1977).

21 Nathan Roberts, 'Character in the Mind: Citizenship, Education and Psychology in Britain, 1880–1914', *History of Education*, 33, no. 2 (March, 2004): 196.

22 Roberts, 'Character in the Mind', 197.

23 Harmsworth was made a baronet on 23 June 1904 and accepted a peerage the following December, taking as his title Baron Northcliffe of the Isle of Thanet. He accepted a viscountcy in 1917. He will be referred to here generally as Harmsworth throughout. D. George Boyce, 'Harmsworth, Alfred Charles William, Viscount Northcliffe (1865–1922)', *Oxford Dictionary of National Biography* (Oxford University Press, September 2004), www.oxforddnb.com/view/article/33717, accessed 27 August 2008.

24 Thomas Fisher Rare Book Library, University of Toronto. Souvenir of Banquet – held at the Fleetway House, the Amalgamated Press Ltd., Thursday, 7 November 1912. For Private Circulation Only (G. Pulman, the Cranford Press, 1912). duff f 00130.

25 George Orwell, 'Boy's Weeklies', in *Inside the Whale and Other Essays* (London: Victor Gollancz, 1940), 124.

26 Claudia Nelson, 'Mixed Messages: Authoring and Authority in British Boys' Magazines', *The Lion and the Unicorn*, 21, no. 1 (1997): 14.

27 Charles Garrett, *Lead Them Straight* (London: UK Band of Hope Union, 1894), 2.

28 Callum Brown, *The Death of Christian Britain: Understanding Secularisation, 1800–2000* (London: Routledge, 2001), 72, see also 77.

29 Brown, *Death of Christian Britain*, 88–9.

30 Jesse J. Prinz, *The Emotional Construction of Morals* (Oxford: Oxford University Press, 2007); see also Monique Scheer 'Are Emotions a Kind of Practice (and Is That What Makes Them Have a History)? A Bourdieuian Approach to Understanding Emotion', *History and Theory*, 51 (2012): 193–220.

31 Sympathy has gradually been replaced in common parlance by the word 'empathy', which is strictly a twentieth-century term. See Carolyn Burdett, 'Is Empathy the End of Sentimentality?' *Journal of Victorian Culture*, 16 (2011): 259–74.

32 Adam Smith, *The Theory of Moral Sentiments* [1759], ed. Ryan Patrick Hanley (New York: Penguin, 2009), 13–62; Charles Darwin, *The Descent of Man, and Selection in Relation to Sex* [2nd edn, 1879] (London: Penguin, 2004), 119–72, and especially 151; Thomas Dixon has explored the emotional basis of morality extensively in his *The Invention of Altruism: Making Moral Meanings in Victorian Britain* (Oxford: Oxford University Press, 2008); see also Rob Boddice, 'The Affective Turn: Historicising the Emotions', in *Psychology and History: Interdisciplinary Explorations*, ed. Cristian Tileagă and Jovan Byford (Cambridge: Cambridge University Press, 2014).

33   Ruth Livesey, 'Reading for Character: Women Social Reformers and Narratives of the Urban Poor in Late Victorian and Edwardian London', *Journal of Victorian Culture*, 9 (2004): 43–67; Stefan Collini, 'The Idea of "Character" in Victorian Political Thought', *Transactions of the Royal Historical Society*, 35 (1985): 29–50.

34   Frances Power Cobbe, 'The Education of the Emotions', *Fortnightly Review*, 43 (1888): 223–36, at 223, 225.

35   Cobbe, 'Education of the Emotions', 225.

36   Cobbe, 'Education of the Emotions', 226.

37   Cobbe, 'Education of the Emotions', 226.

38   Cobbe, 'Education of the Emotions', 226–7.

39   Cobbe, 'Education of the Emotions', 227.

40   Cobbe, 'Education of the Emotions', 228.

41   Cobbe, 'Education of the Emotions', 229.

42   Cobbe, 'Education of the Emotions', 231.

43   Jose Harris, *Private Lives, Public Spirit: Britain 1870–1914* (London: Penguin, 1994), 248–9.

44   J. A. Mangan, *Athleticism in the Victorian and Edwardian Public School: The Emergence and Consolidation of an Educational Ideology* (Cambridge: Cambridge University Press, 1981); John Springhall, 'Building Character in the British Boy: The Attempt to Extend Christian Manliness to Working-Class Adolescents, 1880–1914', in *Manliness and Morality: Middle-Class Masculinity in Britain and America, 1800–1940*, ed. J. A. Mangan and James Walvin (Manchester: Manchester University Press, 1987).

45   Michael Roper, 'Between Manliness and Masculinity: The "War Generation" and the Psychology of Fear in Britain, 1914–1950', *Journal of British Studies*, 44 (2005): 361.

46   John Tosh, 'What Should Historians Do With Masculinity? Reflections on Nineteenth-Century Britain', *History Workshop Journal*, 38 (1994): 183; Martin Francis, 'The Domestication of the Male? Recent Research on Nineteenth and Twentieth-Century British Masculinity', *Historical Journal*, 45 (2002): 639.

47   Tosh, 'What Should Historians Do', 182.

48   Tosh, 'What Should Historians Do', 183.

49   Thomas Hughes, *The Manliness of Christ* (Boston: Houghton, Osgood and Company, 1880), 5–7.

50   Sarah Williams, *Religious Belief and Popular Culture in Southwark c. 1880–1939* (Oxford: Oxford University Press, 1999), 127.

51   In its reclamation of the 'lost' emotional configurations that comprised 'manliness' and 'character', the book conjures with Ute Frevert, *Emotions in History – Lost and Found* (Budapest: Central European University Press, 2011).

52  See Rob Boddice, 'Manliness and the "Morality of Field Sports": E. A. Freeman and Anthony Trollope, 1869–71', *Historian*, 70, no. 1 (2008): 3.

53  Roberts, 'Character in the Mind', 177–97.

54  Roberts, 'Character in the Mind', 178.

55  The classic study is William Reddy, *The Navigation of Feeling: A Framework for the History of Emotions* (Cambridge: Cambridge University Press, 2001); for a discussion of 'emotional regimes' see Barbara Rosenwein, 'Problems and Methods in the History of Emotions', *Passions in Context*, 1 (2010): 1–32, at 21–3; Jan Plamper, 'The History of Emotions: An Interview with William Reddy, Barbara Rosenwein and Peter Stearns', *History and Theory*, 49 (2010): 237–65 at 243.

56  Rosenwein's concept is introduced in 'Worrying about Emotions in History', *American Historical Review*, 107 (2002): 821–45. See also Benno Gammerl, ed., *Emotional Styles – Concepts and Challenges*, special issue of *Rethinking History*, 16 (2012).

57  Brown, *Death of Christian Britain*, 113.

58  Francis, 'Domestication of the Male'; Trev Lynn Broughton and Helen Rogers, eds, *Gender and Fatherhood in the Nineteenth Century* (Houndmills: Palgrave MacMillan, 2007), 1–4; Tosh, *A Man's Place*; P. J. Walker, *Pulling the Devil's Kingdom Down: The Salvation Army in Victorian Britain* (Berkeley: University of California Press, 2001), 10.

59  Anna Clark, 'Rhetoric of Chartist Domesticity: Gender, Language, and Class in the 1830s and 1840', *Journal of British Studies*, 31 (1992): 62–88, and Tosh, *A Man's Place*, chs 1–6.

60  J. Rowbotham, *Good Girls Make Good Wives: Guidance for Girls in Victorian Fiction* (Oxford: Basil Blackwell, 1989), 6.

61  Francis, 'Domestication of the Male', 639. For a wide-ranging discussion of domestic authority, see Lucy Delap, Ben Griffin and Abigail Wills, *The Politics of Domestic Authority in Britain since 1800* (Houndmills: Palgrave MacMillan, 2009).

62  Tosh, *A Man's Place*, 196.

63  Tosh, *A Man's Place*, 170. For an attempt to balance the 'flight' with domestic 'demands' see David B. Marshall, '"A Canoe, and a Tent and God's Great Out-of-Doors": Muscular Christianity and the Flight from Domesticity, 1880s–1930s', in *Masculinity and the Other: Historical Perspectives*, ed. Heather Ellis and Jessica Meyer (Newcastle: Cambridge Scholars Publishing, 2009).

64  *Zoophilist*, 4, n.s. 4, 1 August 1884, 82.

65  See Megan Doolittle, 'Religious Belief and the Protection of Children in Nineteenth-Century English Families', in Broughton and Rogers, *Gender and Fatherhood in the Nineteenth Century*.

66  S. Gill, 'How Muscular Was Victorian Christianity? Thomas Hughes and the Cult of Christian Manliness Reconsidered', in *Gender and Christian Religion*, ed.

R. N. Swanson (Woodbridge, Suffolk: Boydell Press, 1998). See also Carol Christ, 'Victorian Masculinity and the Angel in the House', in *A Widening Sphere: Changing Roles of Victorian Women*, ed. Martha Vicinus (Bloomington: Indiana University Press, 1977); Deborah Gorham, *The Victorian Girl and the Feminine Ideal* (Bloomington: Indiana University Press, 1982).

67  Robert Roberts, *The Classic Slum: Salford Life in the First Quarter of the Century* (Manchester: Manchester University Press, 1971), 35.

68  Heathorn, *For Home, Country and Race*, 158.

69  James and James, *Constructing Childhood*, 36.

70  James and James, *Constructing Childhood*, 35; Jenny Holt, *Public School Literature, Civic Education and the Politics of Male Adolescence* (Farnham: Ashgate, 2008), 6.

71  James and James, *Constructing Childhood*, 36.

72  James and James, *Constructing Childhood*, 35.

73  See Brad Beaven and John Griffiths, 'Creating the Exemplary Citizen: The Changing Notion of Citizenship in Britain, 1870–1939', *Contemporary British History*, 22 (2008): 203–25.

74  Heathorn, *For Home, Country and Race*, 25.

75  Derek Heater, *Citizenship in Britain. A History* (Edinburgh: Edinburgh University Press, 2006), 170–1.

76  J. Welton, *The Psychology of Education* (London: MacMillan, 1911), 475.

# Chapter 1

1  For an important discussion of the historical questions and problems surrounding children's agency see Mary Jo Maynes, 'Age as a Category of Historical Analysis: History, Agency, and Narratives of Childhood', *Journal of the History of Childhood and Youth*, 1, no. 1 (2008): 114–24.

2  John Gillis, 'Transitions to Modernity', *The Palgrave Handbook of Childhood Studies*, ed. Jens Qvortrup, William A. Corsaro and Michael-Sebastian Honig (Basingstoke: Palgrave Macmillan, 2011), 118–19.

3  Roberts, *Making English Morals*, 286.

4  John Springhall, '"Disseminating Impure Literature": The "Penny Dreadful" Publishing Business since 1860', *Economic History Review*, 2nd series, 47 (1994): 567.

5  Springhall, '"Disseminating Impure Literature"', 568.

6  Patrick A. Dunae, 'British Juvenile Literature in an Age of Empire: 1880–1914' (Unpublished Ph.D. Dissertation, Victoria University of Manchester, 1975), 12.

7  Springhall, '"Disseminating Impure Literature"', 582.

8  Since 1935, the Society has been known as the United Society for Christian Literature (USCL). The main repository for the archives of the USCL is the School

of Oriental and African Studies, University of London. The Society's archives contain the surviving records of the Religious Tract Society (RTS) and the Christian Literature Society for India and Africa, founded in 1858 as the Christian Vernacular Education Society for India. Very little original correspondence survives and there are many gaps in publications held. (A fire at the RTS's headquarters in Paternoster Row destroyed most of the Society's archives).

9   Samuel G. Green, *The Story of the Religious Tract Society for One Hundred Years* (London: Religious Tract Society, 1899), 7.

10  *An Account of the Origin and Progress of the London Religious Tract Society* (London, 1803), 9, in Brown, *Death of Christian Britain*, 49.

11  Josef Altholz, *The Religious Press in Britain, 1760–1900* (New York: Greenwood Press, 1989), 39.

12  Brown, *Death of Christian Britain,* 54.

13  Green, *Story of the Religious Tract Society*, 73.

14  Mark W. Turner, *Trollope and the Magazines: Gendered Issues in Mid-Victorian Britain* (London: MacMillan, 2000), 66.

15  *All the Year Round: A Weekly Journal Conducted by Charles Dickens*, 24 (1880): frontispiece.

16  Brown, *Death of Christian Britain,* 54.

17  John Wigley, *The Rise and Fall of the Victorian Sunday* (Manchester: Manchester University Press, 1980).

18  Hugh McLeod, *Religion and Society in England, 1850–1914* (London: MacMillan, 1996), 199.

19  'Family Prayer', *Sunday at Home* (1901–2): 15.

20  Brown, *Death of Christian Britain.*

21  Gordon Hewitt, *Let the People Read: A Short History of the United Society for Christian Literature* (London: Lutterworth Press, 1949), 73.

22  Hewitt. *Let the People Read*, 73–4. Between 1903 and 1938 the annual circulation of the RTS's tracts decreased from 14 million to slightly less than a million.

23  'The Open Door for Christian Literature', *Sunday at Home* (1900–1): 194.

24  Aileen Fyfe, 'Industrialised Conversion: The Religious Tract Society and Popular Science Publishing in Victorian Britain' (Ph.D. Dissertation, History and Philosophy of Science, University of Cambridge, 2000), 233.

25  E. Salmon, *Juvenile Literature as It Is* (London, 1888), 15, 23. The stories of the papers are told in J. Cox, *Take a Cold Tub, Sir!: The story of the* Boy's Own Paper (Guildford: Lutterworth Press, 1982), and W. Forrester, *Great-Grandmama's Weekly: A Celebration of the 'Girl's Own Paper', 1880–1901* (Guildford: Lutterworth Press, 1980).

26  RTS Annual Meeting, speech by Rev. A. W. Gough (Vicar of Brompton), *Religious Tract Society Record of Work at Home and Abroad* (June 1911): 9–10.

27 Green, *Story of the Religious Tract Society*, 127.

28 Kirsten Drotner, *English Children and Their Magazines, 1751–1945* (New Haven: Yale University Press, 1988), 123.

29 Green, *Story of the Religious Tract Society*, 127.

30 'The Boy's Own Paper', *The Religious Tract Society Record of Work at Home and Abroad*, no. 10 (March 1879): 27.

31 'What Are Boys to Read?' *The Religious Tract Society Record of Work at Home and Abroad*, no. 10 (March 1879): 1–3, at 3.

32 Patrick A. Dunae, 'The Boy's Own Paper: Origins and Editorial Policies', *The Private Library*, 2nd series, 9, no. 4 (1976): 134.

33 Dunae, *British Juvenile Literature*, xiii.

34 Dunae, 'The Boy's Own Paper', 151.

35 Dunae, 'The Boy's Own Paper', 151.

36 See, for example, RTS ECM, 3 January 1882 and RTS ECM, 6 February 1900 on the inappropriateness of certain illustrations in the *BOP*.

37 RTS ECM, 20 November 1900, referring to a section in the *Girl's Own Paper*, 17 November 1900.

38 Roberts, *The Classic Slum*, 128.

39 Roberts, *The Classic Slum*, 128–9.

40 Springhall, '"Disseminating Impure Literature"', 568.

41 *Harmsworth Self-Educator Magazine*, 1 (1905): 403.

42 Alfred Harmsworth, letter to Max Pemberton, 1884, quoted in Max Pemberton, *Lord Northcliffe: A Memoir* (London: Hodder and Stoughton, 1922), 30.

43 Alfred Harmsworth, letter to Max Pemberton, 1884, quoted in Pemberton, *Lord Northcliffe*, 30.

44 Kelly Boyd, *Manliness and the Boys' Story Paper in Britain: A Cultural History, 1855–1940* (New York: Palgrave Macmillan, 2003), 9.

45 Edwards to Northcliffe, 17 December 1913, BL, Add. MSS 62182A.

46 Edwards to Northcliffe, 12 December 1920, BL, Add. MSS 62182A.

47 Northcliffe to Edwards, 28 November 1919, BL, Add. MSS 62182A.

48 Edwards to Northcliffe, 13 May 1921 and 26 May 1921, BL, Add. MSS 62182A. Indeed, Hamilton Edwards' life is most mysterious, and it has been only with good fortune that his first name, Robert, has been discovered, in the context of a 'Joint Select Committee of Enquiry on Lotteries and Indecent Advertisements', Twentieth Century House of Commons Sessional Papers, 1908, vol. 9, 478–80 (paper no. 275). His movements after leaving the AP are difficult to ascertain, although it seems he had industrial investments in Ireland and purchased the mansion, park and mineral rights on the Tehidy Estate in Cornwall from A. F. Basset (*Mining Magazine* (1915): 181). According to the scanty biography provided by Scoop, Hamilton Edwards was 'court-martialed in Nov. 1920 for publishing statements "likely to cause disaffection"

viz. reporting the flogging of a youth in Portobello Barracks and the killing of two RIC men by Black & Tans near Tullow', www.scoop-database.com/bio/edwards_robert_hamilton, accessed 27 August 2008. He died in 1932.

49  Hamilton Edwards was editor of the AP boys' papers from 1895, when the *Boys' Friend* was introduced. In 1912, Hamilton Edwards was replaced as editor by Lewis Carlton, who in turn was replaced by seven editors in the next 15 years.

50  For the sake of simplicity, editorial pieces signed by Hamilton Edwards will be referred to as Hamilton Edwards', whether or not he actually wrote them.

51  Jenny Holt, 'The Textual Formations of Adolescence in Turn-of-the-Century Youth Periodicals: The "Boy's Own Paper" and Eton College Ephemeral Magazines', *Victorian Periodicals Review*, 35 (2002): 63–88, at 70.

52  *Boys' Herald*, 5, no. 233 (1908): 400.

53  'Editor's Den – My Readers' Letters', *Boys' Friend*, 8, no. 16 (1901): 244.

54  'Your Editor's Den – Testimony for the BF', *Boys' Friend*, 11, no. 528 (1911): 116.

55  'A Parent's Testimony', *Boys' Herald*, 1, no. 28 (1904): 448.

56  'Your Editor's Den', *Boys' Friend*, 10, no. 509 (1911): 656.

57  George Dilnot, *Romance of the Amalgamated Press* (London: Amalgamated Press, 1925).

58  Northcliffe Papers, BL, Add. MSS 62182A.

59  UK Band of Hope Union 1914, 6. This important movement has been largely ignored by historians. The only notable articles on the Band of Hope are Lilian Shiman, 'The Band of Hope Movement: Respectable Recreation for Working-Class Children', *Victorian Studies*, 17, no. 1 (1973): 49–74 and Annemarie McAllister, 'Picturing the Demon Drink: How Children Were Shown Temperance Principles in the Band of Hope', *Visual Resources*, 28, 4 (2012): 309–323; Brian Harrison, *Drink and the Victorians: The Temperance Question in England, 1815–1872* (Pittsburgh: University of Pittsburgh Press, 1971), 192–4, briefly mentions the organization; Lilian Lewis Shiman, *Crusade against Drink in Victorian England* (London: MacMillan, 1988), 134–55 gives it a bit more attention. Thanks to G. W. Olsen, who shared his unpublished manuscript on the Church of England Temperance Society, 'Drink and the British Establishment'.

60  R. Tayler, *Hope of the Race* (London: Hope Press, 1946), 20–1.

61  Tayler, *Hope of the Race*, 22–3.

62  UK Band of Hope Union Annual Report (1913–14), 5. Only 5 of the County Band of Hope Unions, including Yorkshire – 1865, Dorset – 1864, Lancashire and Cheshire – 1863, Leicestershire and Rutland – 1866, were founded in the 1860s out of 27 total.

63  Tayler, *Hope of the Race*, 55. See also Frederic Smith, ed., *The Band of Hope Jubilee Volume* (London: UK Band of Hope Union, 1897), 222–3.

64  Shiman, *Crusade against Drink*, 153.

65  C. O. Barber, 'A Band of Hope Address: Why Are You a Member of a Band of Hope?' *Quarterly Manual and Band of Hope Reporter for Greenwich and West Kent*, vol. 1, no. 5, October (Greenwich: Borough of Greenwich and West Kent Band of Hope Union, 1880), 9.

66  Tayler, *Hope of the Race*, 15.

67  Smith, *Band of Hope Jubilee Volume*, 8–9.

68  Smith, *Band of Hope Jubilee Volume*, 10–11.

69  UK Band of Hope Union, *Annual Reports* (London: UK Band of Hope, 1914), 5.

70  *The Middlesex Temperance Chronicle. A Quarterly Record of Good Templar, Band of Hope and Other Temperance Work in the County of Middlesex*, August–October (1884): 78.

71  Charles Wakely, *Bands of Hope and Sunday Schools* (London: UK Band of Hope Union, 1894), 4.

72  Tayler, *Hope of the Race*, 40.

73  See NRO FC 74/173, 174: 'When this declaration has been kept for three months you will be acknowledged as a Member of the Band of Hope, and may purchase the Card of Membership.'

74  Sarah Williams, *Religious Belief and Popular Culture in Southwark c. 1880–1939* (Oxford: Oxford University Press, 1999), 156.

75  Annie Young, 'The Parents of Our Members', *Band of Hope Chronicle* (London: UK Band of Hope Union) January (1885): 11.

76  The founder and first editor of the *Band of Hope Review* was T. B. Smithies (1815–83), followed by F. T. Gammon (1849–88). In our period, *Onward* was edited by W. C. Wilson, secretary of the Lancashire and Cheshire Band of Hope and Temperance Union. The paper was renamed the *Workers Onward* in 1910.

77  Harrison, *Drink and the Victorians*, 317.

78  'The Band of Hope Bazaar', *CETS Illustrated*, August (1890): 85.

79  Smith, *Band of Hope Jubilee Volume*, 99.

80  George James Howard, ninth earl of Carlisle (1843–1911) was married to Rosalind Frances Stanley (1845–1921), herself a strong promoter of temperance reform as vice-president of the UK Alliance and president of the National British Women's Temperance Association. Their daughter Lady Cecilia Roberts (d. 1947) succeeded her as president of the NBWTA. See Christopher Ridgway, 'Howard, George James, Ninth Earl of Carlisle (1843–1911)', *Oxford Dictionary of National Biography* (Oxford University Press, 2004), www.oxforddnb.com/view/article/34019, accessed 6 August 2008, and David M. Fahey, 'Howard, Rosalind Frances, Countess of Carlisle (1845–1921)', *Oxford Dictionary of National Biography* (Oxford University Press, September 2004), online edn, May 2006, www.oxforddnb.com/view/article/34022, accessed 6 August 2008.

81  Smith, *Band of Hope Jubilee Volume*, 115–17.

82  Frederic Smith, 'The Juvenile Temperance Organisations in Great Britain and Ireland', *Temperance in All Nations*, ed. J. N. Stearns (New York, 1893) vol. I, 216.

83  Bradford Band of Hope Union, Annual Report, 1895, in Shiman, *Crusade against Drink*, 137.

84  See, for example, questions put to new applicants for workers at the Yorkshire Band of Hope Union, WYAS Leeds, Minute Book, Yorkshire Band of Hope Union, 1904–05, WYL770.

85  Tayler, *Hope of the Race*, 50.

86  Tayler, *Hope of the Race*, 50.

87  For an interesting discussion of the changing moral, medical and scientific understandings of the dangers of drink, see J. Kneale and S. French, '"The Relations of Inebriety to Insurance": Geographies of Medicine, Insurance and Alcohol in Britain, 1840–1911', in *Intoxication: Problematic Pleasures*, ed. Jonathan Herring, Ciaran Regan, Darin Weinberg and Phil Withington (Houndmills: Palgrave Macmillan, 2013), 87–109.

88  William E. A. Axon, *Temperance Teaching in Education, A Paper Read at the Manchester Teachers' Guild. Owens College, 22 October 1891* (Manchester: Brook and Chrystal, 1892), 8.

89  Wakely, *Bands of Hope and Sunday Schools*, 4.

90  See various manuals for instructors, including: *The Band of Hope Blue Book: A Manual of Instruction and Training* (London: UK Band of Hope Union, n.d.) and *Speakers' Self-Help. Outlines of Blackboard and Other Addresses for Band of Hope Meetings* (London: Richard J. James, n.d.).

91  Tayler, *Hope of the Race*, 39.

92  *Speakers' Self-Help*, 1.

93  UK Band of Hope Union, Report of School Scheme (1914–15), 5.

94  UK Band of Hope Union, Report of School Scheme (1907–8), 3.

95  J. R. Diggle, 'Temperance in the Schools', in *Alcohol and Childhood: A Report of Two Conferences*, Church of England Temperance Society (Junior Division) (London: CETS, 1891), 22.

96  C. A. Davis, *The Relation of Sunday School Teachers to the Band of Hope Movement* (London: UK Band of Hope Union, 1894).

97  H. F. Clarke, *The Sunday School in Relation to the Band of Hope* (London: Church of England Temperance Publication Depot, 1892), 3.

98  Clarke, *Sunday School in Relation to the Band of Hope*, 4.

99  CETS leaflet No. 144, 'How to Make the Scriptural Syllabus Interesting to Children', in 'The Scriptural Syllabus: Elementary Lessons on the Bible and Temperance', based on the authorized Syllabus of Instruction by J. Johnson Baker condensed and arranged as a course of instruction for the children of Bands of Hope under 16 years of age by W. Taylor (London: CETS, 1900), 1–2.

100 CETS leaflet No. 144, 2.

101 Wakely, *Bands of Hope and Sunday Schools*, 3.

102 Wakely, *Bands of Hope and Sunday Schools*, 5–6.

103 Davis, *The Relation of Sunday School Teachers*, 2–3.

104 Davis, *The Relation of Sunday School Teachers*, 2–3.

105 Davis, *The Relation of Sunday School Teachers*, 4.

106 Harrison, *Drink and the Victorians*, 171.

107 Smith, *Band of Hope Jubilee Volume*, 300.

108 Smith, *Band of Hope Jubilee Volume*, 301.

109 Smith, *Band of Hope Jubilee Volume*, 301.

110 For example, Sion and Greenfield Congregational Church cooperated and took charge of each other's meetings.

111 WYAS Bradford, Sion Band of Hope and Temperance Society, Harris St Bradford, Programme Book from 12 April 1895–31 January 1906, 28D92 [Anonymous local news cutting, Wed. 7 April 1897].

112 Sion Band of Hope and Temperance Society Programme Book, 16 November 1904; 22 March 1905.

113 Sion Band of Hope and Temperance Society Programme Book, 3 January 1906.

114 WYAS Bradford, Minute Book of Band of Hope Committee Meetings for Girlington Congregational Church, WYB10/3/5/15–16, 'Report of Session, 1895–6'.

115 Minute Book of Band of Hope Committee Meetings for Girlington Congregational Church, 'Report of Session, 1895–6'.

116 Minute Book of Band of Hope Committee Meetings for Girlington Congregational Church, 'Report of Session, 1895–6'.

117 WYAS Bradford, Programme of a Sunday School Rally in Peel Park, in Celebration of the Jubilee of the Bradford Sunday School Union, 1901, WYB10/3/5/16.

118 This figure is around the estimated average for individual societies. See Smith, *Band of Hope Jubilee Volume*, 222.

119 WYAS Bradford, Year Books 1864–1900, containing the annual reports and accounts of the Session, Management, Sunday School, Children's Service, Literary Society, Ladies Sewing Society, Band of Hope and Women's Missionary Association, and list of communicants arranged in Elders' District, for St Andrew's Presbyterian (UR) Church, Bradford, WYB10/5/9/1; and WYAS Bradford, Year Books 1900–1910, containing the annual reports and accounts of the Session, Management, Sunday School, Ladies Sewing Society, Women's Missionary Society, Presbyterian Boys Brigade, Band of Hope, Literary Association, Church Choir, Dorcas Society, Young Women's Guild, Children's Guild, Young Men's Class and list of communicants arranged in Elders' District, for St Andrew's Presbyterian (UR) Church, Bradford, WYB10/5/9/2.

120 Davis, *The Relation of Sunday School Teachers*, 8.

121 Year Books 1900–1910, St Andrew's Presbyterian (UR) Church, Bradford, 9.

122 Year Books 1900–1910, St Andrew's Presbyterian (UR) Church, Bradford, 11.

123 Charles Wakely, 'Essentials in Band of Hope Meetings' (London: UK Band of Hope Union, 1891), 4. [Inserted in Minute Book of Band of Hope Committee Meetings for Girlington Congregational Church.]

124 *Church of England Temperance Chronicle*, 5 (May 1877): 69–70; CETS, *Annual Report*, 20 (1882), 14; CETS, *Annual Report*, 30 (1891), 200.

125 CETS, *Annual Report*, 16 (1887), 14; CETS, *Annual Report*, 19 (1881), 14.

126 G. W. Olsen, 'Church of England Temperance Society', *Alcohol and Temperance in Modern History: An International Encyclopedia* (Santa Barbara, CA: ABC-CLIO, 2003), ed. J. S. Blocker, et al., vol. 1, 155.

127 Harrison, *Drink and the Victorians*, 183.

128 CETS, *Annual Report*, 37 (1898), 49.

129 Olsen, 'Church of England Temperance Society', vol. 1, 156.

130 *CETS Illustrated*, no. 29 (March 1893): 84–5.

131 'A Letter to Our Young Friends – An Industrial Band of Hope', *CETS Illustrated*, 1, n.s. (1890), 41.

132 *CETS Standard Bearer, Special Supplement for Conductors, Members and Supporters of the Juvenile Branches of the CETS*, 8, no. 5 (1888).

133 *CETS Short Manual for the Formation and Guidance of Branches* (London: CETS, 1910), 7.

134 'CETS Work: The Band of Hope', *The Illustrated Temperance Monthly of the Church of England Temperance Society. A Magazine for All Classes* (London: CETS), no. 60 (October 1895): 225.

135 'CETS Work: The Band of Hope', 225.

136 CETS, *Annual Report*, 19 (1881), 22–7.

137 CETS, *Annual Report*, 26 (1887), 57.

138 CETS, *Annual Report*, 42 (1903), 31.

139 CETS, *Annual Report*, 42 (1903), 31.

140 Lambeth Palace Library, Benson Papers, 94, 29–36 (11 September 1891).

141 H. F. Clarke, *How to Avoid Leakage between the Band of Hope and the Adult Society* (London: CETS, 1894), 3.

142 *The Band of Hope Manual: The Formation and Management of the Bands of Hope* (London: UK Band of Hope Union, 1894), 27.

143 *Band of Hope Manual*, 29.

144 *Band of Hope Manual*, 34–6.

145 H. T. James, *Industrial Bands of Hope* (London: CETS, 1891), 3–15.

146 James, *Industrial Bands of Hope*, 8 and 11.

147 James, *Industrial Bands of Hope*, 13.

148   'A letter to our Young Friends', 41.

149   James, *Industrial Bands of Hope*, 13–15.

150   CETS, *Annual Report* (1892), 14.

151   CETS, *Annual Report* (1893), 13.

152   CETS, *Annual Report* (1894), 12–13.

153   CETS, *Annual Report* (1894), 13.

154   CETS, *Annual Report* (1903), 11–12.

155   CETS, *Annual Report* (1907), 18.

156   CETS, *Annual Report* (1912), 21.

157   CETS, *Annual Report* (1913), 15–16.

158   CETS, *Annual Report* (1915), 13.

159   Olsen, 'Drink and the British Establishment', 197.

160   CETS, *Executive Minutes* (November 1912), 22–3.

# Chapter 2

1   Gordon Stables, 'Doings for the Month – June – The Boy Himself, Poultry Run, Pigeon Loft, Aviary, Rabbitry, and Gardens', *Boy's Own*, 27, no. 1376 (27 May 1905): 558. A Scottish-born medical doctor, Stables was a regular contributor to the *BOP*, appearing in almost every monthly issue of the paper from 1884 until his death in 1910. His writings greatly influenced the moral tone of the paper.

2   Stables, 'Doings for the Month', 558, emphasis mine.

3   John Tosh, in his book, *A Man's Place* (170–94) argues that there was a widespread 'flight from domesticity' of men in this era, although he has since nuanced his argument.

4   Miss Forsaith, 'The Secret of Successful Work' (paper read at a conference of the Lancashire and Cheshire Band of Hope Union, held on 25 April 1885) (London: S.W. Partridge & Co.; Manchester: Onward Publishing Office, 1894), 7.

5   Manchester: Lancashire and Cheshire Band of Hope Union, *Annual Reports* (1910), 42.

6   *Workers Onward*, January 1910 (1910–12): 25.

7   Tayler, *Hope of the Race*, 6.

8   Manchester: Lancashire and Cheshire Band of Hope Union, *Annual Reports* (1910), 42.

9   For example, one story declares that the boy 'who wins' is not the one who is governed by his bad habits, but rather the one who is governed by God and whose 'inclinations are in the direction of home'. UK Band of Hope Union 1881, 47.

10   Robert J. Parr, *Willful Waste: The Nation's Responsibility for Its Children* (London: NSPCC, 1910), 70.

11   T. F. Weaving, 'The Coming Men', *The Halfpenny Illustrated Temperance Reciter*, vol. 1. (London: UK Band of Hope Union, 1894), 127.

12   Hesba Stretton, 'Women's Congress of the Chicago Exhibition, 1893', in *Our Future Citizens*, ed. Harriet M. Johnson (London: CETS, 1899), n.p.

13   Francis, 'Domestication of the Male, 637–52; John Tosh, 'Manliness, Masculinities and the New Imperialism', in *Manliness and Masculinities in Nineteenth-Century Britain* (Harlow: Pearson, 2005); Tosh, *A Man's Place*, 196.

14   Thomas Heath, 'Beware', *Young Crusader* (June 1894): 62.

15   Robert Hamilton Edwards, 'Your Editor's Advice', *Boys' Herald*, 1, no. 25 (1904): 400.

16   Hamilton Edwards, 'Teetotalism', *Boys' Herald*, 1, no. 26 (1904): 416; 'Your Editor's Advice', *Boys' Herald*, 1, no. 25 (1904).

17   Edwards, 'Teetotalism', 416.

18   As discussed by G. R. Searle, *The Quest for National Efficiency: A Study in British Politics and Political Thought, 1899–1914* (Berkeley: University of California Press, 1971).

19   John Tosh, 'The Old Adam and the New Man: Emerging Themes in the History of English Masculinities, 1750–1850', in *English Masculinities 1600–1800*, ed. Tim Hitchcock and Michèle Cohen (London: Longman, 1999), 23.

20   Apples of Gold, 'Keep On', *Band of Hope Review* (1914): 96.

21   Hamilton Edwards, 'Editor's Den', *Boys' Friend*, 3, no. 115 (1903): 176.

22   Edward Salmon, 'What Boys Read', *Fortnightly Review*, 45, February (1886): 248.

23   Salmon, 'What Boys Read', 248.

24   W. Scott King, 'The Boy: What He Is and What Are We Going to Make of Him', *Sunday at Home* (1913): 818.

25   King, 'The Boy', 818.

26   *The Religious Tract Society Record of Work at Home and Abroad*, no. 27 (June 1883): 39–40.

27   Buxton, grandson of the abolitionist of the same name, led by example, as it is noted that he was a 'man of high principle', who 'put family concerns above office', see Elizabeth Baigent, 'Buxton, Sir (Thomas) Fowell, Third Baronet (1837–1915)', *Oxford Dictionary of National Biography* (Oxford University Press, 2004), www.oxforddnb.com/view/article/32225, accessed 31 December 2007.

28   *The Religious Tract Society Record of Work at Home and Abroad*, no. 43 (June 1887).

29   *The Religious Tract Society Record of Work at Home and Abroad*, no. 91 (June 1899): 37.

30   David Williamson, 'How to Succeed in Life: Some Finger-Posts for Boys', *Boy's Own*, 32, no. 1633 (30 April 1910): 487.

31   *Seed Time and Harvest*, June (1910).

32   Rev. J. Reid Howatt, 'For the Young', *Sunday at Home* (1902–3): 134.

33   Frederick Blight, 'What Boys Say about Reading', *Band of Hope Annual* (1908): 50.

34   King, 'The Boy', 820.

35   Hamilton Edwards, 'The Penny Dreadful', *Boys' Herald*, 9, no. 460 (1912): 70.

36   Howatt, 'For the Young', 134.

37   *Young Standard Bearer*, 29, no. 10 (September 1909): 75.

38   'Uprooting the Passions', *Young Crusader*, no. 197 (March 1908): 52.

39   'Which Path Will You Take', *Seed Time and Harvest* (1908): 17.

40   'Which Path Will You Take', 17.

41   J. Rogers Rees, 'Men and Manliness', *Leisure Hour* (1890): 111.

42   Church of England Temperance Society c.1900, 33–4.

43   C. W. Saleeby, 'Emotions and Instincts', *Harmsworth Self-Educator* (19 August 1906): 2399.

44   Victor G. Vecki, *Sexual Impotence*. 4th edn (Philadelphia and London: W.B. Saunders, 1912), 219.

45   W. Frank Glenn, 'Impotence in the Male', *Southern Practitioner*, June (1892): 241.

46   Alfred S. Dyer, *Safeguards to Moral Purity and Facts That Men Ought to Know* (London: Dyer Brothers, n.d. [1890s]), 5. For more on the White Cross League (Purity Society before 1891), sexual science and masturbation, see Lesley Hall, 'Hauling Down the Double Standard: Feminism, Social Purity and Sexual Science in Late Nineteenth-Century Britain', *Gender & History*, 16, no. 1 (2004): 36–56; Alan Hunt, 'The Great Masturbation Panic and the Discourses of Moral Regulation in Nineteenth- and Early Twentieth-Century Britain', *Journal of the History of Sexuality*, 8, no. 4 (1998): 575–615; Sue Morgan, 'Knights of God: The White Cross Army 1883–95', in R. N. Swanson, ed. *Gender and the Christian Religion. Studies in Church History* (London: Boydell and Brewer, 1998); Sue Morgan, '"Wild Oats or Acorns?" Social Purity, Sexual Politics and the Response of the Late-Victorian Church', *Journal of Religious History*, 31, no. 2 (2007): 151–68.

47   Dyer, *Safeguards to Moral Purity*, 8.

48   Dyer, *Safeguards to Moral Purity*, 9–10.

49   *Boys' Herald*, 6 (1909): 592.

50   Hamilton Edwards, 'Your Editor's Advice – A Bad Habit', *Boys' Herald*, 1, no. 41 (1904): 668.

51   Gordon Stables, 'Doings for the Month', *Boy's Own*, 22, no. 1102 (1900): 335; 25, no. 1263 (1903): 414–15; 27, no. 1376 (1905): 558.

52   'Boys That Are Wanted', *Young Crusader* (June 1892): 63.

53   John Searson, ed., *The Young Socialist: A Magazine of Love and Service* (Owned by the Glasgow and District Sunday School Union, 1901–16).

54   Uncle Archie, 'Little Things', *Young Socialist*, 2, no. 8 (August 1902): 4.

55   'Helping One Another by Lucie from Huddersfield School', *Young Socialist*, 8, no. 1 (January 1908): 172.

56 Tom Robinson, 'What Daddy Told Dolly', *Young Socialist*, 8, no. 7 (August 1908): 79.

57 John Trevor (?), 'Labour Day and the Children', *Labour Prophet*, May (1895): 73.

58 Some examples are Keir Hardie, 'Jack Clearhead: A Story for Crusaders, and to be Read by Them to Their Fathers and Mothers', *Labour Leader* (8 September 1894): 11 (serial story); 'A Story for Young People', *Labour Leader* (5 January 1895): 2–3; 'To My Little Daughter', *Labour Leader* (30 July 1895): 12; 'The Child Heart', *Labour Leader* (12 June 1897): 198; 'Come to Me, O Ye Children', *Labour Leader* (31 August 1895): 12.

59 Keir Hardie, 'Jim: A Story for Young People', *Young Socialist*, 10, no. 7 (July 1910).

60 *Clarion* (May 19, 1900): 153.

61 'Good and Bad Boys', *Labour Prophet*, July (1893): 65–6.

62 *Clarion* (8 May 1914): 3 (reports about these schools were frequent).

63 ILP Year Book, in Mrs St Clare Norriss, 'Watchman Awake! Save the Children!', Pamphlet (1911), 3.

64 John Trevor, 'Labour Day and the Children', *Labour Prophet*, May (1895): 73.

65 D. J. Rider, 'The Children's May-Day Souvenir, With Designs by Walter Crane. May-Day 1903 Socialist Festival, Alexandra Palace'. [Issued by the Children's Committee, First of May Demonstration, Hon. Sec. Mary Gray, 72, Este Road, Battersea, S. W.]

66 Alan Moore, 'The Child Heart', *Labour Leader* (12 June 1897): 198.

67 Norriss, 'Watchman Awake!' 4.

68 Norriss, 'Watchman Awake!' 4.

69 Norriss, 'Watchman Awake!' 2.

70 Stephen Heathorn and David Greenspoon, 'Organizing Youth for Partisan Politics in Britain, 1918–c.1932', *Historian*, 68, no. 1 (2006): 97 n. 38.

71 Heathorn and Greenspoon 'Organizing Youth for Partisan Politics', 89–119.

72 Harriet M. Johnson, *Our Future Citizens* (London: Church of England Temperance Society, 1899), 15.

73 Apples of Gold, 'Keep On', 96.

# Chapter 3

1 'Mother and Home', *Boy's Own*, n.s., part 1 (1911): 16.

2 'Home', *Young Crusader* (September 1897): 88.

3 'Do You Write to the People at Home?' *Boys' Herald*, 9, no. 443 (1912): 428.

4 'Scouts and Obedience to Parents', *Boys' Herald*, 7, no. 328 (30 October 1909): 244.

5 'Home Politeness', *Band of Hope Review* (1884): 151.

6 *Young Standard Bearer*, n.s. 29, no. 7 (June 1909): 51.

7 Robert Hamilton Edwards, 'Editor's Den', *Boys' Friend*, 2, no. 94 (1903): 709.

8 'Temperance Wives', *Young Crusader*, no. 70 (September 1898): 68.

9 P. Jalland, *Women, Marriage and Politics, 1860–1914* (Oxford: Clarendon Press, 1986), 7.

10 See Tosh, *A Man's Place*, esp. 170–94. Although this chapter explores an argument in contradistinction to that of Tosh in *A Man's Place*, it nevertheless owes a great deal to this work and to Tosh's corpus in general, since it has done more, perhaps, than anything else to establish the question of manliness in the domestic space as an important area of academic research.

11 Outline Addresses, seasonable addresses by M. A. Paull, No. 6, Flower Gathering. – 'For Whom We Gather', *Band of Hope Chronicle*, June (1882): 84.

12 'For Whom We Gather', 84.

13 Anon., 'Don't Marry a Drunkard', *The Marylebone Band of Hope Monthly Visitor*, 2, no. 6 (1883): n.p., emphasis mine.

14 Anne Fellowes, 'A Deliberate Choice', *Leisure Hour* (1893): 124–8.

15 Fellowes, 'A Deliberate Choice', 126.

16 Fellowes, 'A Deliberate Choice', 126.

17 See M. Cohen, 'Manliness, Effeminacy and the French: Gender and the Construction of National Character in Eighteenth-Century England', in *English Masculinities 1660–1800*, ed. Tim Hitchcock and Michèle Cohen (London and New York: Longman, 1999). Cohen charts an important transition from masculine politeness to sincerity; J. Mason, 'Silent Men', *Leisure Hour* (1889): 48–51.

18 Author of How to be Happy Though Married, 'Between School and Marriage', *Girl's Own Paper*, 7, no. 4 (September 1886): 770.

19 'Woman Our Angel', *Yorkshire Factory Times*, 6 October (1899): 2.

20 Countess de Boerio, 'Some Marriage Thorns and How to Avoid Them', *Girl's Own Paper*, 14 (1893): 659.

21 Boerio, 'Some Marriage Thorns', 659.

22 For an archetypical example of this trend, see Agnes Giberne, 'Kathleen: The Story of a Home', *The Sunday at Home Annual* (1882), and the discussion in Stephanie Olsen, 'The Authority of Motherhood in Question: Fatherhood and the Moral Education of Children in England, c. 1870–1900', *Women's History Review*, 18 (2009): 765–80.

23 J. R. Gillis, 'Gender and Fertility Decline Among the British Middle Classes', in *The European Experience of Declining Fertility*, ed. J. R. Gillis, L. A. Tilly and D. Levine (Blackwell: Oxford, 1992), 43.

24 J. W. Kirton (1897 [1870]) *Happy Homes and How to Make Them; or, Counsels on Love, Courtship and Marriage* (London: John Kempster), 88.

25 Sylvanus Stall, *What a Young Husband Ought to Know* (London: Vir Publishing, 1897), 58.

26 Stall, *What a Young Husband Ought to Know*, 262.

27 H. S. Thompson, 'Home and the Choice of a Wife: To Young Men', *Onward*, 17 (1882): 127.

28 Dyer, *Safeguards to Moral Purity*, 11.

29 'True Family Life the Gift of Christ', *Sunday at Home* (London: RTS, 1903–4): 56.

30 'True Family Life the Gift of Christ', 56.

31 Charles Darwin, *The Descent of Man, and Selection in Relation to Sex*, 2nd edn (London: Penguin, 2004 [1879]), 166–7.

32 Kirton, *Happy Homes*, 104.

33 Stall, *What a Young Husband Ought to Know*, 260.

34 H. Jones, 'The Man Who Rises, and the Man Who Falls', *Leisure Hour* (1886): 166.

35 Anon., 'A Search for a Wayward Son', *Marylebone Band of Hope Monthly Visitor*, 1, no. 3 (1881): n.p.

36 'Bob Hilmore's Escape', *CETS Illustrated*, August (1890): 89.

37 Anon., 'Recitation – Following Father', *Young Crusader* (July 1892): 67.

38 Although the *Young Crusader* was targeted at middle-class boys, the CETS and other branches of the Band of Hope had difficulty recruiting above the working classes.

39 *Sunday at Home* (1880): 508–9.

40 'The Little Boy's Faith in God', *Sunday at Home* (1854): 176.

41 'A Discontented Boy', *Sunday at Home* (1887): 638–72.

42 'A Discontented Boy', 672.

43 'A Lost Son', *Leisure Hour* (1885): 4.

44 'A Lost Son', 194.

45 'A Lost Son', 77.

46 'A Lost Son', 155.

47 'A Lost Son', 221.

48 'A Lost Son', 224.

49 'A Lost Son', 227.

50 Hamilton Edwards, 'Your Editor's Chat', *Boys' Herald*, 9, no. 442 (1912): 413.

51 Popular A. S. Hardy, 'Two Drummer Boys', *Boys' Herald*, 1, no. 24 (1904): 386.

52 Robert J. Parr, *Wilful Waste: The Nation's Responsibility for Its Children* (London: NSPCC, 1910), 55–6.

53 Magic Lantern Slide, University of Central Lancashire, Livesey Collection, ID Code: 5837.

54 Stall, *What a Young Husband Ought to Know*, 274.

55 J. Tunnicliff. *The Band of Hope Annual* (London: Simpkin, Marshall and Co., 1865), 24.

56 'Father's Chat on Alcohol', *Onward* (1904): 119–20.

57  E. Showalter, *Sexual Anarchy: Gender and Culture at the Fin de Siècle* (New York: Viking, 1990), 9.

58  J. M. Scott-Moncrieff, 'A Plea for More Womanly Women', *Leisure Hour* (1893): 120.

59  Scott-Moncrieff, 'Plea for More Womanly Women', 122.

60  Scott-Moncrieff, 'Plea for More Womanly Women', 121.

61  Scott-Moncrieff, 'Plea for More Womanly Women', 121, emphasis mine.

62  Lady St Helier, 'The Ideal Husband', *Leisure Hour* (1905): 626.

63  St Helier, 'Ideal Husband', 627–8.

64  G. S. Hall, *The New Woman* (London: Houlston and Sons, c.1900), 6.

65  For an important discussion of lower middle-class men's focus on domesticity, see A. James Hammerton, 'Pooterism or Partnership?: Marriage and Masculine Identity in the Lower Middle Class, 1870–1920', *Journal of British Studies*, 38, no. 3 (1999): 291–321. For a literary description of this problem, see George Gissing, *The Odd Women* (1893; Oxford: Oxford University Press, 2000).

66  Phyllis Browne, 'A Committee of the Whole House – The Home Life', *Leisure Hour* (1895): 401.

67  Tosh, 'Manliness, Masculinities and the New Imperialism', 206. Tosh maintains that the 'turn away from marriage was class-specific', the professional and business classes, which is a useful clarification of his earlier work.

68  F. L. Henderson, 'Why Bob Was a Bachelor: A Story for Mothers and Daughters', *Church of England Temperance Tracts* (Westminster: CETS), no. 5, series H (after 1891): n.p.

69  By the author of 'Occupations of a Retired Life', 'Voices from the Highways and Hedges – A House Beautiful', *Leisure Hour* (1888): 243.

70  Goss, *Husband, Wife and Home*, 20.

71  Stall, *What a Young Husband Ought to Know*, 54.

72  See Kristine Moruzi, *Constructing Girlhood through the Periodical Press, 1850–1915* (Farnham: Ashgate, 2012), 2, 12.

73  Cf. Tosh, *A Man's Place*, 170–94; Olsen, 'Authority of Motherhood in Question'.

# Chapter 4

1  Margaret Watson, 'A Nonentity', *The Church Friendly* (London: Church of England Temperance Benefit Society), 6, no. 65 (March 1901).

2  Watson, 'A Nonentity', 113.

3  Watson, 'A Nonentity', 113.

4  Watson, 'A Nonentity', 114.

5  Watson, 'A Nonentity', 114.

6  Watson, 'A Nonentity', 117.

7   See, for example, Michael Paris, *Warrior Nation: Images of War in British Popular Culture, 1850–2000* (London: Reaktion, 2000), 104–6; Allen Warren, 'Citizens of Empire: Baden-Powell, Scouts and Guides and an Imperial Idea, 1900–1940', in *Imperialism and Popular Culture*, ed. John Mackenzie (Manchester: Manchester University Press, 1986), 232–56; John Springhall, 'The Boy Scouts, Class and Militarism in Reaction to British Youth Movements', *International Review of Social History*, 16, no. 2 (1971): 131–2; John Springhall, Brian Fraser and Michael Edward Hoare, *Sure and Stedfast: A History of the Boys' Brigade, 1883–1983* (London: Collins, 1983). One notable exception is Allen Warren, 'Popular Manliness: Baden-Powell, Scouting and the Development of Manly Character', *Manliness and Morality, Middle Class Masculinity in Britain and America, 1880–1940*, ed. J. A. Mangan and James Walvin (Manchester University Press, 1987).

8   *Boy's Own*, 23 (1905): 558.

9   Robert Baden-Powell, *Rovering to Success: A Guide for Young Manhood* (1922; London: Herbert Jenkins, 1959).

10  Robert Baden-Powell, *Scouting for Boys* (London: C.A. Pearson, 1908).

11  Hamilton Edwards, 'Scouts and Obedience to Parents', *Boys' Herald*, 7, no. 328 (1909): 244; *Boys' Herald*, 5 (1908): 758.

12  Hamilton Edwards, *Boys' Herald*, 6 (1909): 814–15.

13  Edwards to Northcliffe, June 3, 1910, BL, Add. MSS 62182A.

14  Hamilton Edwards, *Boys' Herald*, 1 (1904): 562.

15  Hamilton Edwards, *Boys' Herald*, 2 (1906): 432.

16  *Onward*, 40 (1905): 30.

17  *Boy's Own*, 22 (1900): 270.

18  WYAS Bradford, St Andrew's Presbyterian Church of England, Infirmary Street, Bradford, Year Books, 1904–5, Third Bradford Company Boys' Brigade, WYB10/5/9/2, 11.

19  Edith S. R. Williamson, 'Child Nature from the Band of Hope Standpoint, II', *Onward*, 16 (1906) (Read at the National Band of Hope Conferences, Oxford, 27 September 1905).

20  Williamson, 'Child Nature from the Band of Hope Standpoint, II', 17.

21  William Doak, 'The Band of Hope Movement in Its Relation to Sunday School Work', *The Church of England Temperance Chronicle* (1883): 618–19.

22  James Edmunds, 'A Talk to the Young', *The Church of England Temperance Chronicle* (1882): 88. [Address delivered at the New Year's soirée of the UK Band of Hope Union by Edmunds, a senior physician.]

23  *Liverpool Telegraph*, in *Band of Hope Review* (1880): inside cover.

24  *Leeds Times*, in *Band of Hope Review* (1880): inside cover.

25  Rev. James Fletcher, *The Abstainer: An Illustrated Temperance Monthly*, 1, no. 1 (October 1884): 1.

26  For more on penny dreadfuls see Patrick A. Dunae, 'Penny Dreadfuls: Late 19th-Century Boys' Literature and Crime', *Victorian Studies*, 22, no. 2 (1979): 133–50.

27  'What Are Boys to Read?' *The Religious Tract Society Record of Work at Home and Abroad*, no. 10 (March 1879): 1–3.

28  'Our Monthly Letter' [no date] Special Supplement for: Conductors, Members and Supporters of the Juvenile Branches of the CETS, *Young Standard Bearer* (1881).

29  *Boys' Friend*, 5, no. 205 (1898): 411.

30  Robert Hamilton Edwards, 'A Warning to Boys. The Evil Influence of the Penny Dreadful', *Boys' Friend*, 3, no. 61 (1896): 69.

31  Hamilton Edwards, 'The Penny Dreadful', *Boys' Herald*, 9, no. 460 (1912): 70.

32  Hamilton Edwards, 'A Prejudiced Teacher', *Boys' Friend*, 5, no. 205 (1898): 411.

33  Hamilton Edwards, 'Your Editor's Den', *Boys' Friend*, 3, no. 69 (1896): 131.

34  Hamilton Edwards, 'Editor's Den – A Christian Reader', *Boys' Friend*, 8, no. 28 (1901): 440.

35  Hamilton Edwards, 'Your Editor's Den', *Boys' Friend*, 10, no. 491 (1910): 356; *Boys' Friend*, 5, no. 160 (1898): 27.

36  Hamilton Edwards, *Boys' Herald*, 5, no. 235 (1908): 432.

37  Hamilton Edwards, *Boys' Friend*, 3, no. 98 (1896): 372.

38  *The Religious Tract Society Record of Work at Home and Abroad*, no. 10 (March 1879): 27.

39  'What Are Boys to Read?' 1–3.

40  Hamilton Edwards, *Boys' Herald*, 9, no. 443 (1912): 428.

41  Hamilton Edwards, 'Editor's Den', *Boys' Friend*, 3, no. 115 (1903): 176, emphasis mine.

42  *RTS Record*, no. 11 (June 1879): 36.

43  John Wolffe, 'Cooper, Anthony Ashley-, Seventh Earl of Shaftesbury (1801–1885)', *Oxford Dictionary of National Biography* (Oxford University Press, September 2004); online edn, January 2008, www.oxforddnb.com/view/article/6210, accessed 27 February 2008.

44  Mark Pottle, 'Sandow, Eugen (1867–1925)', *Oxford Dictionary of National Biography* (Oxford University Press, 2004), www.oxforddnb.com/view/article/76284, accessed 18 March 2008.

45  *Young Crusader*, no. 189 (July 1907): 67; and *Young Crusader* (May 1912): 62.

46  Full page ad for new *BOP*, in *The Publisher's Circular: General Record of British and Foreign Literature* (London: Sampson Low, Marston, Searle, & Rivington, 1879), 61.

47  Advertised in the *Boys' Friend*, 204, no. 4 (6 May 1905): 785.

48  In the case of the League of Health and Strength membership conditions included 'No Smoking (until 21 Years of Age); No Drinking of Intoxicants as Beverages; No Swearing; No Gambling; No Evil Habits'. *Boys' Herald*, 5, no. 236 (1908): n.p.

49  Hamilton Edwards, 'Editor's Den – Two Honourable Lads', *Boys' Friend*, 5, no. 219 (1905): 164.

50  RTS ECM, June 6, 1882.

51  Rev. C. F. Tonks, 'My Duty', *Church of England Temperance Society Annual Examination and Inter-Diocesan Competition, 1914–1915* (Westminster: CETS, 1914), 8. Bold in original.

52  Hamilton Edwards, 'Editor's Den', *Boys' Friend*, 8, no. 316 (1901): 39.

53  Hamilton Edwards, 'Your Editor's Advice – Bad Habits and Their Consequences' *Boys' Herald*, 1, no. 27 (1904): 432 and 'Your Editor's Advice – An Extraordinary Gift', *Boys' Herald*, 1, no. 25 (1904): 400.

54  *Young Standard Bearer*, 27 (1907): 42.

55  'The Strong Man's Advice', *Young Crusader* (November 1908): 2; Carey A. Watt, *Serving the Nation: Cultures of Service, Association, and Citizenship in Colonial India* (New Delhi: Oxford University Press, 2005), 51.

56  John Welshman, 'Images of Youth: The Issue of Juvenile Smoking, 1880–1914', *Addiction*, 91, no. 9 (1996): 1379–86.

57  See, for example, Maud Maddick, 'Mr. Boy Next Door: A Story to be Read by, or to, the Children on Sunday Afternoon or at Any Time', *Sunday at Home* (1911): 532; Stephanie Olsen, 'Towards the Modern Man: Edwardian Boyhood in the Juvenile Periodical Press', *Childhood in Edwardian Fiction: Worlds Enough and Time*, ed. Adrienne E. Gavin and Andrew F. Humphries (Houndmills: Palgrave, 2009).

58  Hamilton Edwards, 'A Mistaken Idea', *Boys' Herald*, 1, no. 32 (1904): 512.

59  Edwards, 'A Mistaken Idea', 512.

60  Helen MacDowall, 'My Boys', *Sunday at Home* (1913): 402.

61  'Boys in Big Cities', *Boy's Own*, 25, no. 1282 (8 August 1903): 719.

62  Hamilton Edwards, *Boys' Herald*, 5 (1908): 427.

63  *The Band of Hope Blue Book: A Manual of Instruction and Training* (London: UK Band of Hope Union, 1942), 10.

64  *Speakers' Self-Help*, 21.

65  'Boys That Are Wanted', *Young Crusader* (June 1892): 63.

66  Church of England Temperance Society Annual Report (London, 1913), 15.

67  Harrison, *Drink and the Victorians*, 192.

68  *Speakers' Self-Help*, 11.

69  'Message to Young Men among Our Readers from the Right Hon. The Lord Mayor of Leeds (Ald. J. Hepworth)', *The Workers Onward: The Organ of the Lancashire and Cheshire Band of Hope & Temperance Union* (January 1907): 5.

70  BOC, 'The Two Homes: A Story Founded on Fact', *Quarterly Manual and Band of Hope Reporter for Greenwich and West Kent* (Greenwich: Borough of Greenwich and West Kent Band of Hope Union), 1, no. 2 (January 1880): 7.

71  BOC, 'The Two Homes', *Quarterly Manual and Band of Hope Reporter for Greenwich and West Kent*, 1, no. 3 (April 1880): n.p.

72  'What Children May Do', *Young Crusader* (April 1908): 62.

73  NSPCC Annual Report (1891–2), 65; see also G. K. Behlmer, *Child Abuse and Moral Reform in England, 1870–1908* (Stanford: Stanford University Press, 1982), 185, and C. Sherrington, 'The NSPCC in Transition. 1884–1983: A Study of Organisational Survival' (Ph.D. London University, 1984), 81.

74  See, for example, 'A Little Boy and His Father', S. Knowles, *Every Band of Hope Boy's Reciter: Containing Original Recitations, Dialogues, &C., Written Expressly for Bands of Hope* (Manchester: J. Brook, no. 14, c.1879), 224.

75  D. F. Hannigan, 'The Boy Who Beat His Father', *Onward*, 36 (1901): 27.

76  Hannigan, 'Boy Who Beat His Father', 28.

77  Uncle John, 'Our Willie: A True Story', *Young Standard Bearer*, no. 1 (1881): 2–3.

78  Tayler, *Hope of the Race*, 44.

79  'A Brave Boy', CETS Children's Leaflets (1901).

80  'A Brave Boy', 2.

81  'A Brave Boy', 1.

82  'A Brave Boy', 3.

83  'A Brave Boy', 4.

84  'A Brave Boy', 4.

85  S. U. Cazalet Bloxam, 'The House That Pledge Built', *Temperance Talks with the Children: Twenty Addresses* (London: CETS, n.d.), 151–4.

86  Knowles, *Every Band of Hope Boy's Reciter*, 73.

87  Tonks, 'My Duty', 8.

88  Dr Talmage, 'The Influence of Example', *Band of Hope Chronicle* (December 1885): 194.

89  Talmage, 'The Influence of Example', 194.

90  Tayler, *Hope of the Race*, 45.

91  Tayler, *Hope of the Race*, 41.

92  Tayler, *Hope of the Race*, 42.

93  Tayler, *Hope of the Race*, 38.

94  Church of England Temperance Society, 1892, 63.

95  Apples of Gold, 'A Manly Boy', *Band of Hope Review* (1913): 78.

96  George W. Bungay, 'The Boy Who Dared to Say No', *Young Crusader* (1897): 52.

97  'How to Be a Man', *Onward* (1881): 46.

98  'Boys Wanted', *Band of Hope Review* (1915): 64.

# Chapter 5

1  Angelique Richardson, *Love and Eugenics in the Late Nineteenth Century* (Oxford: Oxford University Press, 2003), 74.

2  See an interesting discussion of this duality in Satadru Sen, *Colonial Childhoods: The Juvenile Periphery of India, 1850–194* (London: Anthem Press, 2005), 51.

3  Elizabeth Buettner, 'Fatherhood Real, Imagined, Denied: British Men in Imperial India', in Broughton and Rogers, *Gender and Fatherhood in the Nineteenth Century*, 185.

4  A. R. Ashwell and R. G. Wilberforce, *Life of Samuel Wilberforce* (1880), ii, 197, quoted in David Newsome, *Godliness and Good Learning: Four Studies on a Victorian Ideal* (London: John Murray, 1961), 90.

5  Newsome; J. A. Mangan, *The Games Ethic and Imperialism: Aspects of the Diffusion of an Ideal* (Harmondsworth: Viking, 1985); J. A. Mangan, 'Noble Specimens of Manhood: Schoolboy Literature and the Creation of a Colonial Chivalric Code', in *Imperialism and Juvenile Literature*, ed. Jeffery Richards (Manchester: Manchester University Press, 1989); J. A. Mangan, *Athleticism in the Victorian and Edwardian Public School: The Emergence and Consolidation of an Educational Ideology* (Cambridge: Cambridge University Press, 1981) Donald Hall, ed., *Muscular Christianity: Embodying the Victorian Age* (Cambridge: Cambridge University Press, 1994).

6  Tosh, *A Man's Place*.

7  Tosh, 'Manliness, Masculinities and the New Imperialism', 209; see also, Roper and Tosh, *Manful Assertions*; Norman Vance, *The Sinews of the Spirit: The Ideal of Christian Manliness in Victorian Literature and Religious Thought* (Cambridge: Cambridge University Press, 1985), 166–206.

8  G. J. Barker-Benfield, *The Culture of Sensibility: Sex and Society in Eighteenth-Century Britain* (Chicago and London: University of Chicago Press, 1992), 98–103; Philip Carter, *Men and the Emergence of Polite Society, Britain 1660–1800* (Harlow: Longman, 2001); Clark, 'Rhetoric of Chartist Domesticity, 62–88; Leonore Davidoff and Catherine Hall, *Family Fortunes: Men and Women of the English Middle Class, 1780–1850* (London: Hutchinson, 1987), ch.7; John Tosh, 'Authority and Nurture in Middle-Class Fatherhood: The Case of Early and Mid-Victorian England', *Gender & History*, 8, no. 1 (1996): 48–64.

9  For example, Davidoff & Hall, *Family Fortunes*, ch. 7; P. Jalland, *Marriage and Politics, 1860–1914* (Oxford: Clarendon Press, 1986); Ellen Ross, *Love and Toil: Motherhood in Outcast London, 1870–1918* (New York: Oxford University Press, 1993).

10 For a range of approaches to 'imperial masculinities', see Tosh, *Manliness and Masculinities*; J. Rutherford, *Forever England: Reflections on Masculinity and Empire* (London: Lawrence & Wishart, 1997); J. M. MacKenzie, ed., *Imperialism and Popular Culture* (Manchester: Manchester University Press, 1986); Patrick A. Dunae, 'Boys' Literature and the Idea of Empire, 1870–1914', *Victorian Studies*, 24 (1980): 105–21.

11 Francis, 'Domestication of the Male', 643.

12 Hammerton, 'Pooterism or Partnership?' 295.

13 Hammerton, 'Pooterism or Partnership?' 320.

14 For a seminal discussion of the former, see Mrinalini Sinha, *Colonial Masculinity: The Manly Englishman and the Effeminate Bengali in the Late Nineteenth Century* (New York: Manchester University Press, 1995). On the latter, see Elizabeth Elbourne's interesting discussion of the eighteenth- and early nineteenth-century Cape in 'Domesticity and Dispossession: The Ideology of "Home" and the British Construction of the "Primitive" from the Eighteenth to the Early Nineteenth Century', in *Deep HiStories: Gender and Colonialism in Southern Africa*, ed. Wendy Woodward, Patricia Hayes and Gary Minkley (Amsterdam: Rodopi, 2002), 27–54. For a discussion of similar dynamics in our period, see, for example, Sarah Carter, *Capturing Women: The Manipulation of Cultural Imagery in Canada's Prairie West* (Montreal and Kingston: McGill-Queen's University Press, 1997), esp. ch. 5.

15 There is a vast historiography on the Rebellion of 1857. See, for example, Biswamoy Pati, ed., *The 1857 Rebellion* (New Delhi: Oxford University Press, 2007).

16 Watt, *Serving the Nation*, 5.

17 Watt, *Serving the Nation*, 5, 7, 14.

18 Stephanie Olsen, 'The Authority of Motherhood in Question: Fatherhood and the Moral Education of Children in England, c. 1870–1900', *Women's History Review*, 18, no. 5 (November 2009): 765–80.

19 Watt, *Serving the Nation*, 49.

20 Watt, *Serving the Nation*, 142.

21 Ashis Nandy, *Traditions, Tyranny and Utopias* (New Delhi: Oxford University Press, 1987), 66.

22 Indian religious or cultural understandings of morality are not the focus here. See Shobna Nijhawan, 'Civilizing Sisters: Writings on How to Save Women, Men, Society and the Nation'. *From Improvement to Development. 'Civilizing Missions' in Colonial and Postcolonial South Asia*, ed. Carey Watt and Michael Mann (London and New York: Anthem Press, 2011), 193–215; Margrit Pernau, 'Maulawi Muhammad Zaka Ullah: Reflections of a Muslim Moralist on the Compatibility of Islam, Hinduism and Christianity', in *Convictions religieuses et engagement en Asie du Sud depuis 1850*, ed. C. Clémentin-Ojha (Paris: École française d'Extrême-Orient), 31–47.

23 For a discussion of how understandings of the racial other were used to define class in the metropole, see Susan Thorne, '"The Conversion of Englishmen and the Conversion of the World Inseparable": Missionary Imperialism and the Language of Class, 1750–1850'. *Tensions of Empire: Colonial Cultures in a Bourgeois World*, ed. Frederick Cooper and Ann Laura Stoler (Berkeley: University of California Press, 1997).

24  For a convincing account of how modern, missionary-driven vernacular education reinforced the place of religion in colonial India, see Parna Sengupta, *Pedagogy for Religion: Missionary Education and the Fashioning of Hindus and Muslims in Bengal* (Berkeley: University of California Press, 2011).

25  Vasanthi Raman, 'The Diverse Life-Worlds of Indian Childhood', in *Family and Gender: Changing Values in Germany and India*, ed. Margrit Pernau, Imtiaz Ahmad and Helmut Reifeld (New Delhi: Sage, 2003), 93.

26  White Cross League, *Annual Reports* (1910–11): 19.

27  Katherine Mullin, 'Dyer, Alfred Stace (1849–1926)', *Oxford Dictionary of National Biography* (Oxford University Press, October 2008), www.oxforddnb.com/view/article/94647, accessed 13 February 2013.

28  Lucy Carroll, 'Origins of the Kayastha Temperance Movement', *Indian Economic Social History Review*, 11 (1974): 432–47, 433.

29  Lucy Carroll, 'The Temperance Movement in India: Politics and Social Reform', *Modern Asian Studies*, 10, no. 3 (1976), 417–47, 419.

30  Carroll, 'The Temperance Movement in India', 426–7.

31  Carroll, 'The Temperance Movement in India', 434 and 430–1.

32  John Murdoch, *My Duties: A Junior Moral Text-Book, with an Address to Teachers* (London and Madras: Christian Literature Society, 1908), 27.

33  Watt, 'Boy Scout Movement in India', *South Asia*, 12, no. 2 (1999), 39, 37–62. The YMCA seems to have fared better in terms of official support. See M. D. David, 'The Missionary Muscular Culture in Modern India', *Discoveries, Missionary Expansion and Asian Cultures*, ed. T. R. De Souza (New Delhi: Concept, 1994), 195–209.

34  'Dr. Murdoch's Jubilee', *Religious Tract Society Record*, March 1895, 4. Linked societies, for example, were the Calcutta, Punjab Religious Book Society; Gujarat Tract Society; North India Tract and Book Society; Ceylon Religious Tract Society. The name of the society, originally the Christian Vernacular Education Society, was shortened in 1891.

35  Watt, *Serving the Nation*, 32.

36  Deana Heath, *Purifying Empire: Obscenity and the Politics of Moral Regulation in Britain, India and Australia* (Cambridge: Cambridge University Press, 2010), 148–9.

37  'A Bengali BOP', *Seed Time and Harvest* (March 1912), 16.

38  *Religious Tract Society Record* (March 1898): 25–7.

39  Heath, *Purifying Empire*, 6.

40  John Murdoch, *The Training of Children for Indian Parents* (3rd edn, London and Madras: Christian Literature Society for India, 1897).

41  Murdoch, *Training of Children for Indian Parents*, 88–9.

42  John Murdoch, *The Indian Young Man in the Battle of Life . Hints to Students on Leaving College* (London and Madras: Christian Literature Society for India, 1903).

43   John Murdoch, *The Indian Student's Manual: Hints on Studies, Moral Conduct, Religious Duties and Success in Life* (Madras: Christian Vernacular Society, 1875), 1.

44   Murdoch, *The Indian Student's Manual*, 1–2.

45   Murdoch, *The Indian Student's Manual*, 107.

46   Murdoch, *The Indian Student's Manual*, 108.

47   For an interesting discussion of how this moral education was thought to lead to a 'moral crisis' for Indian students see Sanjay Seth, *Subject Lessons: The Western Education of Colonial India* (Durham: Duke University Press, 2007), 47–78.

48   Murdoch, *The Indian Young Man in the Battle of Life*.

49   Heath, *Purifying Empire*, 162.

50   Murdoch, *Indian Student's Manual*, 113.

51   Carroll, 'The Temperance Movement in India', 417–47, and Carroll, 'Origins of the Kayastha Temperance Movement', 432–47.

52   Murdoch, *My Duties*, 7.

53   John Murdoch, *Hints on Government Education in India* (Madras: Foster, 1873), 98–9.

54   The sentiment is echoed in the preface to *The Training of Children for Indian Parents*, in which Murdoch states that husbands must guide 'uneducated wives' and puts the onus on training the 'children in the way they should go' in order to ensure both their and the parents' happiness.

55   Murdoch, *Indian Student's Manual*, 166.

56   Gauri Viswanathan, *Masks of Conquest* (New York: Columbia University Press, 1989), 97.

57   Florence Nightingale to Murdoch, BL Manuscripts: Nightingale Papers vol. lxxi MSS/Additional/ -45809 ff. 234 (copy of letter to Dr Murdoch, December 1889) and vol. lxxi MSS/Additional/ -45809 ff. 90 (4 January 1889). Murdoch in turn praised Nightingale, noting that 'Millions will benefit from Miss Nightingale's efforts who never heard her name [. . .] It is a blessed thing to have some unselfish work to do in the world. Few can be as useful as Miss Nightingale; but all, if they try, can find many ways of doing good to those around them'. Murdoch, *My Duties*, 144.

58   Sudhir Chandra, 'The Loyalty of Educated Indians to British Rule (1858–85)', *Continuing Dilemmas, Understanding Social Consciousness* (Delhi: Tulika, 2002), 18–28 and Murdoch, *Hints on Government Education*, 23.

59   Murdoch, *Hints on Government Education*, 20–1, quotes Adam's Report on Vernacular Education in Bengal and Behar, 94.

60   Murdoch, *Hints on Government Education*, 20–1, quotes Adam's Report on Vernacular Education in Bengal and Behar, 101.

61   India, Calcutta University Commission. Vol. I, Part I (1917–19), 23.

62   India, Indian Education Commission, 1882. Calcutta: Superintendent of Government Printing, India (1883), 295.

63   Indian Education Commission, 205.

64 Indian Education Commission, 312.

65 Susannah Wright, 'Citizenship, Moral Education and the English Elementary School', *Mass Education and the Limits of State Building*, ed. Laurence Brockliss and Nicola Sheldon (Basingstoke: Palgrave, 2012), 21–45.

66 Citing a number of chapter titles from Murdoch's *Indian Young Man in the Battle of Life*.

67 Samuel Satyanatha, *Sketches of Indian Christians* (London and Madras: Christian Literature Society for India, 1896), xiii–xvii.

68 F. B. Meyer, 'An Array of Facts', *Religious Tract Society Record* (June 1899): 86.

69 'Calcutta Christian Tract and Book Society', *Religious Tract Society Record* (December 1899): 175.

70 Hayden J. A. Bellenoit, 'Missionary Education, Religion and Knowledge in India, c. 1880–1915', *Modern Asian Studies*, 41, no. 2 (2007): 389.

71 S. Shabbir, *History of Educational Development in Vidarbha from 1882 to 1923* (New Delhi: Northern Book Centre, 2005), 280–1. The first significant backlash against British education in India and a declaration of a national and universal alternative, which represented Indian values and educational goals, was at the Calcutta Congress of 1906. This movement was short-lived, however, almost disappearing by the beginning of the First World War and only springing up again in the 1920s in Mohandas Gandhi's Non-Cooperation Movement. See J. P. Naik, *Educational Planning in India* (Bombay: Allied Publishers, 1965), 66.

72 J. H. Budden, *Prasanna and Kamini: The Story of a Young Hindu* (London: Religious Tract Society, 1885) [translated from a Hindi adaptation of H. C. Mullens' story *Faith and Victory* (London: James Nisbet, 1865)].

73 'Balak: The Bengali BOP', *Seed Time and Harvest* (March 1913): 1.

74 'Chenna and His Friends, Hindu and Christian by Edwin Lewis', *Religious Tract Society Record* (September 1899): 160.

75 'Nuru the Shepherd Boy by Rev. Arthur Le Feuvre', *Religious Tract Society Record* (December 1900): 165.

76 A. D. *Seed-Time and Harvest. A Tale of the Punjab*, 2nd edn (London: Christian Literature Society for India, 1899).

77 *Seed-Time and Harvest*, 46–8.

78 *Seed-Time and Harvest*, 43–5.

79 *Seed-Time and Harvest*, 48.

80 Samuel Satyanatha, *Sketches of Indian Christians* (London and Madras: Christian Literature Society for India, 1896), vii.

81 Satyanatha, *Sketches of Indian Christians*, xiii–xvii.

82 G. Everard, *Religious Tract Society Record* (June 1892): 62–3.

83 R. Wright Hay, 'Testimony from Bengal', *Religious Tract Society Record* (June 1899): 89.

84  India, Report of the Indian Universities Commission (Simla: Government Central Printing Office, 1902). 'Note of Dissent' by the Honourable Mr Justice Gooroo Dass Banerjee, 84–5.

85  India, Indian Education Commission, 1882 (Calcutta, India: Superintendent of Government Printing, 1883), 209–11.

86  Naik, *Educational Planning in India*, 66. For an interesting discussion connecting Hindu nationalism, universal education and national efficiency in this period see Carey A. Watt, 'Education for National Efficiency: Constructive Nationalism in North India, 1909–1916', *Modern Asian Studies*, 31, no. 2 (May 1997): 339–74.

87  J. Knowles, *Our Duty to India and Indian Illiterates* (London and Madras: Christian Literature Society for India, 1910), 2.

88  Hayden J. A. Bellenoit, 'Missionary Education, Religion and Knowledge in India, c. 1880–1915', *Modern Asian Studies*, 41, no. 2 (2007), 392.

89  W. Nassau Lees, *Indian Musalmans* (London: Williams and Norgate, 1871), v.

90  Lionel Alexander Ritchie, 'Mitchell, John Murray (1815–1904)', *Oxford Dictionary of National Biography* (Oxford University Press, 2004); online edn, October 2006, www.oxforddnb.com/view/article/35043, accessed 7 February 2013; John M. Mitchell, *Letters to Indian Youth on the Evidences of the Christian Religion: With a Brief Examination of the Evidences of Hinduism, Pārsīism and Muhammadanism*, 3rd edn (Bombay: Bombay Tract and Book Society, 1857), 4.

91  Mitchell, *Letters to Indian Youth*, 184.

92  Mitchell, *Letters to Indian Youth*, 127.

93  Murdoch, 'Dr. Murdoch's Jubilee', 4.

94  *Christian Literature Society's Quarterly Bulletin*, 4, no. 3 (January 1910): 5.

95  Samuel Smiles, *Self-Help; With Illustrations of Character and Conduct* (London: John Murray, 1859).

96  'Dr. Murdoch's Jubilee', 3.

97  Ashis Nandy, *Traditions, Tyranny and Utopias* (Delhi: Oxford University Press, 1987), 66.

98  For an excellent discussion of British working-class subjecthood, loyalty and dutifulness in elementary schools, see especially Heathorn, *For Home, Country and Race* and Wright, 'Citizenship, Moral Education and the English Elementary School', 21–45.

99  Nita Kumar, 'Provincialism in Modern India: The Multiple Narratives of Education and Their Pain', *Modern Asian Studies*, 40, no. 2 (May 2006), 414.

100  Nita Kumar, *The Politics of Gender, Community and Modernity: Essays on Education* (New Delhi: Oxford University Press, 2007), 238–9.

101  See, for example, Swapna M. Banerjee, 'Children's Literature in Nineteenth Century India: Some Reflections and Thoughts', in 'Stories for Children, Histories of Childhood', *GRAAT* (2007): 337–51.

102  Raman, 'The Diverse Life-Worlds of Indian Childhood', 89–91.

103  Banerjee, 'Children's Literature in Nineteenth Century India', 337–51.

104  Pradip Bose, 'Sons of the Nation: Child Rearing in the New Family', *Texts of Power: Emerging Disciplines in Colonial Bengal*, ed. Partha Chatterjee (Minneapolis: University of Minnesota Press, 1995), 118–19.

105  Gail Minault, *Secluded Scholars: Women's Education and Muslim Social Reform in Colonial India* (Delhi: Oxford University Press, 1998), 4–5.

106  Bose, 'Sons of the Nation', 118–19.

107  Dipesh Chakrabarty, 'The Difference-Deferral of (A) Colonial Modernity: Public Debates on Domesticity in British Bengal', *History Workshop Journal*, 36 (1993), 6.

108  Watt, *Serving the Nation*, 44–5.

109  David W. Savage, 'Murdoch, John (1819–1904)', *Oxford Dictionary of National Biography* (Oxford University Press, 2004); online edn, May 2008, www.oxforddnb.com/view/article/53175, accessed 7 February 2013.

# Chapter 6

1   Quoted in Johnson, *Our Future Citizens*, 9.

2   Report on the Inter-Departmental Committee on Physical Deterioration, Cd. 2175, (*Parliamentary Papers* 32) vol. 1 (1904), (hereafter, Physical Deterioration) 72–6, for adolescence.

3   Physical Deterioration, i, 73.

4   Physical Deterioration, i, 74.

5   Pick, *Faces of Degeneration, A European Disorder, c. 1848–c. 1918* (Cambridge: Cambridge University Press, 1989), 174.

6   Physical Deterioration, i, 34–8.

7   Physical Deterioration, i, 72.

8   Johnson, *Our Future Citizens*, 15.

9   Quoted in George K. Behlmer, *Child Abuse and Moral Reform in England 1870–1908* (Stanford: Stanford University Press, 1982), 52.

10  NSPCC, *A History of the NSPCC* (London: NSPCC, 2000), 3.

11  1 Edw. VII, c. 20 (1901).

12  Bernard Wasserstein, *Herbert Samuel: A Political Life* (Oxford: Clarendon Press, 1992), 104.

13  Wasserstein, *Herbert Samuel*, 98–100.

14  M. K. Inglis, *The Children's Charter: A Sketch of the Scope and Main Provisions of the Children Act, 1908* (London: T. Nelson, 1909), 13.

15  Inglis, *Children's Charter*, 9.

16  *Hansard Parliamentary Debates*, 4th series, vol. 194 (1908), col. 48.

17  *Hansard Parliamentary Debates*, 4th series, vol. 186 (1908), col. 1286.

18  *Hansard Parliamentary Debates*, 4th series, vol. 183 (1908), col. 181.

19  Bernard Wasserstein, 'Samuel, Herbert Louis, First Viscount Samuel (1870–1963)', *Oxford Dictionary of National Biography* (Oxford University Press, September 2004), www.oxforddnb.com/view/article/35928, accessed 26 April 2008.

20  Inglis, *Children's Charter*, 10 and 11.

21  Inglis, *Children's Charter*, 52.

22  Inglis, *Children's Charter*, 11 and 51.

23  Herbert Samuel, *Memoirs* (London: Cresset Press, 1945), 54.

24  Inglis, *Children's Charter*, 9.

25  For a discussion of the resistance of the Band of Hope to other legislation that was intended to aid children (i.e. the 1889 Act for the Prevention of Cruelty to Children) because of feared restrictions on the employment of children in public entertainments, see Behlmer, *Child Abuse*, 52.

26  'Band of Hope Entertainments and The Cruelty to Children Act', UK Band of Hope Union *Annual Reports* (1904–05), 25.

27  Cunningham, *Children and Childhood*, 162. See also S. Pooley, 'Childcare and Neglect: A Comparative Local Study of Late Nineteenth-Century Parental Authority' and D. Thom, '"Beating Children Is Wrong": Domestic Life, Psychological Thinking and the Permissive Turn', both in *The Politics of Domestic Authority in Britain since 1800*, ed. Lucy Delap, Ben Griffin and Abigail Wills (Houndmills: Palgrave, 2009).

28  Parr, *Wilful Waste*, 70.

29  Nicholas Malton, 'Parr, Sir Robert John (1862–1931)', *Oxford Dictionary of National Biography* (Oxford University Press, 2004), www.oxforddnb.com/view/article/69002, accessed 26 August 2008.

30  NSPCC Reports (1898–9), 48.

31  Robert J. Parr, *Benjamin Waugh: An Appreciation* (publisher not given, [1909]) 9.

32  Parr, *Benjamin Waugh*, 8–9.

33  Benjamin Waugh (1894) in, NSPPC, *A History of the NSPCC*, 1.

34  Roberts, *Making English Morals*, 278.

35  *A History of the NSPCC*, 2.

36  Anne Beale, 'Cruelty to Children', *Leisure Hour* (1889): 627.

37  Behlmer, *Child Abuse*, 188.

38  Sherrington, 'NSPCC in Transition', 224.

39  *Child's Guardian: The Official Organ of the National Society for the Prevention of Cruelty to Children*, January (1890).

40  Sherrington, 'NSPCC in Transition', 224; NSPCC Annual Report (1884), 61.

41  Johnson, *Our Future Citizens*, 7.

42  Autumnal Conference at Manchester: A statement in the *Child's Guardian*,
    November (1910): 129. Mr. Harold Agnew (vice-chairman of Society, presiding).

43  *The Child's Guardian*, February (1914): 16.

44  1,200 children were removed from parental custody out of a total of 754,732
    children on whose behalf the NSPCC intervened. *Inebriate Mothers and Their
    Reform*. NSPCC Twenty-Ninth Annual Report (1903), 4–5.

45  Parr, *Wilful Waste*, 51–2.

46  For more on cruelty men, see Monica Flegel, *Conceptualizing Cruelty to Children in
    Nineteenth-Century England* (Farnham: Ashgate, 2009), 181–94.

47  For example, the paper for officers of the NSPCC stated that 'Inspector Butler, of
    Newcastle-on-Tyne, is to be congratulated on the success attained by his son Sidney
    John Butler, who, as a student at the evening classes of the Education Committee,
    has passed with distinction his second-year course in the subjects of practical
    mathematics, physics and machine drawing. His son has been equally successful in
    two examinations at Armstrong College, in engineering and shipbuilding subjects.
    The Inspector's 11-year-old daughter has also gained a four years' free scholarship
    at Rutherford College, the value being £6 per year.' *The Inspectors' Quarterly*, 1,
    no. 1 (29 September 1913): 2.

48  Behlmer, *Child Abuse*, 163.

49  NSPCC, *A History of the NSPCC*, 4.

50  *The Inspectors' Quarterly*, 1, no. 2 (25 December 1913): 6.

51  NSPCC Annual Report (1889), 22, in Sherrington, 'NSPCC in Transition', 93.

52  *Child's Guardian*, May (1914): 52.

53  *Child's Guardian*, January (1914): 7.

54  Parr, *Wilful Waste*, 55.

55  'Drinking and Gambling', *The Child's Guardian*, May (1914): 53.

56  Johnson, *Our Future Citizens*, 7.

57  Tonks, 'My Duty', 8.

58  Photography was also frequently used, mainly to convey the extremes of abuse and
    to encourage feelings of pity in the viewer. For an excellent discussion of this topic,
    see Monica Flegel, 'Changing Faces: The NSPCC and the Use of Photography in the
    Construction of Cruelty to Children', *Victorian Periodicals Review*, 39, no. 1 (2006):
    1–20.

59  *The Power of the Children Being the Report of the National Society for the Prevention
    of Cruelty to Children* (1895–6), 45–6.

60  NSPCC Annual Report, *Inebriate Mothers and Their Reform* (1902–3), 5.

61  Parr, *Wilful Waste*, 60.

62  'Adolescence', *Oxford English Dictionary Online*, http://dictionary.oed.com/cgi/
    entry/50002958?query_type=word&queryword=adolescence&first=1&max_to_
    show=10&single=1&sort_type=alpha, accessed 7 August 2008. G. Stanley Hall.

*Adolescence: Its Psychology and Its Relations to Physiology, Anthropology, Sociology, Sex, Crime, Religion and Education* (2 vols, New York: D. Appleton, 1904).

63   Welton, James. *Psychology of Education* (London: Macmillan, 1911), 232.

64   Inglis, *Children's Charter*, 13.

65   Hall, *Adolescence*, i, x.

66   Sylvanus Stall, *What a Young Boy Ought to Know* (London: Vir Publishing, 1897), 185.

67   Robert Hamilton Edwards, 'Editor's Den – A Very Excellent Book', *Boys' Friend*, 2, no. 82 (1903): 505.

68   Robert Baden-Powell, *Scouting for Boys* (London: C.A. Pearson, 1908), 203.

69   Charles Frederic Goss, *Husband, Wife and Home*, introduction by Sylvanus Stall (London: Vir Publishing, 1905), and Stall, *What a Young Husband Ought to Know*.

70   Sylvanus Stall, *Parental Honesty* (London and Philadelphia: Vir Publishing, 1905).

71   Stall, *Parental Honesty*, 16–18.

72   Stall, *Parental Honesty*, 44.

73   Stall, *Parental Honesty*, 23–4.

74   Stall, *Parental Honesty*, 45–8.

75   Stall, *Parental Honesty*, 50–2.

76   Stall, *Parental Honesty*, 60–1.

77   Clarke, *How to Avoid Leakage*, 4. Clarke was the Honorary Secretary for the Junior Division of the Church of England Temperance Society.

78   Roberts, 'Character in the Mind', 177–97. See Noah W. Sobe, 'Researching Emotion and Affect in the History of Education', *History of Education*, 41 (2012): 689–95.

79   Roberts, 'Character in the Mind', 181.

80   Francis Galton, *Inquiries into Human Faculty and Its Development* (London: Macmillan, 1883), 199.

81   Charles Darwin, *The Descent of Man, and Selection in Relation to Sex*, 2nd edn (London: Penguin, 2004 [1879]), 115, 166, 169.

82   See Thomas E. Jordan, *The Degeneracy Crisis and Victorian Youth* (Albany: State University of New York Press, 1993), 252 for a discussion on the moral impact of degeneration. Also, G. R. Searle, *Eugenics and Politics in Britain, 1900–1914* (Leyden: Noordhoff, 1976).

83   Angelique Richardson, *Love and Eugenics in the Late Nineteenth Century: Rational Reproduction and the New Woman* (Oxford: Oxford University Press, 2003), 72–4.

84   Robert J. Richards, *Darwin and the Emergence of Evolutionary Theories of Mind and Behavior* (Chicago: University of Chicago Press, 1987), 123–4.

85   Pick, *Faces of Degeneration*, 180.

86   Pick, *Faces of Degeneration*, 201.

87   Pick, *Faces of Degeneration*, 185.

88   Pick, *Faces of Degeneration*, 202.

89  Pick, *Faces of Degeneration*, 210.

90  Roger Smith, 'The Physiology of the Will: Mind, Body, and Psychology in the Periodical Literature, 1855–1875', *Science Serialized: Representation of the Sciences in Nineteenth-century Periodicals*, ed. Geoffrey N. Cantor and Sally Shuttleworth (Cambridge: MIT Press, 2004), 83.

91  Sally Shuttleworth, *The Mind of the Child: Child Development in Literature, Science, and Medicine, 1840–1900* (Oxford: Oxford University Press, 2010), ch. 14: 'Child Study in the 1890s'.

92  Hall, *Adolescence*, i, xiii.

93  Hall, *Adolescence*, i, xiv.

94  Arnold Freeman, *Boy Life and Labour: The Manufacture of Inefficiency* (London: P.S. King & Son, 1914), 102, cites Hall, *Adolescence*, ii, 74.

95  Hall, *Adolescence*, i.

96  Hall, *Adolescence*, i, 469. See Chapter VI: 'Sexual Development: Its Dangers and Hygiene in Boys', 411–71.

97  Ransom A Mackie and G. S. Hall, *Education during Adolescence: Based Partly on G. Stanley Hall's Psychology of Adolescence* (New York: E.P. Dutton, 1920), 17, cites Stanley Hall, 'The Ideal School as Based on Child Study', *Forum*, 32 (1901): 24–9.

98  Hall, *Adolescence*, i, 465.

99  Hall, *Adolescence*, i, xiv.

100 Dorothy Ross, 'Hall, Granville Stanley'; www.anb.org/articles/14/14–00254.html; *American National Biography Online*, February 2000, accessed 24 August 2008.

101 G. Stanley Hall, *Youth: Its Education, Regimen and Hygiene* (London: Sidney Appleton, 1908 [1904]).

102 For a discussion of the establishment of the professional discipline of Psychology in Britain, see Harry Hendrick, *Images of Youth: Age, Class and the Male Youth Problem, 1880–1920* (Oxford: Clarendon Press, 1990), 98–101. Michael Roper has shown that new social sciences like sociology and psychology were increasingly influential in the first decades of the twentieth century in Britain. Michael Roper, 'Between Manliness and Masculinity: The "War Generation" and the Psychology of Fear in Britain, 1914–1950', *Journal of British Studies*, 44 (2005): 343–62.

103 Hendrick, *Images of Youth*, 98.

104 J. W. Slaughter, *The Adolescent* (London: Swan Sonnenschein, 1911), 11.

105 Slaughter, *The Adolescent*, 86.

106 Slaughter, *The Adolescent*, 87.

107 Freeman, *Boy Life and Labour*, ix.

108 Urwick, Edward J. *Studies of Boy Life in Our Cities: Written by Various Authors for the Toynbee Trust* (London, 1904), xii.

109 Freeman, *Boy Life and Labour*, 105 (again cites Hall, *Adolescence*, i, 163).

110  C. W. Saleeby, *Harmsworth Self-Educator*, no. 19, 30 August 1906, 2399–240.

111  G. R. Searle, 'Saleeby, Caleb Williams Elijah (1878–1940)', *Oxford Dictionary of National Biography* (Oxford University Press, 2004), www.oxforddnb.com/view/article/47854, accessed 6 February 2013.

112  National Birth-Rate Commission, *The Declining Birth-Rate: Its Causes and Effects* (London: Chapman & Hall, 1916), vi.

113  Lancashire and Cheshire Band of Hope Union Minute Book, 29 October 1913–12 May 1917, M285/1/1/10.

114  C. W. Saleeby, 'Introduction', in Frederick James Gould, *On the Threshold of Sex: A Book for Readers Aged 14–21* (London: C. W. Daniel, 1909), 9–10.

115  C. W. Saleeby, *Health, Strength, and Happiness: A Book of Practical Advice* (London: Grant Richards, 1908), xi.

116  C. W. Saleeby, 'The Human Intellect', *Harmsworth Self-Educator* (20 September 1906): 2548.

117  Thomas Dixon, 'Educating the Emotions from Gradgrind to Goleman', *Research Papers in Education*, 27, no. 4 (2012): 481–95.

118  James Welton, *Psychology of Education* (London: Macmillan, 1911), 42.

119  See, for example, James Sully, 'The New Study of Children', in *Fortnightly Review*, 58 (November 1895): 723–37.

120  James Sully, *Children's Ways* (London: Longmans, Green, and Co., 1897), 134.

121  James Sully, *Studies of Childhood* (London: Longmans, Green, and Co., 1896), 53.

122  Sully, 'The New Study of Children', 727.

123  Sully, *Studies of Childhood*, 266.

124  G. Stanley Hall and M. E. Sadler, eds, *Moral Instruction and Training in Schools*, 95, in Roberts, 'Character in the Mind', 195. Roger Smith has noted that 'discussion of the mind and brain came out of religious and moral preoccupations', 'Physiology of the Will', 84.

125  Freeman, *Boy Life and Labour*, 107.

126  See Chapter 2, note 46.

127  Church of England, *Purity Society Preliminary Report* (London: Harrison and Sons, 1883), 17.

128  Church of England. *Purity Society Preliminary Report*, 18.

129  National Council of Public Morals, 1911–12, 59.

130  National Council of Public Morals, 1911–12, 59.

131  Freeman, *Boy Life and Labour*, 3.

132  Freeman, *Boy Life and Labour*, 232.

133  Physical Deterioration, i, 73.

134  Physical Deterioration, i, 74.

135  Slaughter, *The Adolescent*, 89.

# Conclusion

1   C. W. Saleeby, *Saving the Future: The War and the Coming Race* (National Baby Week Council, 1917), 6.

2   Jenny Holt has said with reference to the school genre that 'from the postwar period onwards, the political and pedagogical confidence of writers was so shaken that it is often hard to identify any coherent message at all.' *Public School Literature, Civic Education and the Politics of Male Adolescence* (Farnham: Ashgate, 2008), 209.

3   RTS Annual Report (1916), 125.

4   Gordon Hewitt, *Let the People Read* (London: Lutterworth Press, 1949), 76–8.

5   RTS Annual Report (1919), 3.

6   RTS Annual Report (1916), 126.

7   RTS Annual Report (1916), 126.

8   *Boys' Friend*, 14, no. 701 (1914): cover.

9   Church of England Temperance Society Annual Report, 1914, 9–10.

10  Rev. Henry Trueman, *Temperance in War-Time* (2nd edn, Westminster: CETS, 1915): back cover.

11  Trueman, *Temperance in War-Time*, 7.

12  'Eric's Resolve', *The Band of Hope Annual* (*Band of Hope Review*), August (1913): 57.

13  'How I Came to Enlist: How Ella, after All, Sent a Man to the Front', *Empire Annual for Girls* (Religious Tract Society, 1915), 87.

14  UK Band of Hope Union, *Annual Reports* (1917–18), 5.

15  UK Band of Hope Union, *Annual Reports* (1918–19), 7.

16  Sara Josephine Baker, *Fighting for Life* (1939; Huntingdon: R.E. Krieger, 1980), 165, in Joanna Bourke, *Dismembering the Male: Men's Bodies, Britain and the Great War* (Chicago: University of Chicago Press), 17.

17  Nicoletta F. Gullace, '*The Blood of Our Sons': Men, Women, and the Renegotiation of Citizenship during the Great War* (New York: Palgrave MacMillan, 2002), 36–50, 68–9.

18  George F. Shee, *The Briton's First Duty* (London: Grant Richards, 1901), 252, quoted in Gullace, '*The Blood of Our Sons*', 41. See also Michael Roper's reminder of the importance of the emotional bonds of family, and the army as a 'domestic institution': *The Secret Battle: Emotional Survival in the Great War* (Manchester: Manchester University Press, 2009), 162.

19  Bourke, *Dismembering the Male*, 163–4. See also Ute Frevert, 'Honor, Gender, and Power: The Politics of Satisfaction in Pre-War Europe', in *An Improbable War: The Outbreak of World War I and European Political Culture before 1914*, ed. Holger Afflerbach and David Stevenson (New York: Berghahn Books, 2007), 248.

20  For the difficulties faced by those men returning to a 'domesticated masculinity'
    see Jessica Meyer, *Men of War: Masculinity and the First World War in Britain*
    (Houndmills: Palgrave MacMillan, 2009), ch. 4.

21  Thomas Hughes, *The Manliness of Christ* (Boston: Houghton, Osgood and
    Company, 1880), 31–3.

22  Hughes, *The Manliness of Christ*, 30. For the Christian context of these passages,
    see Allen J. Frantzen, *Bloody Good: Chivalry, Sacrifice and the Great War* (Chicago:
    Chicago University Press, 2004), 142–4.

23  BBC, 'Student Protests: The Morning after the Night before', www.bbc.co.uk/news/
    uk-11969349, accessed 9 December 2011.

24  Barnardo's, 'Scandal of Britons Who Have Given Up on Children', www.barnardos.
    org.uk/news/media_centre/press_releases.htm?ref=74051, accessed 3 November
    2011.

25  BBC Radio 4, 'Feral Kids and Feckless Parents', broadcast 14 December 2011.

26  BBC, 'England Riots: Broken Society Is Top Priority – Cameron', www.bbc.co.uk/
    news/uk-politics-14524834, accessed 9 December 2011.

27  BBC, 'Were the Riots Caused by Bad Manners?' www.bbc.co.uk/news/uk-
    16035543, accessed 9 December 2011.

28  BBC, 'Archbishop: Rescue Young or Face Further Riots', www.bbc.co.uk/news/uk-
    16039951, accessed 9 December 2011.

29  BBC, 'Riots "Results of Me-First Society" – Bishop', www.bbc.co.uk/news/uk-
    14520074, accessed 9 December 2011.

30  *Guardian*, 'Archbishop of Canterbury says riots will return unless we reach out to
    the young', www.guardian.co.uk/uk/2011/dec/05/riots-return-young-archbishop-
    canterbury?INTCMP=SRCH, accessed 9 December 2011.

31  BBC, 'England Rioters "Poorer, Younger, Less Educated"', www.bbc.co.uk/news/uk-
    15426720, accessed 9 December 2011.

# Bibliography

## Primary sources

### Unpublished and institutional primary sources

#### *Birmingham City Archives*

Quinton Parish Band of Hope (Church of England Temperance Society Juvenile branch), EP 72/16.

#### *British Library, London*

Northcliffe Papers.
Lancashire and Cheshire Band of Hope Union Annual Reports.
NSPCC Annual Reports.

#### *Lambeth Palace Library, London*

Benson Papers.
Church of England Temperance Society, *Annual Reports.*
Church of England Temperance Society, *Executive Minutes.*

#### *Manchester City Archives*

Lancashire and Cheshire Band of Hope Union Collection, GB127.M285.

#### *School of Oriental and African Studies (SOAS), London*

Religious Tract Society, Additional Deposits.
Religious Tract Society, *Annual Reports.*
Religious Tract Society, Copyright Committee Minutes.
Religious Tract Society, Correspondence.
Religious Tract Society, Executive Committee Minutes.
Religious Tract Society, Finance Committee Minutes.
Religious Tract Society, List of New Publications.

### Thomas Fisher Rare Book Library, University of Toronto

Souvenir of Banquet – held at the Fleetway House, the Amalgamated Press Ltd, Thursday, 7 November 1912. For Private Circulation only. G. Pulman, Cranford Press, 1912. duff f 00130.

### West Yorkshire Archive Service (WYAS), Leeds

Leeds and District Band of Hope, Demonstration Leaflets, 1883–1885 with other papers. WYL1476.
Minute Book, Yorkshire Band of Hope Union (Halifax, Bradford, Leeds, Hull, Huddersfield, Dewsbury, York, Batley, Ossett), 1904–5. WYL770.

### WYAS, Bradford

Bradford Harris Street Sion Band of Hope and Temperance Society, Minutes, 28D92.
Girlington, Little Lane Church and Predecessors, Records, WYB10.

### Norfolk Record Office (NRO)

Diss Wesleyan-Methodist Band of Hope abstinence Declaration Booklet, FC 74/173.
Shetford Congregational Temperance Society and Band of Hope Minute Book, 1890–1908, FC 120/98.

## Printed British government documents

### Statutes

Act for Regulating the Sale of Intoxicating Liquors, 35 & 36 Vict., c. 94 (1872).
Children Act, 8 Edw. VII, c. 67 (1908).
Elementary Education Act, 33 & 34 Vict., c. 75 (1870).
Elementary Education Act, 43 & 44 Vict., c. 23 (1880).
Elementary Education Act, 54 & 55 Vict., c. 56 (1891).
Intoxicating Liquors (Sale to Children) Act, 49 & 50 Vict., c. 56 (1886).
Intoxicating Liquors (Sale to Children) Act, 1 Edward VII, c. 27 (1901).
Licensing Act, 2 Edw. VII, c. 28 (1902).
Licensing Act, 4 Edw. VII, c. 23 (1904).
Licensing Act, 35 & 36 Vict., c. 94 (1872).
Metropolitan Police Act, 2 & 3 Vict., c. 47 (1839).
Youthful Offenders Act, 1 Edw. VII, c. 20 (1901).

### Debates

*Hansard Parliamentary Debates*, 3rd series, vol. 204 (1872).
*Hansard Parliamentary Debates*, 4th series, vol. 91 (1901).
*Hansard Parliamentary Debates*, 4th series, vol. 183 (1908).

*Hansard Parliamentary Debates*, 4th series, vol. 186 (1908).
*Hansard Parliamentary Debates*, 4th series, vol. 194 (1908).

## Parliamentary sessions and papers

*British Parliamentary Papers. Social Problems, Drunkenness.* [1834–99] 4 vols. Microform. Shannon: Irish University Press, 1968.
House of Commons. 'A Bill to Amend the Laws Relating to the Sale of Intoxicating Liquors'. *Parliamentary Papers*, 1872. Vol. 2, pp. 303–97.
—. *Report from the Select Committee on Habitual Drunkards Together with the Proceedings of the Committee Minutes of Evidence*, 1872.
—. *Report from the Select Committee on Public Houses*, 1854.
House of Lords. *Report of the Select Committee of the House of Lords Appointed for the Purpose of Inquiring into the Prevalence of Habits of Intemperance*, 1879.
—. Select Committee of the House of Lords on Intemperance. *First, Second, Third, Fourth Report[s], Together with Minutes of Evidence*, 1877. *Final Report*, 1878–9, X (113).
'Intoxicating Liquor Laws Amendment Bill'. *Parliamentary Papers*, 1872. Vol. 2, p. 346.
'Intoxicating Liquor (Licensing Bill)'. *Parliamentary Papers*, 1871. Vol. 2, pp. 489–588.
Joint Select Committee of Enquiry on Lotteries and Indecent Advertisements, Twentieth Century House of Commons Sessional Papers, 1908, vol. 9.
'Permissive Prohibitory Liquor Bill'. *Parliamentary Papers*, 1871. Vol. 4, pp. 449–52.
*Religious Worship, England and Wales, 1851. Parliamentary Papers*, 1852–3. Vol. 79, pp. 188–238, 301.
Report of the Inter-Departmental Committee on Physical Deterioration, Cd. 2175, 1904.
Royal Commission on Liquor Licensing Laws. *Minutes of Evidence*. 9 vols. *Final Report*, 1897–9.
*Spirituous Liquors Licensing Bill. Parliamentary Papers*, 1872. Vols 5–6, pp. 243–342.

## Other government sources

India, Report of the Indian Universities Commission. Simla: Government Central Printing Office, 1902.
India, Indian Education Commission, 1882. Calcutta: Superintendent of Government Printing, India, 1883.

## Newspapers and journals

### Amalgamated Press

*Answers to Correspondents.*
*Boys' Friend.*

*Boys' Herald.*
*Boys' Realm.*
*Champion.*
*Comic Cuts.*
*Harmsworth Self-Educator.*
*Home Circle.*
*Illustrated Chips.*
*Marvel.*
*Sunday Circle.*
*Sunday Companion.*

## Band of Hope

*Band of Hope Annual.*
*Band of Hope Review.*
*Borough of Marylebone and North-West Middlesex Band of Hope Union Quarterly Manual.*
*Comrades: A Band of Hope, Temperance and Family Magazine. Journal of the Ashton under Lyne & District United Temperance Association.*
*Every Band of Hope Boy's Reciter: Containing Original Recitations, Dialogues, &C., Written Expressly for Bands of Hope.*
*Halfpenny Illustrated Temperance Reciter.*
*Marylebone Band of Hope Monthly Visitor.*
*Onward.*
*Our Boys and Girls Band of Hope Journal,* to aid young people in Band of Hope and temperance work.
*Quarterly Manual and Band of Hope Reporter for Greenwich and West Kent.*
*Sion Chapel Band of Hope Monthly Visitor.*
*Workers Onward: The Organ of the Lancashire and Cheshire Band of Hope & Temperance Union.*

## Church of England Temperance Society

*Boys' & Girls' Companion: An Illustrated Magazine for Boys and Girls.*
*Church of England Illustrated Temperance Magazine.*
*Church of England Temperance Chronicle.*
*Church of England Temperance Tracts.*
*Young Crusader.*
*Young Standard Bearer.*

## Religious Tract Society

*Boy's Own Paper.*
*Chatterbox.*

*Children's Friend.*

*Child's Companion or Sunday Scholar's Reward.*

*Church Friendly.*

*Empire Annual for Girls.*

*Girl's Own Paper.*

*Leisure Hour.*

*Religious Tract Society Record of Work at Home and Abroad.*

*Seed Time and Harvest: Records of Religious Tract Society Work among the Nations of over 250 Languages.*

*Sunday at Home.*

*Tract Magazine and Christian Miscellany.*

## Socialist papers

*Clarion.*

*Daily Herald: The Labour Daily Newspaper.*

*Labour Leader: A Weekly Record of Social and Political Progress.*

*Labour Prophet.*

*Yorkshire Factory Times.*

*Young Socialist: A Magazine of Love and Service.*

## Other

*Abstainer: An Illustrated Temperance Monthly.*

*All the Year Round: A Weekly Journal Conducted by Charles Dickens.*

*Chums.*

*Child's Companion or Sunday Scholar's Reward.*

*Children's Friend. A Magazine for Boys and Girls at Home and School.*

*Child's Guardian: The Official Organ of the National Society for the Prevention of Cruelty to Children.*

*Family Friend.*

*Fortnightly Review.*

*Inspector's Quarterly.*

*Lancet.*

*Middlesex Temperance Chronicle, A Quarterly Record of Good Templar, Band of Hope and Other Temperance Work in the County of Middlesex.*

*Mining Magazine.*

*Zoophilist.*

## Published primary sources

Anon. *The Band of Hope Blue Book: A Manual of Instruction and Training, Preparing for Citizenship.* Westminster: UK Band of Hope Union, 1942.

Anon. *Church of England Temperance Society Annual Examination and Inter-Diocesan Competition, 1914–1915.* Westminster: Church of England Temperance Society, 1914.

—. *The Proceedings of the Twelfth International Congress on Alcoholism.* London: Paternoster House, 1909.

—. *The Publisher's Circular: General Record of British and Foreign Literature.* London: Sampson Low, Marston, Searle, & Rivington, 1879.

—. *Socialist Sunday Schools: A Manual.* Gateshead: National Council of British Socialist Sunday Schools, 1924.

—. *The Socialist Sunday Schools Song Book.* Glasgow: S.L. Press, 1917 [1911].

A. D. *Seed-Time and Harvest. A Tale of the Punjab.* 2nd edn. London: Christian Literature Society for India, 1899.

Baden-Powell, Robert. *Rovering to Success: A Guide for Young Manhood.* 1922; London: Herbert Jenkins, 1959.

—. *Scouting for Boys.* London: C.A. Pearson, 1908.

Band of Hope Review Office. *Speakers' Self-Help: Outlines of Blackboard and Other Addresses for Band of Hope Meetings.* London: Richard J. James, n.d.

Budden, J. H. *Prasanna and Kamini: The Story of a Young Hindu.* London: Religious Tract Society, 1885.

Church of England Purity Society. *Preliminary Report.* London, 1883.

Church of England Temperance Society. *Short Manual for the Formation and Guidance of Branches.* London: Church of England Temperance Society, 1910.

Clarke, H. F. *How to Avoid Leakage between the Band of Hope and the Adult Society.* London: Church of England Temperance Society, 1894.

—. *The Sunday School in Relation to the Band of Hope.* London: Church of England Temperance Publication Depot, 1892.

Darwin, Charles. *The Descent of Man, and Selection in Relation to Sex* [2nd edn, 1879]. London: Penguin, 2004.

Davis, C. A. *The Relation of Sunday School Teachers to the Band of Hope Movement.* London: UK Band of Hope Union, 1894.

Diggle, J. R. 'Temperance in the Schools', in *Alcohol and Childhood: A Report of Two Conferences*, Church of England Temperance Society (Junior Division). London: Church of England Temperance Society, 1891.

Dilnot, George (compiler). *Romance of the Amalgamated Press.* London: Amalgamated Press, 1925.

Dyer, Alfred S. *Plain Words to Young Men upon an Avoided Subject.* London: Dyer Brothers, n.d.

—. *Safeguards to Moral Purity and Facts That Men Ought to Know.* London: Dyer Brothers, n.d. [1890s].

Eccles, William McAdam. *The Relation of Alcohol to Physical Deterioration and National Efficiency. Eighth Lees and Raper Memorial Lecture.* London: Church of England Temperance Society, 1908.

Fielding, W. 'What Shall I Do with My Son?' *The Nineteenth Century*, April (1883): 578–86.

Forsaith, Miss. 'The Secret of Successful Work' (paper read at a conference of the Lancashire and Cheshire Band of Hope Union, held on 25 April 1885). London: S.W. Partridge & Co.; Manchester: Onward Publishing Office.

Freeman, Arnold. *Boy Life and Labour: The Manufacture of Inefficiency*. London: P.S. King & Son, 1914.

Galton, Francis, *Inquiries into Human Faculty and Its Development*. London: Macmillan, 1883.

Garrett, Charles. *Lead Them Straight*. London: UK Band of Hope Union, 1894.

Glenn, W. Frank. 'Impotence in the Male', *Southern Practitioner*, June (1892).

Gissing, George. *The Odd Women* [1893]. Oxford: Oxford University Press, 2000.

Goss, Charles Frederic. *Husband, Wife and Home*. With intro by Sylvanus Stall. London: Vir Publishing, 1905.

Gosse, Edmund. *Father and Son*. London: William Heinemann, 1907.

Gould, James. *On the Threshold of Sex: A Book for Readers Aged 14–21*. London, 1909.

Green, Samuel G. *The Story of the Religious Tract Society for One Hundred Years*. London: Religious Tract Society, 1899.

Hall, George Scarr. *The New Woman*. London: Houlston and Sons, c. 1900.

Hall, Granville Stanley. *Adolescence: Its Psychology and Its Relations to Physiology, Anthropology, Sociology, Sex, Crime, Religion and Education*. 2 vols. New York: D. Appleton, 1904.

—. *Youth: Its Education, Regimen and Hygiene*. London: Sidney Appleton, 1908 [1904].

Hercod, R. 'La protection de l'enfant dans la lutte contre l'alcoolisme', *The Proceedings of the Twelfth International Congress on Alcoholism*. London: National Temperance League, 1909.

Hughes, Thomas. *Tom Brown's Schooldays* [1857]. London: Collins' Clear-Type Press, n.d.

—. *The Manliness of Christ* [1879]. Boston: Houghton, Osgood and Company, 1880.

Inglis, M. K. *The Children's Charter: A Sketch of the Scope and Main Provisions of the Children Act, 1908*. London: T. Nelson, 1909.

James, H. T. *Industrial Bands of Hope*. London: Church of England Temperance Society, 1891.

Johnson, Harriet M. *Our Future Citizens*. London: Church of England Temperance Society, 1899.

Key, Ellen. *Barnets århundrade* [The Century of the Child]. Stockholm, 1900.

Kirton, J. W. *Happy Homes and How to Make Them; or, Counsels on Love, Courtship, and Marriage*. London: John Kempster [first published, 1870; Kempster editions in 1874, 1879 and 1897.].

Knowles, J. *Our Duty to India and Indian Illiterates*. London and Madras: Christian Literature Society for India, 1910.

Knowles, S. *Every Band of Hope Boy's Reciter: Containing Original Recitations, Dialogues, &c., Written Expressly for Bands of Hope.* Manchester: J. Brook, c.1903.

Lees, W. Nassau. *Indian Musalmans.* London: Williams and Norgate, 1871.

Mackie, Ransom A. and G. S. Hall. *Education during Adolescence: Based Partly on G. Stanley Hall's Psychology of Adolescence.* New York: E.P. Dutton, 1920.

Meyer, F. B. 'An Array of Facts', *Religious Tract Society* (1899).

Mitchell, John M. *Letters to Indian Youth on the Evidences of the Christian Religion: With a Brief Examination of the Evidences of Hinduism, Pārsīism and Muhammadanism.* Bombay: Bombay Tract and Book Society, 1857.

Murdoch, John. *Hints on Government Education in India.* Madras: Foster, 1873.

—. *The Indian Student's Manual: Hints on Studies, Moral Conduct, Religious Duties and Success in Life.* Madras: Christian Vernacular Society, 1875.

—. *The Indian Young Man in the Battle of Life. Hints to Students on leaving College.* London & Madras: Christian Literature Society for India, 1903.

—. *The Training of Children for Indian Parents.* London and Madras: Christian Literature Society for India, 1897.

National Birth-Rate Commission, *The Declining Birth-Rate: Its Causes and Effects.* London: Chapman & Hall, 1916.

Norris, Mrs St Clare. 'Watchman Awake! Save the Children!' Pamphlet (1911).

Parr, Robert J. *Benjamin Waugh: An Appreciation* [1909].

—. *Wilful Waste: The Nation's Responsibility for Its Children.* London: NSPCC, 1910.

Pemberton, Max. *Lord Northcliffe: A Memoir.* London: Hodder and Stoughton, 1922.

Saleeby, C. W. *Health, Strength, and Happiness: A Book of Practical Advice.* London: Grant Richards, 1908.

—. *Saving the Future: The War and the Coming Race.* National Baby Week Council, 1917.

Salmon, E. *Juvenile Literature As It Is.* London, 1888.

Samuel, Herbert. *Memoirs.* London: Cresset Press, 1945.

Satyanatha, Samuel. *Sketches of Indian Christians.* London and Madras: Christian Literature Society for India, 1896.

Shee, George F. *The Briton's First Duty.* London: Grant Richards, 1901.

Slaughter, J. W. *The Adolescent.* London: Swan Sonnenschein, 1911.

Smiles, Samuel. *Self-Help; With Illustrations of Character and Conduct.* London: John Murray, 1859.

Smith, Adam. *The Theory of Moral Sentiments* [1759], ed. Ryan Patrick Hanley. New York: Penguin, 2009.

Smith, Frederic, ed. *The Band of Hope Jubilee Volume.* London: UK Band of Hope Union, 1897.

—. 'The Juvenile Temperance Organisations in Great Britain and Ireland', in *Temperance in All Nations, History of the Cause in all Countries of the Globe, Together with Papers and Essays, Addresses and Discussions of the World's Temperance Congress Held by the National Temperance Society, Chicago, June, 1893* [World's Temperance Congress, 1893], ed. J. N. Stearns. New York: National Temperance Society, 1893.

Stall, Sylvanus. *Parental Honesty*. London and Philadelphia: Vir Publishing, 1905.

—. *What a Young Boy Ought to Know*. London: Vir Publishing, 1909 [1897].

—. *What a Young Husband Ought to Know*. London: Vir Publishing, 1897.

—. *What a Young Man Ought to Know*. London: Vir Publishing, 1909 [1897].

—. *With the Children on Sundays: Through the Eye-Gate and Ear-Gate into the City of Child-Soul*. Philadelphia: Uplift Publishing, 1911.

Sully, James. *Children's Ways*. London: Longmans, Green, and Co., 1897.

—. *Studies of Childhood*. London: Longmans, Green, and Co., 1896.

Tonks, C. F. 'My Duty, to God, to My Country, to My Home, to Myself', in *CETS Annual Examination and Inter-Diocesan Competition* (1914–15).

Trueman, Rev. Henry, *Temperance in War-Time*. 2nd edn, Westminster: Church of England Temperance Society, 1915.

UK Band of Hope Union. *Annual Reports*. London: UK Band of Hope, 1914.

—. *The Band of Hope Blue Book: A Manual of Instruction and Training*. London: UK Band of Hope Union, 1942.

—. Report of School Scheme [annual].

Urwick, Edward J. *Studies of Boy Life in Our Cities: Written by Various Authors for the Toynbee Trust*. London, 1904.

Vecki, Victor G. *Sexual Impotence*. 4th edn. Philadelphia and London: W.B. Saunders, 1912.

Wakely, Charles. *Bands of Hope and Sunday Schools*. London: UK Band of Hope Union, 1894.

—. *Essentials in Band of Hope Meetings*. London: UK Band of Hope Union, 1891.

—. *The Temperance Manual for the Young*. London: UK Band of Hope Union, 1891.

—. *Temperance Teaching in Schools throughout the World*. London: UK Band of Hope Union, n.d.

Welton, James. *Psychology of Education*. London: Macmillan, 1911.

White Cross League. *Annual Reports* (1910–11).

Williamson, David. *From Boyhood to Manhood*. London: Religious Tract Society, 1910.

## Secondary sources

### Books and articles

Alderson, David. *Mansex Fine: Religion, Manliness and Imperialism in Nineteenth-Century British Culture*. Manchester: Manchester University Press, 1998.

Allender, Tim. 'Anglican Evangelism in North India and the Punjabi Missionary Classroom: The Failure to Educate "the Masses", 1860–77', *History of Education*, 32, no. 3 (2003): 273–88.

—. 'Surrendering a Colonial Domain: Educating North India, 1854–1890', *History of Education*, 36, no. 1 (2007): 45–63.

Altholz, Josef. *The Religious Press in Britain, 1760–1900*. New York: Greenwood Press, 1989.

Ariès, Philippe. *Centuries of Childhood*. London: Cape, 1962.

Avery, Gillian. *Childhood's Pattern: A Study of Heroes and Heroines of Children's Fiction, 1790–1950*. London: Hodder and Stoughton, 1975.

Baker, Gordon. 'The Romantic and Radical Nature of the 1870 Education Act', *History of Education*, 30, no. 3 (2001): 211–32.

Banerjee, Swapna M. 'Children's Literature in Nineteenth Century India: Some Reflections and Thoughts', in *Stories for Children, Histories of Childhood* (*GRAAT*, 2007): 337–51.

—. *Men, Women, and Domestics: Articulating Middle-Class Identity in Colonial Bengal*. New Delhi: Oxford University Press, 2008.

Bantock, G. H. 'Educating the Emotions: An Historical Perspective', *British Journal of Educational Studies*, 34, no. 2 (1986): 122–41.

Barker-Benfield, G. J. *The Culture of Sensibility: Sex and Society in Eighteenth-Century Britain*. Chicago and London: University of Chicago Press, 1992.

Barthes, Roland. *The Rustle of Language*. New York: Farrar Straus & Giroux, 1986.

Beaven, Brad and John Griffiths. 'Creating the Exemplary Citizen: The Changing Notion of Citizenship in Britain 1870–1939', *Contemporary British History*, 22, no. 2 (2008), 203–25.

Behlmer, George K. 'Character Building and the English Family: Continuities in Social Casework, ca. 1870–1930', in *Singular Continuities: Tradition, Nostalgia, and Identity in Modern British Culture*, ed. George K. Behlmer and Fred M. Leventhal. Stanford: Stanford University Press, 2000.

—. *Child Abuse and Moral Reform in England, 1870–1908*. Stanford: Stanford University Press, 1982.

—. *Friends of the Family: The English Home and Its Guardians, 1850–1940*. Stanford: Stanford University Press, 1998.

Bellenoit, Hayden J. A. *Missionary Education and Empire in Late Colonial India, 1860–1920*. London: Pickering & Chatto, 2007.

—. 'Missionary Education, Religion and Knowledge in India, c.1880–1915', *Modern Asian Studies*, 41, no. 2 (2007): 369–94.

Berry, Laura C. *The Child, the State and the Victorian Novel*. Charlottesville: University Press of Virginia, 1999.

Bibbings, L. 'Images of Manliness: The Portrayal of Soldiers and Conscientious Objectors in the Great War', *Social and Legal Studies*, 12 (2003): 335–58.

Boddice, Rob. 'The Affective Turn: Historicising the Emotions', in *Psychology and History: Interdisciplinary Explorations*, ed. Cristian Tileagă and Jovan Byford. Cambridge: Cambridge University Press, 2014.

—. 'In Loco Parentis? Public-School Authority, Cricket and Manly Character, 1855–62', *Gender and Education*, online edition, 4 July (2008).

—. 'Manliness and the "Morality of Field Sports": E. A. Freeman and Anthony Trollope, 1869–71', *The Historian*, 70, no. 1 (2008): 1–29.

Bose, Pradip Kumar. 'Sons of the Nation, Childrearing in the New Family', in *Texts of Power: Emerging Disciplines in Colonial Bengal*, ed. Partha Chatterjee. Minneapolis: University of Minnesota, 1995.

Bourke, Joanna. *Dismembering the Male: Men's Bodies, Britain and the Great War*. Chicago: University of Chicago Press, 1996.

—. 'Fear and Anxiety: Writing about Emotion in Modern History', *History Workshop Journal*, no. 55 (2003): 111–33.

Boyd, Kelly. 'Exemplars and Ingrates: Imperialism and the Boys' Story Paper, 1880–1930', *Historical Research*, 67 (1994): 143–55.

—. '"Half-Caste Bob" or Race and Caste in the Late-Victorian Boy's Story Paper', in *Negotiating India in the Nineteenth Century Media*, ed. David Finkelstein and Douglas Beers. Basingstoke and New York: St. Martin's Press, 2000.

—. 'Knowing Your Place: The Tension of Manliness in Boys' Story Papers, 1918–39', in *Manful Assertions: Masculinities in England since 1800*, ed. Michael Roper and John Tosh. London: Routledge, 1991.

—. *Manliness and the Boys' Story Paper in Britain: A Cultural History, 1855–1940*. New York: Palgrave Macmillan, 2003.

Bradley, Ian. *The Call to Seriousness: The Evangelical Impact on the Victorians*. New York: MacMillan, 1976.

Bradstock, Andrew, ed. *Masculinity and Spirituality in Victorian Culture*. New York: St. Martin's Press, 2000.

Brantlinger, Patrick. *Rule of Darkness: British Literature and Imperialism, 1830–1914*. Ithaca: Cornell University Press, 1988.

Bratton, J. S. *The Impact of Victorian Children's Fiction*. London: Croom Helm, 1981.

—. 'Of England, Home and Duty: The Image of England in Victorian and Edwardian Juvenile Fiction', in *Imperialism and Popular Culture*, ed. John M. MacKenzie. Manchester: Manchester University Press, 1986. 73–93.

Bristow, Joseph. *Empire Boys: Adventures in a Man's World*. London: HarperCollins, 1991.

Broughton, Trev Lynn and Helen Rogers. *Gender and Fatherhood in the Nineteenth Century*. Houndmills: Palgrave MacMillan, 2007.

Brown, Callum. *The Death of Christian Britain: Understanding Secularisation, 1800–2000*. London: Routledge, 2001.

Buettner, Elizabeth. *Empire Families: Britons and Late Imperial India*. Oxford: Oxford University Press, 2004.

—. 'Fatherhood Real, Imagined, Denied: British Men in Imperial India', in *Gender and Fatherhood in the Nineteenth Century*, ed. Helen Rogers and Trev Broughton. London: Palgrave Macmillan, 2007.

—. 'Parent-Child Separations and Colonial Careers: The Talbot Family Correspondence in the 1880s and 1890s', in *Childhood in Question, Children, Parents and the State*, ed. Anthony Fletcher and Stephen Hussey. Manchester: Manchester University Press, 1999.

Burdett, Carolyn. 'Is Empathy the End of Sentimentality?', *Journal of Victorian Culture*, 16 (2011): 259–74.

Callan, Eamonn. *Creating Citizens: Political Education and Liberal Democracy*. Oxford: Clarendon Press, 1997.

Carroll, Lucy. 'Origins of the Kayastha Temperance Movement', *Indian Economic Social History Review*, 11 (1974): 432–47.

—. 'The Temperance Movement in India: Politics and Social Reform', *Modern Asian Studies*, 10, no. 3 (1976): 417–47.

Carter, Philip. *Men and the Emergence of Polite Society, Britain 1660–1800*. Harlow: Longman, 2001.

Chakrabarty, Dipesh. 'The Difference – Deferral of (A) Colonial Modernity: Public Debates on Domesticity in British Bengal', *History Workshop Journal*, 36, no. 1 (1993): 1–34.

Chandra, Sudhir. 'The Loyalty of Educated Indians to British Rule', in *Continuing Dilemmas. Understanding Social Consciousness*. Delhi: Tulika, 2002.

Childs, Michael. *Labour's Apprentices: Working-Class Lads in Late Victorian and Edwardian England*. Montreal: McGill-Queen's University Press, 1992.

Christ, Carol. 'Victorian Masculinity and the Angel in the House', in *A Widening Sphere: Changing Roles of Victorian Women*, ed. M. Vicinus. Bloomington: Indiana University Press, 1977.

Clark, Anna. 'The Rhetoric of Chartist Domesticity: Gender, Language, and Class in the 1830s and 1840s', *Journal of British Studies*, 31 (1992): 62–88.

Cohen, Michèle. *Fashioning Masculinity: National Identity and Language in the Eighteenth Century*. London: Routledge, 1996.

—. 'Manliness, Effeminacy and the French: Gender and the Construction of National Character in Eighteenth-Century England', in *English Masculinities, 1660–1800*, ed. Tim Hitchcock and Michèle Cohen. London: Longman, 1999.

Collini, Stefan. 'The Idea of "Character" in Victorian Political Thought', *Transactions of the Royal Historical Society*, 35, no. 5 (1985): 29–50.

Connell, R. W. *Masculinities*. Berkeley: University of California Press, 1995.

Cooter, Roger, ed. *In the Name of the Child: Health and Welfare, 1880–1940*. Oxfordshire: Routledge, 2012.

Coppock, David A. 'Respectability as a Prerequisite of Moral Character: The Social and Occupational Mobility of Pupil Teachers in the Late Nineteenth and Early Twentieth Centuries', *History of Education*, 26, no. 2 (1997): 165–86.

Cox, Jack. *Take a Cold Tub, Sir! The Story of the Boy's Own Paper*. Guildford: Lutterworth Press, 1982.

Cunningham, Hugh. 'Childhood Histories', *Journal of Victorian Culture*, 9, no. 1 (2004): 90–6.

—. *Children and Childhood in Western Society since 1500*. Harlow: Longman, 1995.

Cutt, Margaret Nancy. *Ministering Angels: A Study of Nineteenth-Century Evangelical Writing for Children*. Wormley, Hertfordshire: Five Owls Press, 1979.

David, M. D. 'The Missionary Muscular Culture in Modern India', in *Discoveries, Missionary Expansion and Asian Cultures*, ed. T. R. De Souza. New Delhi: Concept, 1994.

Davidoff, Leonore and Catherine Hall. *Family Fortunes: Men and Women of the English Middle Class, 1780–1850*. London: Hutchinson, 1987.

Davies, Jonathan. 'Education for Citizenship: The Joseph Rowntree Charitable Trust and the Educational Settlement Movement', *History of Education*, 32, no. 3 (2003): 303–18.

Davin, Anna. *Growing Up Poor: Home, School and Street in London, 1870–1914*. London: Rivers Oram, 1996.

—. 'Waif Stories in Late Nineteenth-Century England', *History Workshop Journal*, 52 (2001): 67–98.

—. 'What Is a Child?' in *Childhood in Question, Children, Parents and the State*, ed. Anthony Fletcher and Stephen Hussey. Manchester: Manchester University Press, 1999.

Dawson, Graham. *Soldier Heroes: British Adventure, Empire and the Imagining of Masculinity*. New York: Routledge, 1994.

Delap, Lucy, Ben Griffin and Abigail Wills, eds. *The Politics of Domestic Authority in Britain since 1800*. Houndmills: Palgrave MacMillan, 2009.

Digby, Ann and Peter Searby. *Children, School and Society in Nineteenth-century England*. London: MacMillan, 1981.

Dixon, Diana. 'From Instruction to Amusement: Attitudes of Authority in Children's Periodicals before 1914', *Victorian Periodicals Review*, 19 (Summer 1986): 63–7.

Dixon, Thomas. 'Educating the Emotions from Gradgrind to Goleman', *Research Papers in Education*, 27, no. 4 (2012): 481–95.

—. *From Passions to Emotions: The Creation of a Secular Psychological Category*. Cambridge: Cambridge University Press, 2006.

—. *The Invention of Altruism: Making Moral Meanings in Victorian Britain*. Oxford: Oxford University Press, 2008.

Doolittle, Megan. 'Close Relations? Bringing Together Gender and Family in English History', *Gender & History*, 11, no. 3 (1999): 542–54.

—. 'Religious Belief and the Protection of Children in Nineteenth-Century English Families', in *Gender and Fatherhood in the Nineteenth Century*, ed. Trev Lynn Broughton and Helen Rogers. Houndmills: Palgrave MacMillan, 2007.

Dror, Yuval. 'Zionist Cultural Transfer through Ties between Schools and Informal Education Frameworks in the British Mandate Period (1918–1948)', *History of Education Review*, 26 (1997): 56–71.

Drotner, Kirsten. *English Children and Their Magazines, 1751–1945*. New Haven: Yale University Press, 1988.

Dudink, Stefan, Karen Hagemann and Anna Clark, eds. *Representing Masculinity: Male Citizenship in Modern Western Culture*. New York: Palgrave Macmillan, 2007.

Dunae, Patrick. 'Boys' Literature and the Idea of Empire, 1870–1914', *Victorian Studies*, 24 (Autumn 1980): 105–21.

—. 'The Boy's Own Paper: Origins and Editorial Policies', *Private Library*, 2nd series, 9, no. 4 (1976): 123–58.

—. 'Education, Emigration and Empire: The Colonial College 1887–1905', in *'Benefits Bestowed'? Education and British Imperialism*, ed. J. A. Mangan. Manchester: Manchester University Press, 1988.

—. 'Penny Dreadfuls: Late Nineteenth Century Boys' Literature and Crime', *Victorian Studies*, 22 (1979): 133–50.

Dyhouse, Carol. *Girls Growing Up in Late Victorian and Edwardian England*. London: Routledge & Kegan Paul, 1981.

Ecclestone, Kathryn. 'From Emotional and Psychological Well-Being to Character Education: Challenging Policy Discourses of Behavioural Science and "Vulnerability"', *Research Papers in Education*, 27, no. 4 (2012): 463–80.

Elbourne, Elizabeth. 'Domesticity and Dispossession: The Ideology of "Home" and the British Construction of the "Primitive" from the Eighteenth to the Early Nineteenth Century', in *Deep HiStories: Gender and Colonialism in Southern Africa*, ed. Wendy Woodward, Patricia Hayes and Gary Minkley. Amsterdam: Rodopi, 2002.

Ellis, Heather and Jessica Meyer, eds. *Masculinity and the Other: Historical Perspectives*. Newcastle upon Tyne: Cambridge Scholars Publishing, 2009.

Erikson, Erik H. *Childhood and Society*. 1950; New York and London: W.W. Norton, 1985.

Fahrmeir, Andreas. *Citizenship: The Rise and Fall of a Modern Concept*. New Haven and London: Yale University Press, 2007.

Fass, Paula. 'The World Is at Our Door: Why Historians of Children and Childhood Should Open Up', *Journal of the History of Childhood and Youth*, 1, no. 1 (2008): 11–31.

Flegel, Monica. 'Changing Faces: The NSPCC and the Use of Photography in the Construction of Cruelty to Children', *Victorian Periodicals Review*, 39, no. 1 (2006): 1–20.

—. *Conceptualizing Cruelty to Children in Nineteenth-Century England: Literature, Representation, and the NSPCC*. Surrey: Ashgate, 2009.

Forrester, W. *Great-Grandmama's Weekly: A Celebration of the 'Girl's Own Paper', 1880–1901*. Guildford: Lutterworth Press, 1980.

Francis, Martin. 'The Domestication of the Male? Recent Research on Nineteenth and Twentieth-Century British Masculinity', *Historical Journal*, 45 (2002): 637–52.

Frantzen, Allen J. *Bloody Good: Chivalry, Sacrifice and the Great War*. Chicago: Chicago University Press, 2004.

Freeden, Michael. 'Civil Society and the Good Citizen: Competing Conceptions of Citizenship in Twentieth-Century Britain', in *Civil Society in British History:*

*Ideas, Identities, Institutions*, ed. Jose Harris. Oxford: Oxford University Press, 2003.

Frevert, Ute. *Emotions in History: Lost and Found*. Budapest: Central European University Press, 2011.

—. 'Honor, Gender, and Power: The Politics of Satisfaction in Pre-War Europe', in *An Improbable War: The Outbreak of World War I and European Political Culture before 1914*, ed. Holger Afflerbach and David Stevenson. New York: Berghahn Books, 2007.

Galbraith, Gretchen. *Reading Lives: Reconstructing Childhood, Books, and Schools in Britain, 1870–1920*. New York: St. Martin's Press, 1997.

Gammerl, Benno, ed. *Emotional Styles – Concepts and Challenges*, special issue of *Rethinking History*, 16 (2012).

Gay, Peter. 'The Manliness of Christ', in *Religion and Irreligion in Victorian Society*, ed. R. W. Davis and R. J. Helmstadter. London: Routledge, 1992.

Ghosh, Suresh Chandra. '"English in Taste, in Opinions, in Words and Intellect": Indoctrinating the Indian through Textbook, Curriculum and Education', in *The Imperial Curriculum*, ed. J. A. Mangan. New York: Routledge, 1993.

Gilbert, Alan D. *The Making of Post-Christian Britain: A History of the Secularization of Modern Society*. London: Longman, 1980.

Gilbert, Arthur N. 'Masturbation and Insanity: Henry Maudsley and the Ideology of Sexual Repression', *Albion*, 12, no. 3 (1980): 268–82.

Gill, S. 'How Muscular Was Victorian Christianity? Thomas Hughes and the Cult of Christian Manliness Reconsidered', in *Gender and Christian Religion*, ed. R. N. Swanson. Woodbridge, Suffolk: Boydell Press, 1998.

Gillis, John R. 'Ritualization of Middle-Class Family Life in Nineteenth Century Britain', *International Journal of Politics, Culture, and Society*, 3, no. 2 (1989): 213–35.

—. 'Transitions to Modernity', in *The Palgrave Handbook of Childhood Studies*, ed. Jens Qvortrup, William A. Corsaro and Michael-Sebastian Honig. Basingstoke: Palgrave Macmillan, 2011.

—. *A World of Their Own Making: Myth, Ritual, and the Quest for Family Values*. New York: Basic Books, 1996.

—. *Youth and History*. New York: Academic Press, 1974.

Gordon, Eleanor and Gwyneth Nair. 'Domestic Fathers and the Victorian Parental Role', *Women's History Review*, 15, no. 4 (2006): 551–9.

Gorham, Deborah. *The Victorian Girl and the Feminine Ideal*. Bloomington: Indiana University Press, 1982.

Gorman, Daniel. *Imperial Citizenship: Empire and the Question of Belonging*. Manchester: Manchester University Press, 2006.

Gullace, Nicoletta F. *'The Blood of Our Sons' Men, Women, and the Renegotiation of Citizenship during the Great War*. New York: Palgrave MacMillan, 2002.

Gutzke, David W. '"The Cry of the Children". The Edwardian Campaign against Maternal Drinking', *British Journal of Addiction*, 79 (1984): 71–84.

Haggis, Jane and Margaret Allen. 'Imperial Emotions: Affective Communities of Mission in British Protestant Women's Missionary Publications c1880–1920', *Journal of Social History*, 41, no. 3 (2008): 691–716.

Hall, Catherine. *Civilising Subjects: Metropole and Colony in the English Imagination, 1830–1867*. Chicago: University of Chicago Press, 2002.

—. 'Making Colonial Subjects: Education in the Age of Empire', *History of Education*, 37, no. 6 (2008): 773–87.

Hall, Donald, ed. *Muscular Christianity: Embodying the Victorian Age*. Cambridge: Cambridge University Press, 1994.

Hall, Lesley A. 'Birds, Bees and General Embarrassment: Sex Education in Britain, from Social Purity to Section 28', in *Public or Private Education?: Lessons from History*, ed. Richard Aldrich. Woburn education series; London: Woburn, 2004.

—. 'Hauling Down the Double Standard: Feminism, Social Purity and Sexual Science in Late Nineteenth-Century Britain', *Gender & History*, 16, no. 1 (2004): 36–56.

Hammerton, A. James. 'Pooterism or Partnership?: Marriage and Masculine Identity in the Lower Middle Class, 1870–1920', *Journal of British Studies*, 38, no. 3 (1999): 291–321.

Harris, Jose. *Private Lives, Public Spirit: Britain 1870–1914*. London: Penguin, 1994.

Harrison, Brian. *Drink and the Victorians: The Temperance Question in England, 1815–1872*. Pittsburgh: University of Pittsburgh Press, 1971.

Heater, Derek. *Citizenship in Britain: A History*. Edinburgh: Edinburgh University Press, 2006.

Heath, Deana. *Purifying Empire: Obscenity and the Politics of Moral Regulation in Britain, India and Australia*. Cambridge: Cambridge University Press, 2010.

Heathorn, Stephen. *For Home, Country and Race: Constructing Gender, Class and Englishness in the Elementary School, 1880–1914*. Toronto: University of Toronto Press, 2000.

Heathorn, Stephen and David Greenspoon, 'Organizing Youth for Partisan Politics in Britain, 1918–c.1932', *Historian*, 68, no. 1 (2006): 89–119.

Hendrick, Harry. *Children, Childhood, and English Society, 1880–1990*. Cambridge: Cambridge University Press, 1997.

—. *Images of Youth: Age, Class and the Male Youth Problem, 1880–1920*. Oxford: Clarendon Press, 1990.

Heredia, Rudolf C. 'Education and mission: The School as an Agent of Evangelisation in India', in *Discoveries, Missionary Expansion and Asian Cultures*, ed. Teotonio R. De Souza. New Delhi: Concept, 1994.

Hewitt, Gordon. *Let the People Read*. London: Lutterworth Press, 1949.

Hilton, Matthew. 'Leisure, Politics, and the Consumption of Tobacco in Britain since the Nineteenth Century', in *Histories of Leisure*, ed. Rudy Koshar. Oxford: Berg, 2002.

—. *Smoking in British Popular Culture, 1800–2000: Perfect Pleasures*. Manchester: Manchester University Press, 2000.

—. '"Tabs", "Fags" and the "Boy Labour Problem" in Late Victorian and Edwardian England', *Journal of Social History*, 28 (1995): 587–607.

Hitchcock, Tim and Michèle Cohen, eds. *English Masculinities, 1660–1800*. London: Longman, 1999.

Hogan, Anne and Andrew Bradstock, eds. *Women of Faith in Victorian Culture: Reassessing the Angel of the House*. New York: St. Martin's Press, 1998.

Holt, Jenny. *Public School Literature, Civic Education and the Politics of Male Adolescence*. Farnham: Ashgate, 2008.

—. 'The Textual Formations of Adolescence in Turn-of-the-Century Youth Periodicals: The *Boy's Own Paper* and Eton College Ephemeral Magazines', *Victorian Periodicals Review*, 35 (2002): 63–88.

Honey, J R de S. *Tom Brown's Universe: The Development of the Victorian Public School*. London: Millington, 1977.

Howell, Sara and Jane Humphries. 'The Origins and Expansion of the Male Breadwinner Family: The Case of Nineteenth Century Britain', *International Review of Social History*, 42 (supplement 5) (1997): 25–64.

Huggins, Mike J. 'More Sinful Pleasures? Leisure, Respectability and the Male Middle Classes in Victorian England', *Journal of Social History*, 33, no. 3 (2000): 585–600.

Hunt, Alan, 'The Great Masturbation Panic and the Discourses of Moral Regulation in Nineteenth- and Early Twentieth-Century Britain', *Journal of the History of Sexuality*, 8, no. 4 (1998): 575–615.

Inglis, Fred. *The Promise of Happiness: Value and Meaning in Children's Fiction*. Cambridge: Cambridge University Press, 1981.

James, Allison and Adrian James. *Constructing Childhood: Theory, Policy and Social Practice*. Houndmills: Palgrave Macmillan, 2004.

Jordan, Thomas E. *The Degeneracy Crisis and Victorian Youth*. Albany: State University of New York Press, 1993.

Kneale, J. and S. French, '"The Relations of Inebriety to Insurance": Geographies of Medicine, Insurance and Alcohol in Britain, 1840–1911', in *Intoxication: Problematic Pleasures*, ed. Jonathan Herring, Ciaran Regan, Darin Weinberg and Phil Withington. Houndmills: Palgrave Macmillan, 2013.

Kumar, Nita. *The Politics of Gender, Community, and Modernity*. Oxford: Oxford University Press, 2008.

—. 'Provincialism in Modern India: The Multiple Narratives of Education and Their Pain', *Modern Asian Studies*, 40, no. 2 (2006): 397–423.

LaRossa, Ralph. *The Modernization of Fatherhood: A Social and Political History*. Chicago: University of Chicago Press, 1997.

Lee, Lesley Fox. 'The Dalton Plan and the Loyal, Capable Intelligent Citizen', *History of Education*, 29, no. 2 (2000): 129–38.

Livesey, Ruth. 'Reading for Character: Women Social Reformers and Narratives of the Urban Poor in Late Victorian and Edwardian London', *Journal of Victorian Culture*, 9 (2004): 43–67.

Lovett, Laura L. 'Age: A Useful Category of Historical Analysis', *Journal of Childhood and Youth*, 1, no. 1 (2008): 89–90.

McAllister, Annemarie. 'Picturing the Demon Drink: How Children Were Shown Temperance Principles in the Band of Hope', *Visual Resources*, 28, no. 4 (2012): 309–23.

McCann, Phillip, ed. *Popular Education and Socialization in the Nineteenth Century*. London: Methuen, 1977.

McClelland, Keith and Sonya O. Rose. 'Citizenship and Empire, 1867–1928', in *At Home with the Empire*, ed. Catherine Hall and Sonya O. Rose. Cambridge: Cambridge University Press, 2006.

McDonald, Ellen E. 'English Education and Social Reform in Late 19th Century Bombay', *Journal of Asian Studies*, 25 (1966): 453–70.

MacDonald, Robert H. *The Language of Empire: Myths and Metaphors of Popular Imperialism, 1880–1918*. Manchester: Manchester University Press, 1994.

—. 'Reproducing the Middle-Class Boy: From Purity to Patriotism in the Boys' Magazines, 1892–1914'. *Journal of Contemporary History*, 24 (1989): 519–39.

—. *Sons of Empire: The Frontier and the Boy Scout Movement 1890–1910*. Toronto: University of Toronto Press, 1993.

MacKenzie, John M., ed. *Imperialism and Popular Culture*. Manchester: Manchester University Press, 1986.

McLeod, Hugh. *Religion and Society in England, 1850–1914*. London: MacMillan, 1996.

Mahood, Linda. *Policing Gender, Class and Family: Britain, 1850–1940*. Edmonton: University of Alberta Press, 1995.

Mangan, J. A. *Athleticism in the Victorian and Edwardian Public School: The Emergence and Consolidation of an Educational Ideology*. Cambridge: Cambridge University Press, 1981.

—. *The Games Ethic and Imperialism: Aspects of the Diffusion of an Ideal*. Harmondsworth: Viking, 1985.

—. 'Noble Specimens of Manhood: Schoolboy Literature and the Creation of a Colonial Chivalric Code', in *Imperialism and Juvenile Literature*, ed. Jeffery Richards. Manchester: Manchester University Press, 1989.

—. *The Imperial Curriculum: Racial Images and Education in the British Colonial Experience*. London: Routledge, 1993.

Mangan, J. A. and James Walvin, eds. *Manliness and Morality: Middle-Class Masculinity in Britain and America, 1800–1940*. Manchester: Manchester University Press, 1987.

Marshall, David B. '"A Canoe, and a Tent and God's Great Out-of-Doors": Muscular Christianity and the Flight from Domesticity, 1880s–1930s', in *Masculinity and the Other: Historical Perspectives*, ed. Heather Ellis and Jessica Meyer. Newcastle: Cambridge Scholars Publishing, 2009.

Maynes, Mary Jo. 'Age as a Category of Historical Analysis: History, Agency, and Narratives of Childhood', *Journal of the History of Childhood and Youth*, 1, no. 1 (2008): 114–24.

Meyer, Jessica. *Men of War: Masculinity and the First World War in Britain.* Houndmills: Palgrave MacMillan, 2009.

Mintz, Steven. *A Prison of Expectations: The Family in Victorian Culture.* New York: New York University Press, 1983.

—. 'Reflections on Age as a Category of Historical Analysis', *Journal of Childhood and Youth*, 1, no. 1 (2008): 91–4.

Mitchell, Sally. *The New Girl: Girls' Culture in England, 1880–1915.* New York: Columbia University Press, 1995.

Morgan, Sue. 'Knights of God: The White Cross Army 1883–95', in *Gender and the Christian Religion. Studies in Church History*, ed. R. N. Swanson. London: Boydell and Brewer, 1998.

—. '"Wild Oats or Acorns?" Social Purity, Sexual Politics and the Response of the Late-Victorian Church', *Journal of Religious History*, 31, no. 2 (2007): 151–68.

Moruzi, Kristine. *Constructing Girlhood through the Periodical Press, 1850–1915.* Farnham: Ashgate, 2012.

Murdoch, Lydia, *Imagined Orphans: Poor Families, Child Welfare, and Contested Citizenship in London.* New Brunswick, NJ: Rutgers University Press, 2006.

Mutch, Deborah. *English Socialist Periodicals, 1880–1900.* Farnham: Ashgate, 2005.

Myers, Kevin. 'Marking Time: Some Methodological and Historical Perspectives on the "Crisis of Childhood"', *Research Papers in Education*, 27, no. 4 (2012): 409–22.

Naik, J. P. *Educational Planning in India.* New Delhi: Allied Publishers, 1965.

Nandy, Ashis. 'Reconstructing Childhood: A Critique of the Ideology of Adulthood', in *Traditions, Tyranny and Utopias, Essays in the Politics of Awareness.* Delhi: Oxford University Press, 1987.

—. *Traditions, Tyranny and Utopias.* New Delhi: Oxford University Press, 1987.

Nelson, Claudia. *Boys Will Be Girls: The Feminine Ethic and British Children's Fiction, 1857–1917.* New Brunswick, NJ: Rutgers University Press, 1991.

—. *Invisible Men: Fatherhood in Victorian Periodicals, 1850–1910.* Athens, Georgia: University of Georgia Press, 1995.

—. 'Mixed Messages: Authoring and Authority in British Boys' Magazines', *The Lion and the Unicorn*, 21, no. 1 (1997): 1–19.

—. 'Sex and the Single Boy: Ideals of Manliness and Sexuality in Victorian Literature for Boys', *Victorian Studies*, 32 (1989): 525–50.

Neubauer, John. *The Fin-de-Siecle Culture of Adolescence.* New Haven: Yale University Press, 1992.

Newsome, David. *Godliness and Good Learning: Four Studies on a Victorian Ideal.* London: John Murray, 1961.

Nijhawan, Shobna. 'Civilizing Sisters: Writings on How to Save Women, Men, Society and the Nation', in *From Improvement to Development. Civilizing Missions' in Colonial and Post-Colonial South Asia*, ed. Carey Watt and Michael Mann. London and New York: Anthem Press, 2011.

Olsen, G. W. 'Church of England Temperance Society', in *Alcohol and Temperance in Modern History: An International Encyclopedia*, ed. J. S. Blocker, D. M. Fahey and I. R. Tyrrell. Santa Barbara, CA: ABC-Clio, 2003.

—. 'Drink and the British Establishment – the Church of England Temperance Society, 1873–1919'. Unpublished manuscript.

Olsen, Stephanie. 'The Authority of Motherhood in Question: Fatherhood and the Moral Education of Children in England, c. 1870–1900', *Women's History Review*, 18, no. 5 (2009): 765–80.

—. 'Daddy's Come Home. Evangelicalism, Fatherhood and Lessons for Boys in Late Nineteenth-Century Britain', *Fathering*, 5 (2007): 174–96.

—. 'Towards the Modern Man: Edwardian Boyhood in the Juvenile Periodical Press', in *Childhood in Edwardian Fiction: Worlds Enough and Time*, ed. Adrienne Gavin and Andrew Humphries. New York: Palgrave Macmillan, 2009.

Orwell, George, 'Boy's Weeklies', *Horizon*, 1 (1940): 174–200.

Paisley, Fiona. 'Childhood and Race: Growing Up in the Empire', in *Gender and Empire*, ed. Philippa Levine. Oxford: Oxford University Press, 2004.

Paris, Michael. *Warrior Nation: Images of War in British Popular Culture, 1850–2000*. London: Reaktion, 2000.

Pati, Biswamoy. *The 1857 Rebellion*. New Delhi: Oxford University Press, 2007.

Pernau, Margrit. 'Maulawi Muhammad Zaka Ullah. Reflections of a Muslim Moralist on the Compatibility of Islam, Hinduism and Christianity', in *Convictions religieuses et engagement en Asie du Sud depuis 1850 (Études Thématiques No. 25)*, ed. Clémentin-Ojha. Paris: École française d'Extrême-Orient, 2011.

—. 'Teaching Emotions. The Encounter between Victorian Values and Indo-Persian Concepts of Civility in 19th Century Delhi', in *Knowledge Production, Pedagogy, and Institutions in Colonial India*, ed. Indra Sengupta, Daud Ali and Javed Majeed. New York: Palgrave Macmillan, 2011.

Phillips, Simon. '"Character, Grit and Personality": Continued Education, Recreation and Training at Boots Pure Drug Company 1918–45', *History of Education*, 32, no. 6 (2003): 627–43.

Pick, Daniel. *Faces of Degeneration. A European Disorder, c. 1848–c. 1918*. Cambridge: Cambridge University Press, 1989.

Plamper, Jan. 'The History of Emotions: An Interview with William Reddy, Barbara Rosenwein, and Peter Stearns', *History and Theory*, 49, no. 2 (2010): 237–65.

Pollock, Linda. *Forgotten Children: Parent-Child Relations from 1500 to 1900*. Cambridge: Cambridge University Press, 1983.

Prinz, Jesse J. *The Emotional Construction of Morals*. Oxford: Oxford University Press, 2008.

Proctor, Tammy M. '"Patriotism Is Not Enough": Women, Citizenship, and the First World War', *Journal of Women's History*, 17, no. 2 (2005), 169–76.

Pryke, Sam. 'The Control of Sexuality in the Early British Boy Scouts Movement', *Sex Education*, 5, no. 1 (2005): 15–28.

Raman, Vasanthi. 'The Diverse Life-Worlds of Indian Childhood', in *Family and Gender: Changing Values in Germany and India*, ed. Margrit Pernau, Imtiaz Ahmad and Helmut Reifeld. New Delhi, Thousand Oaks and London: Sage, 2003.

Randall, Don. *Kipling's Imperial Boy: Adolescence and Cultural Hybridity*. Houndmills: Palgrave, 2000.

Reddy, William M. *The Navigation of Feeling: A Framework for the History of Emotions*. Cambridge and New York: Cambridge University Press, 2001.

Reynolds, Kimberley. *Girls Only? Gender and Popular Fiction in Britain, 1880–1914*. Philadelphia: Temple University Press, 1990.

Richards, Jeffrey. *Happiest Days: The Public Schools in English Fiction*. New York: St. Martin's Press, 1988.

—, ed. *Imperialism and Juvenile Literature*. New York: Manchester University Press, 1989.

Richards, Robert J. *Darwin and the Emergence of Evolutionary Theories of Mind and Behavior*. Chicago: University of Chicago Press, 1987.

Richardson, Angelique. *Love and Eugenics in the Late Nineteenth Century: Rational Reproduction and the New Woman*. Oxford: Oxford University Press, 2003.

Roberts, M. J. D., *Making English Morals: Voluntary Association and Moral Reform in England, 1787–1886*. Cambridge: Cambridge University Press, 2004.

Roberts, Nathan. 'Character in the Mind: Citizenship, Education and Psychology in Britain, 1880–1914', *History of Education*, 33, no. 2 (March 2004): 177–97.

Roberts, Robert. *The Classic Slum: Salford Life in the First Quarter of the Century*. Manchester: Manchester University Press, 1971.

Roper, Michael. 'Between Manliness and Masculinity: The "War Generation" and the Psychology of Fear in Britain, 1914–1950', *Journal of British Studies*, 44 (2005): 343–62.

—. 'Maternal Relations: Moral Manliness and Emotional Survival in Letters Home during the First World War', in *Masculinities in Politics and War: Gendering Modern History*, ed. Stefan Dudink, Karen Hagemann and John Tosh. New York: Palgrave, 2004.

—. *The Secret Battle: Emotional Survival in the Great War*. Manchester: Manchester University Press, 2009.

Roper, Michael and John Tosh, eds. *Manful Assertions: Masculinities in Britain since 1800*. London: Routledge, 1991.

Rose, Jonathan. *The Edwardian Temperament, 1895–1919*. Athens: Ohio University Press, 1986.

—. 'The History of Education as the History of Reading', *History of Education*, 36, no. 4 (2007): 595–605.

—. *The Intellectual Life of the British Working Classes*. New Haven: Yale University Press, 2001.

Rose, Lionel. *The Erosion of Childhood: Child Oppression in Britain, 1860–1918*. London: Routledge, 1991.

Rosenthal, Michael. *The Character Factory: Baden Powell and the Origins of the Boy Scout Movement*. London: Collins, 1986.

Rosenwein, Barbara. 'Problems and Methods in the History of Emotions', *Passions in Context*, 1 (2010): 1–32.

—. 'Worrying about Emotions in History', *American Historical Review*, 107 (2002): 821–45.

Ross, Ellen. *Love and Toil: Motherhood in Outcast London, 1870–1918*. New York: Oxford University Press, 1993.

Rowbotham, Judith. *Good Girls Make Good Wives: Guidance for Girls in Victorian Fiction*. Oxford: Basil Blackwell, 1989.

Rutherford, Jonathan. *Forever England: Reflections on Masculinity and Empire*. London: Lawrence & Wishart, 1997.

Scheer, Monique. 'Are Emotions a Kind of Practice (and Is That What Makes Them Have a History)? A Bourdieuian Approach to Understanding Emotion', *History and Theory*, 51, no. 2 (2012): 193–220.

Searle, G. R. *The Quest for National Efficiency: A Study of British Politics and Political Thought, 1899–1914*. Berkeley: University of California Press, 1971.

—. *Eugenics and Politics in Britain 1900–1914*. Leyden: Noordhoff International Publishing, 1976.

Sen, Satadru. *Colonial Childhoods: The Juvenile Periphery of India, 1850–1945*. London: Anthem Press, 2005.

Sengupta, Parna. *Pedagogy for Religion: Missionary Education and the Fashioning of Hindus and Muslims in Bengal*. Berkeley: University of California Press, 2011.

Seth, Sanjay. *Subject Lessons: The Western Education of Colonial India*. Durham and London: Duke University Press, 2007.

Shabbir, S. *History of Educational Development in Vidarbha*. New Delhi: Northern Book Centre, 2005.

Sherington, Geoffrey. '"A Better Class of Boy": The Big Brother Movement, Youth Migration and Citizenship of Empire', *Australian Historical Studies*, 34, no. 120 (2002): 267–85.

Shiman, Lilian Lewis. 'The Band of Hope Movement: Respectable Recreation for Working-Class Children', *Victorian Studies*, 17, no. 1 (1973): 49–74.

—. *Crusade against Drink in Victorian England*. London: MacMillan, 1988.

Showalter, Elaine. *Sexual Anarchy: Gender and Culture at the Fin de Siècle*. New York: Viking, 1990.

Shuttleworth, Sally. *The Mind of the Child: Child Development in Literature, Science, and Medicine, 1840–1900*. Oxford: Oxford University Press, 2010.

—. 'Victorian Childhood', *Journal of Victorian Culture*, 9, no. 1 (2004): 107–13.

Simon, Brian. *The Two Nations and the Educational Structure, 1780–1870*. London: Lawrence & Wishart, 1960.

Simon, Brian and Ian Bradley, eds. *The Victorian Public School: Studies in the Development of an Educational Institution*. Dublin: Gill and Macmillan, 1975.

Sinha, Mrinalini. *Colonial Masculinity: The 'Manly Englishman' and the 'Effeminate Bengali' in the Late Nineteenth Century*. New York: Manchester University Press, 1995.

Smith, John T. 'The Beginnings of Citizenship Education in England', *History of Education Society Bulletin*, 69, no. 1 (2002): 6–16.

Smith, Roger. 'The Physiology of the Will: Mind, Body, and Psychology in the Periodical Literature, 1855–1875', *Science Serialized: Representation of the Sciences in Nineteenth-Century Periodicals*, ed. Geoffrey N. Cantor and Sally Shuttleworth. Cambridge: MIT Press, 2004.

Smuts, Alice Boardman. *Science in the Service of Children, 1883–1935*. New Haven: Yale University Press, 2006.

Sobe, Noah W. 'Researching Emotion and Affect in the History of Education', *History of Education*, 41 (2012): 689–95.

Springhall, John. 'The Boy Scouts, Class and Militarism in Relation to British Youth Movements, 1908–30', *International Review of Social History*, 16 (1971): 121–58.

—. 'Building Character in the British Boy: The Attempt to Extend Christian Manliness to Working-Class Adolescents, 1880–1914', in *Manliness and Morality: Middle-Class Masculinity in Britain and America, 1800–1940*, ed. J. A. Mangan and James Walvin. Manchester: Manchester University Press, 1987.

—. *Coming of Age: Adolescence in Britain, 1860–1960*. Dublin: Gill and MacMillan, 1986.

—. '"Disseminating Impure Literature": The "Penny Dreadful" Publishing Business since 1860', *Economic History Review*, 2nd series, 47 (1994): 567–84.

—. '"Healthy Papers for Manly Boys": Imperialism and Race in the Harmsworths' Halfpenny Boys' Papers of the 1890s and 1900s', in *Imperialism and Juvenile Literature*, ed. Jeffrey Richards. New York: Manchester University Press, 1989.

— *Youth, Empire and Society: British Youth Movements, 1883–1940*. London: Croom Helm, 1977.

—. *Youth, Popular Culture and Moral Panics: Penny Gaffs to Gansta-Rap, 1830–1996*. Basingstoke: Macmillan, 1998.

Springhall, John, Brian Fraser and Michael Edward Hoare. *Sure and Stedfast: A History of the Boys' Brigade, 1883–1983*. London: Collins, 1983.

Srinivasan, Prema. *Children's Fiction in English in India: Trends and Motifs*. Chennai: T.R. Publications, 1998.

Stearns, Peter N. 'Challenges in the History of Childhood', *Journal of the History of Childhood and Youth*, 1, no. 1 (2008): 35–42.

—. 'Defining Happy Childhoods Assessing a Recent Change', *Journal of the History of Childhood and Youth*, 3, no. 2 (2010): 165–86.

Tayler, R. *Hope of the Race*. London: Hope Press, 1946.

Thorne, Susan. *Congregational Missions and the Making of an Imperial Culture in Nineteenth-Century England*. Stanford: Stanford University Press, 1999.

—. "'The Conversion of Englishmen and the Conversion of the World Inseparable":
    Missionary Imperialism and the Language of Class, 1750–1850', in *Tensions of*
    *Empire: Colonial Cultures in a Bourgeois World*, ed. Frederick Cooper and Ann Laura
    Stoler. Berkeley: University of California Press, 1997.

Tosh, John. 'Authority and Nurture in Middle-Class Fatherhood: The Case of Early and
    Mid-Victorian England', *Gender & History*, 8, no. 1 (1996): 48–64.

—. 'Gentlemanly Politeness and Manly Simplicity in Victorian England', *Transactions of*
    *the Royal Historical Society*, 6th series, 12 (2002): 455–72.

— *Manliness and Masculinities in Nineteenth-Century Britain: Essays on Gender, Family,*
    *and Empire*. Harlow and New York: Pearson Longman, 2005.

—. *A Man's Place: Masculinity and the Middle-Class Home in Victorian England*. New
    Haven: Yale University Press, 1999.

—. 'Masculinities in an Industrializing Society: Britain, 1800–1914', *Journal of British*
    *Studies*, 44, no. 2 (2005): 330–42.

—. 'Methodist Domesticity and Middle-Class Masculinity in Nineteenth-Century
    England', *Studies in Church History*, 34 (1998): 323–45.

— 'The Old Adam and the New Man: Emerging Themes in the History of English
    Masculinities, 1750–1850', in *English Masculinities 1600–1800*, ed. Tim Hitchcock
    and Michèle Cohen. London: Longman, 1999.

—. 'What Should Historians Do With Masculinity? Reflections on Nineteenth-Century
    Britain', *History Workshop Journal*, 38 (1994): 179–202.

Turner, Mark W. *Trollope and the Magazines: Gendered Issues in Mid-Victorian Britain*.
    London: MacMillan, 2000.

Vance, Norman. *The Sinews of the Spirit: The Ideal of Christian Manliness in Victorian*
    *Literature and Religious Thought*. Cambridge: Cambridge University Press, 1985.

Veldman, Meredith. 'Dutiful Daughter versus All-Boy: Jesus, Gender, and the
    Secularization of Victorian Society', *Nineteenth Century Studies*, 11 (1997): 1–24.

Viswanathan, Gauri. *Masks of Conquest: Literary Study and British Rule in India*. New
    York: Columbia University Press, 1989.

Volk, Anthony. 'The Evolution of Childhood', *Journal of the History of Childhood and*
    *Youth*, 4, no. 3 (2011): 470–94.

Walker, Pamela J. *Pulling the Devil's Kingdom Down: The Salvation Army in Victorian*
    *Britain*. Berkeley: University of California Press, 2001.

Walvin, James. *A Child's World: A Social History of English Childhood, 1800–1914*.
    Harmondsworth, Middlesex: Pelican, 1982.

Warner, Philip. *The Best of British Pluck: The Boy's Own Paper*. London: MacDonald and
    Jane's, 1976.

Warren, Allen. 'Citizens of Empire: Baden-Powell, Scouts and Guides and an Imperial
    Idea, 1900–1940', in *Imperialism and Popular Culture*, ed. John Mackenzie.
    Manchester: Manchester University Press, 1986.

—. 'Sir Robert Baden-Powell, the Scout Movement and Citizen Training in Great
    Britain, 1900–1920', *English Historical Review*, 101 (1986): 376–98.

Wasserstein, Bernard. *Herbert Samuel: A Political Life*. Oxford: Clarendon Press, 1992.

Watt, Carey A. 'Boy Scout Movement in India', *South Asia*, 7, no. 2 (1999): 37–62.

—. 'Education for National Efficiency: Constructive Nationalism in North India, 1909–1916', *Modern Asian Studies*, 31, no. 2 (1997): 339–74.

—. *Serving the Nation: Cultures of Service, Association, and Citizenship*. New Delhi: Oxford University Press, 2005.

Watt, Carey A. and Michael Mann, eds. *Civilizing Missions in Colonial and Postcolonial South Asia. From Improvement to Development*. London: Anthem Press, 2011.

Welshman, John. 'Child Health, National Fitness, and Physical Education in Britain, 1900–1940', in *Cultures of Child Health in Britain and the Netherlands in the Twentieth Century*, ed. Marijke Gijswijt-Hofstra and Hilary Marland. Amsterdam, NY: Rodopi, 2003.

—. 'Images of Youth: The Issue of Juvenile Smoking, 1880–1914', *Addiction*, 91, no. 9 (1996): 1379–86.

Whitehead, Clive. *Colonial Educators: The British Indian and Colonial Education Service, 1858–1983*. London: I.B. Tauris, 2003.

—. 'The Historiography of British Imperial Education Policy, Part I: India', *History of Education*, 34, no. 3 (2005): 315–29.

Wigley, John. *The Rise and Fall of the Victorian Sunday*. Manchester: Manchester University Press, 1980.

Williams, Sarah. *Religious Belief and Popular Culture in Southwark c. 1880–1939*. Oxford: Oxford University Press, 1999.

Windholz, Anne M. 'An Emigrant and a Gentleman: Imperial Masculinity, British Magazines, and the Colony That Got Away', *Victorian Studies*, 42, no. 4 (2000): 631–58.

Wood, Diana. *The Church and Childhood*. Oxford: Ecclesiastical History Society, 1994.

Wright, Susannah. 'Citizenship, Moral Education and the English Elementary School', in *Mass Education and the Limits of State Building*, ed. Laurence Brockliss and Nicola Sheldon. London: Palgrave, 2012.

Wynne, Deborah. *The Sensation Novel and the Victorian Family Magazine*. New York: Palgrave, 2001.

Yeo, Eileen Janes, '"The Boy Is the Father of the Man": Moral Panic over Working-Class Youth, 1850 to the Present', *Labour History Review*, 69, no. 2 (2004): 185–99.

## Unpublished theses

Dunae, Patrick A. 'British Juvenile Literature in an Age of Empire: 1880–1914'. Ph.D. Victoria University of Manchester, 1975.

Fyfe, Aileen. 'Industrialised Conversion: The Religious Tract Society and Popular Science Publishing in Victorian Britain'. Ph.D. History and Philosophy of Science, University of Cambridge, 2000.

Lang, Marjory. 'Children and Society in Eighteenth-Century Children's Literature'. Ph.D. University of British Columbia, 1976.

Sherrington, Christine Anne. 'The NSPCC in Transition. 1884–1983: A Study of Organisational Survival'. Ph.D. London University, 1984.

# Index